THE GILDED AGE AND AFTER

THE GILDED AGE
AND AFTER

Selected Readings in American History

JOHN A. DENOVO, *General Editor*
Contributing Editors: HUGO A. MEIER,
GERALD G. EGGERT, ROGER R. TRASK

CHARLES SCRIBNER'S SONS · NEW YORK

T O

J E A N N E

M Y R L

J E A N

D O R O T H Y

Printed in the United States of America
Library of Congress Catalog Card Number 72–4449
SBN 684–13150–1 (cloth)
SBN 684–13149–8 (paper)

Introduction

The era between the Civil War and the First World War is one of the more important periods of American history, but it is also among the least understood. The so-called Gilded Age too often is thought of simply as a time of political decadence. The significance of this half-century, however, easily becomes evident to those who look beyond the world of politics. During these years occurred basic economic developments that transformed the United States from a predominantly agrarian society into a matured industrial-urban nation. This book concentrates on these developments with their varied social, intellectual, and political ramifications.

Chapter One examines the Darwinian business ethic of the industrial era, which assumed the prizes in the economic race went to the fleetest of foot, who presumably best served the needs of society. After exploring in Chapter Two the process by which large industries developed, along with some of the political and constitutional issues involved, Chapter Three sketches out the changing status of workingmen and the problems of labor-management relations. Chapter Four deals with the distress that industrialization brought to the farmer in the closing days of agricultural expansion and with the prosperity that came in the early twentieth century when agricultural supply and demand approached a balance. The inadequate responses of the Gilded Age's political system to the rapid changes wrought by industrialism and urbanization receive attention in Chapter Five. Finally, because the rise of the city has been so central to modern America, Chapter Six probes such issues as urban housing, transportation, government, and life-styles during the late nineteenth and early twentieth centuries.

We believe that the student can best share the excitement and variety of the American experience by reading contemporary sources. This need not be limited to official documents. Included are materials that convey the flavor of society during this half-century: speeches and petitions; letters of eminent statesmen and ordinary citizens; popular handbooks and magazine articles; memoirs, novels, and poetry. The student should finish this book with a deeper understanding of the Gilded Age and the years that followed. He should also have a better appreciation of the rich variety of sources from which the historian attempts to reconstruct the past.

Contents

THE GILDED AGE AND AFTER

1. Business and American Society, 1865-1914

THE truce concluded at Appomattox Court House in April of 1865 marked more than the military and political victory of the North; it also signified triumph of a new business way of life for Americans. In the half-century separating the Civil War and World War I, the United States moved rapidly from its old largely agrarian and commercial condition toward a new status as an industrial power. By 1914, the nation's economy, its social values, and its political goals differed strikingly from those familiar to Americans in 1860.

This new era was one of enormous opportunity for entrepreneurial energies. Businessman, farmer, laborer, and immigrant alike sensed the new optimism and, enduring present evils, dreamed of bettering their condition. Virgin prairies awaited the plow, there were new western lands for speculation, cities and railroads to build, new inventions and industries to exploit. Multiplier industries such as railroads and construction, in turn, stimulated the growth of complementary ventures in machinery manufacture, iron and steel production, and the business of investing other people's money. That important social invention, the business corporation, achieved new constitutional sanction in belated reinterpretations of the Fourteenth Amendment. The amendment, assumed to be essentially a guarantee of the civil rights of the freedmen, became a new and potent tool for mushrooming economic expansion. It expedited the accumulation of investment capital by offering both wider scope and legal protection for the organizational talents of the captains of industry whose boldness of enterprise increased as their responsibility became depersonalized.

The social and ethical character of this energetic era of business expansion has become a major subject of interpretation by novelists and historians. The earliest major insight was provided by the realistic writers Mark Twain and Charles Dudley Warner in their cooperative novel *The Gilded Age,* published in 1873. Their picture of American society in the immediate postwar years mingled bitterness, sarcasm, and humor. Heavy government wartime expenditures, high tariffs, inflated paper money, and the optimism encouraged by Northern victory brought quick wealth to many Americans and at least the promise of wealth to a great many more. But easy money, a reaction to wartime idealism, and the laissez-faire attitude of government toward business also encouraged a relaxation of morals which was reflected in politics, business, and personal behavior.

The Panic of 1873 dimmed the assurances of the Gilded Age as it had been defined by Twain and Warner, but the buoyant materialism of the era continued into the next century. It became standard practice for historians of the twentieth century to brand American business, society, and culture in the fifty years before World War I as ethically corrupt, economically ruthless, and politically incompetent. Vernon Louis Parrington, a major interpreter of American civilization, writing in the 1920s, stressed the "great barbecue" aspects of the new industrial age and, as a good Progressive, lamented the shift of social and political influence from the people to the new plutocrats. The wrong men, argued Parrington, were reaping the material blessings of American economic growth and offensively flaunting their new wealth in cheap and tawdry self-display.

A second modern interpretation of the period was offered by historian Charles A. Beard, already noted for his emphasis on the economic determinants underlying historical development. To Beard, the Civil War had brought about a second American Revolution, drastically transforming the American economy and society. The influence of the old agrarian-minded statesmen had yielded to that of a new and expanding urban middle class, and in particular to that segment whose considerable wealth was rooted in wartime opportunities and had continued to grow in the burgeoning economy. But Beard also recognized that social and economic opportunity were not yet closed to average Americans. The new economic rulers were not a hereditary class in the sense familiar in European social upheavals for American society still remained flexible.

Less generous to the age was the deterministic analysis of Matthew Josephson, whose continuing best seller of the 1930s about *The Robber Barons* pictured late nineteenth century America as a world exploited by the new breed of entrepreneurs. His interpretation suggested an American equivalent of the Marxist formula, positing an exploiting plutocracy which must eventually be overthrown by the long-suffering proletariat in a society politically and morally corrupt.

Recent historians in our own age of affluence have tended to be more discreet in their interpretations of the business society dominant in the period 1865–1914. A new interest in labor and business history has persuaded some of them, such as the eminent historian of the Civil War era, Allan Nevins, that the rise of big business and its social influence were less a moral catastrophe than a misunderstood and probably necessary phenomenon in our national development. The great industrial captains were often ruthless men, but their energetic and imaginative leadership was in harmony with the demands of the era.

Subsequent chapters will explore the methods and the results of the process of industrial expansion before 1914. Our immediate concern is with the impact of business expansion on American life in general, and more specifically in the arena of social behavior. Underlying this enormous growth of business and industry was a congenial new philosophy compounded of frank materialism, popular science, and ruthless opportunism. It was a philosophy sanctified by pious adaptations of the old Puritan ethic of hard work, devotion to duty, and righteous social behavior.

This chapter first reviews the convergence of the old rural-oriented Calvinist ethic of success with the realities of the new business emphasis. Benjamin Franklin may be credited with popularizing the major tenets of this ethic in America. It glorified individualism, for the self-reliant man led social progress. It honored frugality, for to be sparing of resources made easier the accumulating of reserves for business expansion. Honesty and reliability won special praise, for such qualities won the confidence—and hence patronage—of others. And the ethic's emphasis on the gospel of work as a positive good won hearty acceptance in a society where there was so much to do. All of these qualities encouraged a material success in vocation or "calling" which was evidence to men of God's approval.

The postwar publicists of the business ethic exploited its virtues in sermons, newspaper squibs, the faithful public school reader, and handbooks of homilies aimed at ambitious young men [I and II]. The moral limitations implicit in the old ethic were not always helpful guidance for the young man confronting the jungle environment of a business world where size and power outranked quality and service, and competition became ever more fierce. Business leaders were often guilty of a selective morality in which the gospel of work was devoted less to God than to profit, and speculation proved to be richer in its rewards than was labor [III].

A newer ethic, meanwhile, was eroding the old doctrine of success. Charles Darwin's biological hypothesis conquered American sociology. Darwin believed that nature, by way of uninhibited competition, eliminated the weak and thus "naturally selected" the best qualities for survival among the strong. The translation of a scientific hypothesis into social terms provided a convenient rationalization for irresponsible individualism, ruthless competition, the senseless accumulation of wealth, and uninhibited *laissez-faire.* Such "Social Darwinism" probably was neither understood nor accepted as a philosophy of life by most businessmen of the era. Nonetheless, American disciples of Herbert Spencer, the English popular interpreter of "survival of the fittest" thought, included steelmaker Andrew Carnegie, who contentedly attributed business success and the progress of society to free competition.

A second approach in this chapter relates the rise of business leadership to the reinforcement of materialistic values in American society. Amazing profits and fortunate speculations in this period, 1865–1914, created vast fortunes for a few men and generous wealth for many more. Untaxed, such wealth tempted its possessors to demonstrate social importance by means of ostentatious expenditures. While a newly fledged "captain of business" might himself discount luxury and personal display, he presumed an obligation to his family and to community opinion which encouraged what contemporary sociologist Thorstein Veblen picturesquely termed "conspicuous consumption." Less fortunately situated citizens read with more envy than resentment the society column accounts of Lucullan banquets in the magnificent mansions of the rich which they had passed in awed admiration, and the matrimonial ventures of millionaires occasioned public curiosity and excitement [IV].

Also watching were the critics of such wealth—the representatives of underpaid and overworked labor, the philosophical radical, the moralist fearful of the corrupting influence of great wealth. But they were not typical of the general public, which respected more the pronouncements of such a Social Darwinist as the great scholar William Graham Sumner. Although Sumner may have disapproved of the display, he justified the process by which wealth was accumulated and deprecated those who would curb its growth or tax it away [V].

Conscientious millionaires accepted Andrew Carnegie's "Gospel of Wealth," which urged social responsibility for the redistribution of family fortunes, if not necessarily their acquisition. While the Gospel stressed Christian Stewardship as preached in the old ethic, some churchmen were disturbed because it slighted benefactions for charities and new churches in favor of public libraries and hero awards. For many other critics at home and abroad, not even philanthropies could be reconciled with the low wages and social irresponsibility which had helped to create the fortunes [VI].

Materialist values also influenced the life of the mind. A real need existed for practical education in a nation where science and technology ruled industrial production and required a new class of managers and technicians. Mechanics institutes and technical schools had come into being even before the Civil War, and the Morrill Act of 1862 officially recognized the importance of subsidizing such instruction in so-called land-grant colleges. Now it was heatedly argued that the old classical curriculum merely produced mean-spirited "gentlemen," too falsely proud to prepare for an honest trade [VII]. Accompanying the expansion of business, too, was the growth of popular higher education. With increase in size, however, came pressures threatening to convert higher learning in America into another form of business enterprise, sacrificing humanistic values to the demands of the marketplace [VIII].

Materialism also commercialized aesthetic values. Machine production tended to standardize a culture of bad taste, and for many Americans the only immediate contact with "fine art" was the popular chromolithograph. Men of new wealth, however, joined the connoisseurs of the older mercantile families in vying for status as collectors of fine art, rare books, and other costly evidences of refinement. Abetted by a lingering acquisitiveness, such amateur enthusiasts sought rare paintings with the zeal reminiscent of their capture of another corporation [IX]. Their efforts did yield to the New World a cultural bonus of disemboweled abbeys, rare old masters, and antique artifacts of infinite variety, many of which eventually found their way into museums for all citizens to enjoy. Second and third generations of the wealthy often revealed greater sophistication in cultural interests, and whatever splendor American cultural life could claim owed much to their earnest ministrations and ready purses. In a democracy where few considered it the proper function of government to subsidize culture, it was perhaps fortunate that the tycoons accepted the responsibility, even if unintentionally.

A third aspect of business civilization examined here is the close association of business and government. The quest for tariff protection and subsidies to advance new industrial ventures belied the widely professed admiration for *laissez-faire*. Such association resulted frequently enough in political scandals which provided grist for the busy editorial mills of the popular press. Certainly, Beriah Sellers, Mark Twain's exuberant hero of bold enterprise in *The Gilded Age*, was not unduly disheartened by the corruptibility of public officials whose sense of personal profit impeded their capacity to discriminate between public trust and private gain [X].

There were many critics of this concentration on business values, but the average citizen probably accepted such values as a kind of norm. While he might not admire the boldest abuses of economic power, his own dreams of success and of the good life very likely differed only in scale from those of the Carnegies and Rockefellers. Even farmers, as their own opportunities declined, envied the apparent prosperity and promises of the towns and cities whose ways of life they once had scorned (see Chapter Four). And labor—public pronouncements aside—was not at heart opposed to the business ideals, however much it desired a greater share of the golden loaf (see Chapter Three).

The business ideals thus penetrated almost every aspect of American life. They tended to set a standard for social behavior which probably served very practical requirements in an expanding economy and increasingly complex society. The compulsion toward gain and expansion led to nationalized industries by 1900 (see Chapter Two) and to the penetration of overseas markets by American business. It encouraged as well the "dollar imperialism" which thrived in the Caribbean and elsewhere before 1914 (see Chapter Nine, selection IV).

Were these "business ideals" compatible with the traditional spirit of American democracy? They have been considered by some historians as essential to the rise of the United States as a viable power in a modern industrial world. Perhaps, indeed, the qualities of life explored in this chapter still significantly influence our behavior today. EDITED BY HUGO A. MEIER

I

The success literature of a business age offers young men trusted formulas for finding "room at the top".

FROM: Popular manuals for achieving success in business, 1856, 1876.

THE ambitious young man after the Civil War could draw guidance and inspiration from hundreds of editorials, stories, sermons, and books which attempted to set forth a rationale for achieving success in business. Freeman Hunt, editor of a leading business journal, set the pace in 1856 in his miscellany, *Worth and Wealth,* and in 1858 provided suitable examples in his two-volume *Lives of American Merchants.* Hunt's homiletic efforts were updated in 1876 by a *Scribner's Monthly* editor, Josiah Gilbert Holland, whose *Every-Day Topics* again stressed the opportunities supposedly awaiting young men of temperance, frugality, industry, initiative, perseverance—and perhaps gullibility.

What precepts for "getting ahead" were offered by Hunt and Holland?

Why were these considered especially appropriate for a business career?

How appropriate would such advice be for achieving success in our own day? Suggest revisions which might be required.

FREEMAN HUNT: *THE MAN OF BUSINESS AND THE BUSINESS MAN*

⌇

THE man of business and the *business man* both have business to do; but the *business* man is the one who does it. The business man thinks, moves, acts, and makes himself felt in the world. If a thought comes into his head it is one of breadth and compass—it don't center on self and its narrow world. It reaches away and embraces others. It has a wide range, and does not stop till it touches and affects for good the interests of all. Nor are the thoughts of such men immobile. They become acting, living realities in the wide and busy world. The authors of them make of these business thoughts, actualities—give them "local habitation and a name," and steamboats are built, an ocean is navigated, and distant climes and nations brought together; an electric telegraph springs into being as by enchantment, and lightning becomes garrulous and voluble, and thought out-travels the winged winds; and in a twinkling, the bands and schackles [*sic*] of trade are loosened. Such are the *workings* produced by the *business man.* He awakens the drowsy and helpless multitudes, puts life and thought, energy and action into them, and makes the world leap rejoicing along the path of ages. Where its step before was but a single year, now it strides by scores and fifties.

> "Men of thought, men of action,
> Clear the way."

And they *do clear the way*—their thoughts become tangible, moving, demolishing forces, that break down and crush all opposing barriers,

Freeman Hunt, *Worth and Wealth: A Collection of Maxims, Morals, and Miscellanies for Merchants and Men of Business* (New York: Stringer and Townsend, 1856), pp. 41–43.

opening a pathway of progress, into which the more sluggish and timid portion of humanity may securely travel. But the *man* of business is emphatically what the name indicates. His business is always on his hands. He don't *do* it. He don't know how to go to work in the right way. His thoughts are all measured and slow. He weighs self-made doubts and supposed contingencies, and before he moves the *business man* gets up and runs away from him and wins the race. The man of business won't go ahead, he only eddies round and round—he don't "progress"—his path is a circle. He don't find himself at night many miles on his journey's way, but like the hour hand of a clock just where he started. He is not clear and decided in what he does, but often stands hesitating and puzzled. He ventures and falls back; has a stout heart in *fancy*, but none in *fact*. Such a man may get a living—he may even help others to live, but the throbbing heart of the great world will not be accelerated by his presence nor his work. Thus you will perceive that a man of business is not necessarily a business man.

> "Act—act in the living present,
> Man within, and God o'er head."

JOSIAH G. HOLLAND: *ROOM ENOUGH AT THE TOP* (1876)

TO the young men annually making their entrance upon active life, with great ambitions, conscious capacities and high hopes, the prospect is, in ninety-nine cases in a hundred, most perplexing. They see every avenue to prosperity thronged with their superiors in experience, in social advantages, and in the possession of all the elements and conditions of success. Every post is occupied, every office filled, every path crowded. Where shall they find room? It is related of Mr. Webster that when a young lawyer suggested to him that the profession to which he had devoted himself was overcrowded, the great man replied: "Young man, there is always room enough at the top." Never was a wiser or more suggestive word said. There undoubtedly is always room enough where excellence lives. Mr. Webster was not troubled for lack of room. Mr. Clay and Mr. Calhoun were never crowded. . . .

It is well, first, that all young men remember that nothing will do them so much injury as quick and easy success, and that nothing will do them so much good as a struggle which teaches them exactly what there is in them, educates them gradually to its use, instructs them in personal economy, drills them into a patient and persistent habit of

Josiah G. Holland, *Every-Day Topics: A Book of Briefs* (New York: Scribner, Armstrong and Company, 1876), pp. 106–110.

work, and keeps them at the foot of the ladder until they become strong enough to hold every step they are enabled to gain. . . .

The young men will say that only a few can reach the top. That is true, but it is also true that the further from the bottom one goes, the more scattering the neighborhood. One can fancy, for illustration, that every profession and every calling is pyramidal in its living constituency, and that while only one man is at the top, there are several tiers of men below him who have plenty of elbow-room, and that it is only at the base that men are so thick that they pick the meat out of one another's teeth to keep themselves from starving. If a man has no power to get out of the rabble at the bottom, then he is self-convicted of having chosen a calling or profession to whose duties he has no adaptation.

The grand mistake that young men make, during the first ten years of their business and professional life, is in idly waiting for their chance. . . . The young physicians and young lawyers who sit idly in their offices, and smoke and lounge away the time "waiting for something to turn up," are by that course fastening themselves for life to the lower stratum, where their struggle for a bare livelihood is to be perpetual. The first ten years are golden years, that should be filled with systematic reading and observation. Everything that tends to professional and personal excellence, should be an object of daily pursuit. To such men the doors of success open of themselves at last. . . .

There is another point that ought not to be overlooked in the treatment of this subject. Young men look about them and see a great measure of worldly success awarded to men without principle. They see the trickster crowned with public honors, they see the swindler rolling in wealth, they see the sharp man, the overreaching man, the unprincipled man, the liar, the demagogue, the time-server, the trimmer, the scoundrel who cunningly manages, though constantly disobeying moral law and trampling upon social courtesy, to keep himself out of the clutches of the legal police, carrying off the prizes of wealth and place. All this is a demoralizing puzzle and a fearful temptation; and multitudes of young men are not strong enough to stand before it. They ought to understand that in this wicked world there is a great deal of room where there is integrity. Great trusts may be sought by scoundrels, but great trusts never seek them; and perfect integrity is at a premium even among scoundrels. . . .

In the realm of eminent acquirements and eminent integrity there is always room enough. Let no young man of industry and perfect honesty despair because his profession or calling is crowded. Let him always remember that there is room enough at the top, and that the question whether he is ever to reach the top, or rise above the crowd at the base of the pyramid, will be decided by the way in which he improves the first ten years of his active life in securing to himself a thorough knowledge of his profession, and a sound moral and intellectual culture.

II

The ragged heroes of novelist Horatio Alger, Jr.,
inspire American boys in their quest for fame and fortune.

FROM: *Mark, the Match Boy*, a novel of 1897.

No writer filled eager young minds with grander dreams of success than did Horatio Alger, Jr., who abandoned the Unitarian ministry for a career of writing and pious counsel for American boys. *Ragged Dick*, Alger's first non-literary masterpiece in 1867, led a parade of stereotyped heroes in a procession of novels including *Luck and Pluck, Tattered Tom*, and *Mark, the Match Boy*. In the latter tale, "Ragged Dick" has been guided by Fate, his own solid virtues, and the intercession of a wealthy benefactor to a respectable mercantile position, and hence is qualified to contribute in turn to the rise of another heroic street urchin. As "Richard Hunter," the formerly ragged Dick relieves Alger's stern puritan conscience regarding vain display by explaining why his "handsomely furnished" front room on the third floor was compatible with the success precept of frugality.

What does the "philosophy" of Dick Hunter suggest about the ultimate goal of success as understood in the business age?

What explains the continuing popularity of Alger's novels in the 1920s and their rapid decline in interest for American readers during the 1930s and subsequent decades?

◆§
. . . THOSE who have read "Ragged Dick" and "Fame and Fortune,"—the preceding volumes of this series,—will understand that less than three years before Richard Hunter was an ignorant and ragged bootblack about the streets. . . . By a series of upward steps, partly due to good fortune, but largely to his own determination to improve, and hopeful energy, Dick had now become a book-keeper in the establishment of Rockwell & Cooper, on Pearl Street, and possessed the confidence and good wishes of the firm in a high degree. . . . . .

It may be thought that, considering how recently Richard Hunter had been a ragged bootblack, content to sleep in boxes and sheltered

Horatio Alger, Jr., *Mark, the Match Boy; or Richard Hunter's Ward* (Philadelphia: The John C. Winston Company, 1897), pp. 13, 15–18.

doorways, and live at the cheapest restaurants, he had become very luxurious in his tastes. Why did he not get a cheaper boarding-place, and save up the difference in price? No doubt this consideration will readily suggest itself to the minds of some of my young readers.

As Richard Hunter had a philosophy of his own on this subject, I may as well explain it here. He had observed that those young men who out of economy contented themselves with small and cheerless rooms, in which there was no provision for a fire, were driven in the evening to the streets, theatres, and hotels, for the comfort which they could not find at home. Here they felt obliged to spend money to an extent of which they probably were not themselves fully aware, and in the end wasted considerably more than the two or three dollars a week extra which would have provided them with a comfortable home. But this was not all. In the roamings spent outside many laid the foundation of wrong habits, which eventually led to ruin or shortened their lives. They lost all the chances of improvement which they might have secured by study at home in the long winter evenings, and which in the end might have qualified them for posts of higher responsibility, and with a larger compensation. . . . . .

So Richard Hunter kept on his way, indifferent to the criticisms which his conduct excited in the minds of young men of his own age. He looked farther than they, and knew that if he wanted to succeed in life, and win the respect of his fellow-men, he must do something else than attend theatres, and spend his evenings in billiard saloons.

III

The moral and practical deficiencies of the success ethic bring disillusionment and reappraisal after the turn of the century.

FROM: "A Passing Humbug," a magazine article of 1912.

THE optimism of Hunt, Holland, and Alger was not shared by the more perceptive observers of business society. As early as 1868, E. L. Godkin, journalist and a major social analyst of the Gilded Age, cautioned that "five out of six of the great fortunes are made rapidly, by happy hits or bold and ingenious combinations," rather than by frugality and simple industry.* By 1912 the accumulated mass of success literature was admitted to be mostly simple-minded humbug, an anachronistic attempt to adapt the homilies of Franklin's "Poor Richard" to the Social Darwinist world of cut-throat competition, monopoly, and business corruption, qualities many believed to be more truly characteristic of

---

* E. L. Godkin, "Commercial Immorality and Political Corruption," *North American Review,* 107(July, 1868), 250.

modern American society.

What aspects of the success story were becoming unacceptable after 1900?

Explain this accusation: "Probably they did not turn so many young men into scoundrels . . . though if they turned them into anything it must have been into scoundrels."

∾§

BEAUTIFUL as is the life of the average millionaire, he seldom shows to advantage when explaining to the young how they too may attain greatness. A few years ago that sort of advice constituted rather a formidable body of printed matter. Nowadays it seems, happily, to have shrunk and one seldom finds a whole book of it, though occasionally it flourishes in the magazines when rich folk "in the public eye" or people "in the forefront" tell their interviewers how by their mighty wills and hardy virtues they came to be the men they are. It looks as if our traditional books of success were passing. The book addressed to young men "on the threshhold" by some presumably successful elder, usually a compound of Polonius and Sam Slick, seems to have lost its charm. The time may come when even a country boy will no longer care to learn how John D. Rockefeller made himself. Yet only a few years ago there was apparently an eager demand for the autobiography of every goose who laid a golden egg. Some attribute this change to the prolonged assaults of the muckrakers, impairing the public confidence in millionaire homiletics. People now like to read the story of a millionaire's success told by some one other than himself. It may be less edifying but it is apt to be more piquant.

As one looks back on these success-books now they seem rather quaint than harmful. Probably they did not turn so many young men into scoundrels as might have been supposed, though if they turned them into anything it must have been into scoundrels. "Be practical, young man," these self-made writers used to say, and cut away everything in life that has no money in it. They were always drawing lessons for the young from their own early disadvantages. Start early at your job, young man, remain raw, illiterate, stone-blind, stone-deaf to everything that does not pay. Remember that great motto of success—All's well that sells well. It was the literature of the diamond shirt-stud and it gathered fast in our periodicals and in our books, especially in the goody-goody ones. Along with this frankly immoral advice, to be sure, went many pious platitudes, but they were usually of the limpest gen-

"A Passing Humbug," *The Bookman*, 36 (September, 1912), 18. Reprinted by permission of Dodd, Mead & Company.

erality, freely admitting exceptions if the exceptions paid. Christian principles, said one old success-book we happen to recall, can often be used even in business, and with great moral boldness the writer added, "It may be better to deserve success than to attain it." Strive upward toward the light, young man, said another, choose the right and not the wrong. What you need, said a third in his helpful, concrete way, is individuality; grasp the handle of your being and you will get it. "Self-control is the first rung in the ladder of success." True words, but what hope in this world for the sort of young man who needed them? It is doubtful of course if young men took this advice seriously, for after all, the mind, if one has any, begins to sprout at an early age, and there are plenty of young things of twenty-one or so who are more than half-witted. Yet it did have some bad effects and few will regret that this particular body of humbug has diminished.

In the first place young men must have inferred the haphazard nature of the great rewards when they saw them falling to people who wrote in that manner; and in the second place their cocksure and flatulent old age must have shaken the faith of youth in the wisdom of years and experience. The contributions of the millionaire seemed to fall below even the modest standards of this literature, nonsense from him having the eloquence of his millions. Young men soon began to see that if they would get on in the world they had better waste no time in reading him. Lovable as the rich man always is, we did undoubtedly call him in too often to address the Sunday-school, and let him publish overmuch.

IV

"Mr. Dooley" describes the monetary magnificence of matrimony among the rich.

FROM: A popular humorist's satire on business wealth, 1899.

SPECULATION, industriousness, business skill or whatever the cause, the new age of industry witnessed the rapid increase in number and size of private fortunes. Envious but admiring citizens followed the extravagances of the "idle rich" in newspaper and magazine. Finley Peter Dunne, a newspaper editor and writer of great talent and social perceptiveness, found such matters worthy of comment by his fictional "Martin Dooley"— a loquacious Irish saloon-keeper whom Dunne introduced to the world in the Chicago *Evening Post* in 1893. "Mr. Dooley" soon became a household guide to the fables and foibles of America's business-minded society of the era.

What are special advantages of social commentary expressed in cartoons, dialect caricatures, and similar indirect techniques of communication?

Point out the specific examples of irony and satire employed by Dunne to analyze the society of families of great wealth and the sources of that wealth.

◆ᔈ

"THEY'SE wan thing that always makes me feel sure iv what Hogan calls th' safety iv our dimmycratic institutions," said Mr. Dooley, "an' that's th' intherest th' good people iv New York takes in a weddin' iv th' millyionaires. Anny time a millyionaire condiscinds to enther th' martial state, as Hogan says, an', as Hogan says, make vows to Hyman, which is the Jew god iv marredge, he can fill th' house an' turn people away fr'm th' dure. An' he does. Th' sthreets is crowded. Th' cars can har'ly get through. Th' polis foorce is out, an' hammerin' th' heads iv th' delighted throng. Riprisintatives iv th' free an' inlightened press, th' pollutyem iv our liberties, as Hogan says, bright, intilligent young journalists, iver ready to probe fraud an' sham, disgeesed as waithers, is dashin' madly about, makin' notes on their cuffs. Business is suspinded. They'se no money in Wall Sthreet. It's all at th' sacred scene. Hour be hour, as th' prisints ar-re delivered, th' bank rates go up. Th' Threeasury Departmint has to go on a silver basis, there bein' no goold to mannyfacther into plunks.

"Inside th' house, th' prisints cast a goolden gleam on th' beauchious scene. Th' happy father is seen seated at a table, dictatin' millyion-dollar checks to a stinographer. Th' goold chandeliers is draped with r-ropes iv dimon's an' pearls. Th' hired girl is passin' dhrinks in goolden goblets. Twinty firemen fr'm th' New York Cinthral Railroad is shovellin' di'mon-studded pickle crutes into th' back yard, among th' yachts an' horses. Chansy Depoo enthers an' thrips over a box iv bonds. 'Ar-re these th' holy bonds iv mathrimony?' he says; f'r he is a wild divvle, an' ye can't stop his jokin', avin on solemn occasions.

"Th' soggarth comes in afther a while, carryin' a goold prayer-book, th' gift iv th' Rothscheelds, an' stands behind a small but valyable pree Doo. To th' soft, meelojous chune iv th' Wagner Palace Weddin' March fr'm 'Long Green,' th' groom enthers, simply but ixpinsively attired in government fours, an' fannin' himsilf with a bunch iv first morgedge bonds.

"Th' prayers f'r th' occasion, printed on negotyable paper, is disthributed among th' guests. Th' bride was delayed be th' crowd outside. Women screamed an' waved their handkerchefs, sthrong men cheered

Finley Peter Dunne, *Mr. Dooley in the Hearts of His Countrymen* (Boston: Small, Maynard and Company, 1899), pp. 234–239.

an' wept; an' 'twas not until th' polis had clubbed tin hardy pathrites to death that th' lady cud enther th' house where her fate was to be sealed. But fin'lly she med it; an' th' two happy, happy childher, whose sunshiny youth riprisinted five thousan' miles iv thrack, eight goold mines, wan hundherd millyion dollars' worth iv rollin' stock, an' a majority intherest in th' Chicago stock yards, was r-ready f'r th' nicissary thransfers that wud establish th' com-bination.

"Th' ceremony was brief, but intherestin'. Th' happy father foorced his way through dimon' stomachers; an' they was tears in his eyes as he handed th' clargyman, whose name was Murphy,—but he carried himsilf as well as if he was used to it,—handed him a check f'r tin millyion dollars. I don't blame him. Divvle th' bit! Me own hear-rt is har-rd an' me eyes ar-re dhry, but I'd break down if I had to hand anny wan that much. 'I suppose th' check is good,' says th' clargyman. ' 'Tis certified,' says th' weepin' father. 'Do ye take this check,' says the clargyman, 'to have an' to hold, until some wan parts ye fr'm it?' he says. 'I do,' says th' young man. 'Thin,' says th' clargyman, 'I see no reason why ye shudden't be marrid an' live comfortable,' he says. An' marrid they were, in th' same ol' foolish way that people's been marrid in f'r cinchries. 'Tis a wondher to me th' ceremony ain't changed. Th' time is comin', Hinnissy, whin millyionaires'll not be marrid be Father Murphy, but be th' gov'nors iv th' stock exchange. They'll be put through th' clearin' house, me faith, an' securities'll be issued be th' combination. Twentyyear, goold-secured, four per cint. bonds iv mathrimony! Aha, 'tis a joke that Chansy Depoo might've med!

"Th' crowd outside waited, cheerin' an fightin' the polis. In this here land iv liberty an' akequality, Hinnisy, ivry man is as good as ivry other man, except a polisman. An' it showed how thrue th' people in New York is to th' thraditions iv Jefferson that divvle a wan iv thim 'd move away till th' check 'd been passed fr'm father to son, an' th' important part iv th' sacred ceremony was over. Thin a few iv thim wint home to cook dinner f'r their husbands, who was previnted be their jooties at th' gas-house fr'm attindin' th' function. Th' rest raymained an' see th' two gr-reat fortunes get into their carredge, pursued be th' guests to th' amount iv five hundhred millyions, peltin' thim with seed pearls."

"Sure," said Mr. Hennessy, "meebe 'twasn't as bad as th' pa-apers let on. Ye can't always thrust thim."

"P'rhaps not," said Mr. Dooley. "Th' pa-apers say, 'Two gr-reat fortunes united'; an', if that's it, they didn't need th' sarvices iv a priest, but a lawyer an' a thrust comp'ny. P'rhaps, with all th' certyfied checks, 'twas two rale people that was marrid; an', if that's so, it explains th' prisince iv Father Murphy."

V

A famous scholar defends contemporary "captains of industry" and justifies their fabulous fortunes.

FROM: "The Absurd Effort to Make the World Over," an essay by William Graham Sumner.

WILLIAM GRAHAM SUMNER, an Episcopal minister turned college professor, achieved great renown as the result of his masterly work in social science. A brilliant lecturer, Sumner persuaded Yale students of the virtues of economic *laissez-faire* and of the social appropriateness of Darwinian "natural selection" theory. This scholar had no sympathy for business efforts to influence government on behalf of its own profits, but he rejected social philosophies based on curbing business individualism or free enterprise. He also condemned artificial attempts at social leveling, whether of class status or of wealth, both of which he held to be the fruits of natural abilities to meet competition in the business jungle.

To what legitimate factors does Sumner attribute the accumulation of wealth?

How does he refute the accusation that social danger exists in the ownership by individuals of large fortunes?

IF it is said that there are some persons in our time who have become rapidly and in a great degree rich, it is true; if it is said that large aggregations of wealth in the control of individuals is a social danger, it is not true.

The movement of the industrial organization which has just been described has brought out a great demand for men capable of managing great enterprises. Such have been called "captains of industry." The analogy with military leaders suggested by this name is not misleading. The great leaders in the development of the industrial organization need those talents of executive and administrative skill, power to command, courage, and fortitude, which were formerly called for in military affairs and scarcely anywhere else. The industrial army is also as dependent on its captains as a military body is on its generals. One of the worst features of the existing system is that the employees have a constant risk in their employer. If he is not competent to manage the business with success, they suffer with him. Capital also is dependent on the skill of the captain of industry for the certainty and magnitude of its profits. Under these circumstances there has been a great demand

Albert G. Keller and Maurice R. Davie, eds., *Essays of William Graham Sumner*, I (New Haven: Yale University Press, 1934), 95–99. Reprinted by permission.

for men having the requisite ability for this function. As the organization has advanced, with more impersonal bonds of coherence and wider scope of operations, the value of this functionary has rapidly increased. The possession of the requisite ability is a natural monopoly. Consequently, all the conditions have occurred to give to those who possessed this monopoly excessive and constantly advancing rates of remuneration.

Another social function of the first importance in an intense organization is the solution of those crises in the operation of it which are called the conjuncture of the market. It is through the market that the lines of relation run which preserve the system in harmonious and rhythmical operation. The conjuncture is the momentary sharper misadjustment of supply and demand which indicates that a redistribution of productive effort is called for. The industrial organization needs to be insured against these conjunctures, which, if neglected, produce a crisis and catastrophe; and it needs that they shall be anticipated and guarded against as far as skill and foresight can do it. The rewards of this function for the bankers and capitalists who perform it are very great. The captains of industry and the capitalists who operate on the conjuncture, therefore, if they are successful, win, in these days, great fortunes in a short time. There are no earnings which are more legitimate or for which greater services are rendered to the whole industrial body. The popular notions about this matter really assume that all the wealth accumulated by these classes of persons would be here just the same if they had not existed. They are supposed to have appropriated it out of the common stock. This is so far from being true that, on the contrary, their own wealth would not be but for themselves; and besides that, millions more of wealth, many-fold greater than their own, scattered in the hands of thousands, would not exist but for them. . . . . .

But it is repeated until it has become a commonplace which people are afraid to question, that there is some social danger in the possession of large amounts of wealth by individuals. I ask, why?. . . It would be easy, however, to show what good is done by accumulations of capital in a few hands—that is, under close and direct management, permitting prompt and accurate application; also to tell what harm is done by loose and unfounded denunciations of any social component or any social group. In the recent debates on the income tax the assumption that great accumulations of wealth are socially harmful and ought to be broken down by taxation was treated as an axiom, and we had direct proof how dangerous it is to fit out the average politician with such unverified and unverifiable dogmas as his warrant for his modes of handling the direful tool of taxation.

Great figures are set out as to the magnitude of certain fortunes and the proportionate amount of the national wealth held by a fraction of the population, and eloquent exclamation-points are set against them. If the figures were beyond criticism, what would they prove? . . . Wealth, in itself considered, is only power, like steam, or electricity, or knowledge. The question of its good or ill turns on the question how it will be used. To prove any harm in aggregations of wealth it must be shown that great wealth is, as a rule, in the ordinary course of social affairs, put to a mischievous use. This cannot be shown beyond the very slightest degree, if at all.

VI

A British moralist weighs the justice of the "Gospel of Wealth" against the morality of the fact of wealth.

FROM: The Rev. Hugh Price Hughes' magazine article, "Irresponsible Wealth," 1890.

IF a sense of guilt seldom troubled the accumulators of a great business fortune, the ethical issue of how to use it was more troublesome. Andrew Carnegie, one of the more literate and socially conscious of the tycoons, attempted to settle the issue in a famous essay of 1889, "The Gospel of Wealth." To leave a fortune for charitable distribution after death was wasteful and irresponsible, argued Carnegie. But bequeathing it to one's children might debilitate their characters. Therefore, the enormously affluent steelmaster concluded that rich men should act as trustees of their own wealth, disposing of it carefully by way of socially creative benefactions during their own lifetime. However, worried moralists at home and abroad—while admiring Carnegie's gifts of some $350,-000,000—still questioned the morality of huge fortunes *per se*, regardless of philanthropies.

Why does the otherwise sympathetic Rev. Hughes brand Carnegie as "an anti-Christian phenomenon, a social monstrosity, and a grave political peril"?

How does Hughes refute Sumner's argument regarding the nature of the process by which great fortunes are accumulated?

＆

I AM quite unable to let off Mr. Carnegie in the pleasant and approving way in which Mr. Gladstone dismisses him. I have always believed that Mr. Carnegie is personally a most estimable and generous man, who sets a splendid example to the unhappy class to which he belongs, and is entirely worthy of Mr. Gladstone's praise. But when I contemplate him as the representative of a particular class of million-

The Rev. Hugh Price Hughes, cited in "Irresponsible Wealth," *Nineteenth Century*, 28 (December, 1890), 891–892, 895.

aires, I am forced to say, with all personal respect, and without holding him in the least responsible for his unfortunate circumstances, that he is an anti-Christian phenomenon, a social monstrosity, and a grave political peril. Mr. Gladstone tells us that Mr. Carnegie is of opinion that 'rank, as it exists among us, is a widely demoralising power.' I am bound to say that an American millionaire ironmaster, the artificial product of such measures as the McKinley Bill, is a far greater 'demoralising power.' In a really Christian country—that is to say, in a community reconstructed upon a Christian basis—a millionaire would be an economic impossibility. Jesus Christ distinctly prohibited the accumulation of wealth. I know that expositors can prove anything, and that theologians can explain away anything. But if 'Lay not up for yourselves treasures upon the earth' does not forbid the accumulation of wealth, the New Testament was written on Talleyrand's principle and was intended to 'conceal thought.' No one now argues that millionaires are needed to carry out great public works like the Bridgewater Canal, because modern joint-stock enterprise, and the ever-increasing activity of the State, make us entirely independent of millionaires, and, indeed, capable of enterprises which no millionaire could attempt. They have now no beneficent *raison d'être*. They are the unnatural product of artificial social regulations. They flourish portentously in the unhealthy forcing-house of Protection, but everything else fades and dies beside them. We prefer the fresh air. Millionaires at one end of the scale involve paupers at the other end, and even so excellent a man as Mr. Carnegie is too dear at that price. Whatever may be thought of Mr. Henry George's doctrines and deductions, no one can deny that his facts are indisputable, and that Mr. Carnegie's 'progress' is accompanied by the growing 'poverty' of his less fortunate fellow-countrymen. I say 'less fortunate' because I am sure Mr. Carnegie is much too sensible a man to suppose for a moment that his vast fortune represents a proportionate superiority over the rest of his fellow citizens, or even over those who combined to create his fortune. Thanks to unrestricted competition and the tariff, he has pocketed much more than his equitable share of the joint product of Labour and Capital. If he thinks that he has made this great pile, so to speak off his own bat, let him set up business on a solitary island, and see how much he can net annually without the co-operation of 'his twenty thousand men' and the ceaseless bounties of the vanishing Republican majority in Congress.

In no sense whatever is a Pennsylvania millionaire ironmaster a natural, and therefore an inevitable, product. There is a total fallacy at the very foundation of Mr. Carnegie's argument. He assumes that millionaires are necessary results of modern industrial enterprise, and that consequently the only question ethical writers can discuss is the best

way of enabling these unfortunate persons to get honestly and bene-
ficently rid of their superfluous wealth. But there is a much more important prior question—how to save them from the calamity of finding
themselves the possessors of a huge fortune which is full of most perilous
temptation, both to themselves and to their children. . . . I am greatly surprised that Mr. Gladstone quotes, without demur or protest, Mr. Carnegie's extraordinary delusion that he is a 'normal process,' 'an imperative
condition,' and an 'essential condition of modern society.' Nothing of
the sort. Free trade, free land, and a progressive income tax would relieve him of the greater part of his anxious financial responsibilities, and
such a death-duty as he himself wisely advocates would complete the
emancipation of his children. We must not for a moment forget that all
the evils of excessive wealth which Mr. Carnegie laments, and from
which he nobly desires to protect his children, are artificial and not
necessary evils. . . . . .

. . . Millionaires will continue to be manufactured, and manufactured, as Mr. Gladstone reminds us, in ever-increasing numbers. For
them, when they are already in existence, Mr. Carnegie's advice is truly
a 'gospel'; and all the friends of humanity will greatly rejoice that this
most timely 'gospel' has now been preached by the most eloquent and
persuasive of living voices. If Mr. Gladstone would only persuade the
wealthy of the British Empire and the United States to act upon the
principles of Mr. Carnegie's 'gospel,' his latest service to mankind would
vie with the very greatest in his unparalleled career. It is to be feared
that many of our wealthy and privileged classes are living in a fool's
paradise, and have no conception of the gravity of the social problem.

VII

*Business needs generate demands for practical and
technical instruction to supplement outdated "gentlemanly education."*

FROM: A businessman's answer to an inquiry by a U.S. Commissioner of
Education, 1870.

THE rapid expansion of business and industry brought new demands
for technical schools and the substitution of "practical" subjects for the
"useless" holdovers from the old classical curriculum. The new high
schools, especially, were criticized for their slow introduction of courses
in drawing, the manual arts, and technical subjects. Henry Carey Baird,
an industrial publisher of Philadelphia, stated the case for more practical
education very plainly when responding in 1870 to a questionnaire from
the United States Bureau of Education.

If Baird's view was typical, what was the "business ideal" of the means and goals of a successful education?

Is there any evidence that business interests today exercise any significant influence over school curricula or methods? Are there other types of influence today?

QUESTION 5. Does this and still further acquisitions of knowledge increase the capacity of the workingman to meet the exigency of his labor by new methods or in improvements in implements or machinery; and if so, how much does this inventive skill add to the power of producing wealth?—Answers. (a) Here is a point, in my opinion, for a full, and even hot, controversy. Too much education of a certain sort, such as Greek, Latin, French, German, and especially book-keeping, to a person of humble antecedents, is utterly demoralizing in nine cases out ten, and is productive of an army of mean-spirited "gentlemen," who are above what is called "a trade," and who are only content to follow some such occupation as that of standing behind a counter, and selling silks, gloves, bobbins, or laces, or to "keep books." After a good deal of observation, and more especially during [the] thirteen years past that I have been a pretty close student of social science, I have arrived at the conclusion that our system of education, as furnished by law, when it goes beyond what in Pennsylvania is called a grammar school, is vicious in the extreme—productive of more evil than good. Were the power lodged with me, no boy or girl should be educated at the public expense beyond what he or she could obtain at a grammar school, except for some useful occupation. "The high school" of to-day must, as I believe, under an enlightened system, be supplanted by *the technical school,* with possibly "shops" connected with it. A boy who graduates at the Philadelphia High School is not provided with the means of earning a living at any occupation in which he is likely to engage, except book-keeping, teaching, or shop-keeping, or tending, and possibly law, or theology. We are manufacturing too many "gentlemen" and "ladies," so called, and demoralization is the result. What good do Greek, Latin, French, German, &c., do to a counter-skipper in a retail dry goods shop? Advertise tomorrow in "The Public Ledger" for a book-keeper, and 100 or more answers would come in 24 hours. I did so two or three years since, and at 2 p.m. of the first day I had received 55 replies, and abandoned the search, or rather the Ledger letter-box. The brightest boy who has graduated at the high school for years, was at the head of his classes from his entry into

"The Relations of Education and Labor," *Report of the Commissioner of Education Made to the Secretary of the Interior for the Year 1870* (Washington: Government Printing Office, 1870), p. 459.

the preliminary schools, throughout his course in the high school, and up to the final hour, is now a clerk in a printing office in this city. Such a boy—this boy, and I know him well—has the capacity to work himself up to the head of the largest mining operation, the greatest iron works, or the grandest consolidated railroad monopoly in the country, had he ever been put upon the track, but, thanks to our barbarous system of public education, he will probably finish his career as a clerk, or at best as a successful buyer and seller of merchandise. Were I in the position of General Eaton, I would commence a crusade against the ignorance of our educators, and I would bring the people to a proper recognition of *"what knowledge is most worth,"* as Herbert Spencer has so well and truly sung, or these ignoramuses should have the satisfaction of lopping off my official head.

VIII

Thorstein Veblen berates the "pecuniary values" of business-influenced American higher education.

FROM: Thorstein Veblen's *The Higher Learning in America,* 1918.

A MAJOR foe of the growing business influence on the American way of life was the economist and social analyst Thorstein Veblen, Wisconsin-born son of Norwegian immigrants. An intellectual maverick whose unorthodox conduct and social ideas gave him little popularity among college administrators, Veblen carried on a one-man war against what he believed to be the business perversion of major social organizations, including the universities. Veblen distinguished business from industry, and argued that the pecuniary motives of business brought inefficiency and hypocrisy into those institutions in which it became involved.

What was the nature of the business influence on education as it was described by Veblen?

Are Veblen's charges in any significant degree true of the situation in higher education in our own time?

◆◇

BUSINESS principles take effect in academic affairs most simply, obviously and avowably in the way of a business-like administration of the scholastic routine; where they lead immediately to a bureaucratic organization and a system of scholastic accountancy. . . . The large American schools are primarily undergraduate establishments,—with negligible exceptions; and under these current American conditions, of excessive numbers, such a centralized and bureaucratic administration appears to be indispensable for the adequate control of immature and reluctant students; at the same time, such an organization conduces to an excessive size. The immediate and visible effect of such a large and centralized administrative machinery is, on the whole, detrimental to scholarship, even in the undergraduate work; though it need not be so in all respects and unequivocally, so far as regards that routine training that is embodied in the undergraduate curriculum. But it is at least a necessary evil in any school that is of so considerable a size as to preclude substantially all close or cordial personal relations between the teachers and each of these immature pupils under their charge, as, again, is commonly the case with these American undergraduate establishments. Such a system of authoritative control, standardization, gradation, accountancy, classification, credits and penalties, will necessarily be drawn on stricter lines the more the school takes on the character of a house of correction or a penal settlement; in which the irresponsible inmates are to be held to a round of distasteful tasks and restrained from (conventionally) excessive irregularities of conduct. At the same time this recourse to such coercive control and standardization of tasks has unavoidably given the schools something of the character of a penal settlement.

As intimated above, the ideal of efficiency by force of which a large-scale centralized organization commends itself in these premises is that pattern of shrewd management whereby a large business concern makes money. The underlying business-like presumption accordingly appears to be that learning is a merchantable commodity, to be produced on a piece-rate plan, rated, bought and sold by standard units, measured, counted and reduced to staple equivalence by impersonal, mechanical tests. In all its bearings the work is hereby reduced to a mechanistic, statistical consistency, with numerical standards and units; which conduces to perfunctory and mediocre work throughout, and acts to deter both students and teachers from a free pursuit of knowledge, as contrasted with the pursuit of academic credits. So far as this mechanistic system goes freely into effect it leads to a substitution of salesmanlike proficiency—a balancing of bargains in staple credits—in the place of scientific capacity and addiction to study.

The salesmanlike abilities and the men of affairs that so are drawn into the academic personnel are, presumably, somewhat under grade in their kind; since the pecuniary inducement offered by the schools is rather low as compared with the remuneration for office work of a similar character in the common run of business occupations, and since businesslike employés of this kind may fairly be presumed to go unreservedly to the highest bidder. Yet these more unscholarly members of the staff will necessarily be assigned the more responsible and discretionary positions in the academic organization; since under such a scheme of standardization, accountancy and control, the school becomes primarily a bureaucratic organization, and the first and unremitting duties of the staff are those of official management and accountancy. The further qualifications requisite in the members of the academic staff will be such as make for vendibility,—volubility, tactful affrontery, conspicuous conformity to the popular taste in all matters of opinion, usage and conventions.

The need of such a businesslike organization asserts itself in somewhat the same degree in which the academic policy is guided by considerations of magnitude and statistical renown; and this in turn is somewhat closely correlated with the extent of discretionary power exercised by the captain of erudition placed in control. At the same time, by provocation of the facilities which it offers for making an impressive demonstration, such bureaucratic organization will lead the university management to bend its energies with somewhat more singleness to the parade of magnitude and statistical gains. It also, and in the same connection, provokes to a persistent and detailed surveillance and direction of the work and manner of life of the academic staff, and so it acts to shut off initiative of any kind in the work done.

Intimately bound up with this bureaucratic officialism and accountancy, and working consistently to a similar outcome, is the predilection for "practical efficiency"—that is to say, for pecuniary success —prevalent in the American community. . . .

It appears, then, that the intrusion of business principles in the universities goes to weaken and retard the pursuit of learning, and therefore to defeat the ends for which a university is maintained. This result follows, primarily, from the substitution of impersonal, mechanical relations, standards and tests, in the place of personal conference, guidance and association between teachers and students; as also from the imposition of a mechanically standardized routine upon the members of the staff, whereby any disinterested preoccupation with scholarly or scientific inquiry is thrown into the background and falls into abeyance. Few if any who are competent to speak in these premises will question that such has been the outcome. To offset against this work of mutilation and retardation there are certain gains in expedition, and in the volume of traffic that can be carried by any given equipment and corps of employés. Particularly will there be a gain in the statistical showing, both as regards the volume of instruction offered, and probably also as regards the enrolment; since accountancy creates statistics and its absence does not.

Such increased enrolment as may be due to businesslike management and methods is an increase of undergraduate enrolment. The net effect as regards the graduate enrolment—apart from any vocational instruction that may euphemistically be scheduled as "graduate"—is in all probability rather a decrease than an increase. Through indoctrination with utilitarian (pecuniary) ideals of earning and spending, as well as by engendering spendthrift and sportsmanlike habits, such a businesslike management diverts the undergraduate students from going in for the disinterested pursuit of knowledge, and so from entering on what is properly university work; as witness the relatively slight proportion of graduate students—outside of the professional schools—who come up from the excessively large undergraduate departments of the more expansive universities, as contrasted with the number of those who come into university work from the smaller and less businesslike colleges.

IX

"Mr. Dooley" explains how the self-made man achieves respectability in the world of the higher culture.

FROM: "Art Patronage," a parody by Finley Peter Dunne, 1902.

In the Italian Renaissance the patronage of popes and princes provided an encouraging subsidy for art, music, and letters. During the age of business influence, princes of the purse found it important to ego and social position that their newly-won wealth find concrete expression in flamboyant mansions, occasional monuments to themselves, and costly ventures in fine art and artifacts. Even where their intentions were worthy and generous, enthusiasm and a lack of aesthetic sophistication too often resulted in crudities and bad taste. "Mr. Dooley," saloon-keeper and social commentator, delightfully parodied the raiding expeditions of the wealthy in quest of Old World masterpieces and public esteem.

Trace the steps by which a man of ripening fortune progressed toward the status of "connysoor" of art.

To what degree were the cultural activities of men of wealth in the Gilded Age and its aftermath both helpful and harmful to the development of native American standards in aesthetic matters?

❧

"YE SEE, Hinnissy, whin a man gets hold iv a large hatful iv money, wan iv th' first things he does is to buy some art. Up to th' time whin th' top blew off th' stock market, he bought his art out iv th' front

Finley Peter Dunne, *Observations by Mr. Dooley* (New York: R. H. Russell, 1902), pp. 41–46.

window iv a news an' station'ry shop or had it put in be th' paperhanger.
He took th' Sundah pa-apers that ar-re a gr-reat help if ye're collectin'
art, an' he had some pitchers iv fruit that looks nachral enough to ate,
d'ye mind, a paintin' iv a deer like th' wan he shot at in th' Manotowish
counthry in Eighty-eight, an' a livin' likeness iv a Lake Supeeryor white
fish on a silver plate. That was th' peryod, mind ye, whin th' iron dogs
howled on his lawn an' people come miles an' miles fr to see a grotto
made out iv relics iv th' Chicago fire.

"Manetime his daughter was illustratin' suspinders an' illuminatin'
china plates an' becomin' artistic an' afther awhile whin th' time come
that he had to keep a man at th' dure to sweep out th' small bills, she
give him a good push to'rd betther things. Besides, his pardner down th'
sthreet had begun collectin' pitchers, an' ivry time he wint abroad th'
mannyfacthrers iv picture frames bought new autymobills fr th' Champs
All Easy. So 'twas a soft matther fr our frind Higbie to be persuaded
that he ought to be a pathron iv art, an' he wint abroad detarmined to
buy a bunch iv chromos that'd make people come out iv th' gallery iv
his pardner down th' sthreet stiflin' their laughter in their hands.

"Now ye'd think seein' that he made his money in this counthry,
he'd pathronize American art. Ye'd believe he'd sind wurrd down to his
agent fr to secure forty feet iv Evansville be moonlight an' be con-tint.
But he don't.

"Ye don't catch Higbie changin' iv anny iv his dividends on domestic finished art. He jumps on a boat an' goes sthraight acrost to th' cen-
thral deepo. The first thing he gets is a porthrait iv himsilf be wan iv
th' gr-reat modhren masthers, Sargent be name. This here Sargent, Hogan
tells me, used to live in this counthry, an' faith, if he'd stayed here ye
might see him to-day on a stagin'. But he had a mind in his head an'
he tore off fr Europe th' way a duck hunter goes fr a rice swamp.
Afther awhile, Higbie shows up, an' says he: 'I'm Higbie iv th' Non-
Adhesive Consolidated Glue Company,' he says. 'Can ye do me?' 'I can
an' will,' says Sargent. 'I'll do ye good. How much have ye got?' he says.
'Get some more an' come around,' he says. An' Higbie puts on his
Prince Albert coat an' laves it open so that ye can see his watch charm
—th' crown iv Poland with th' Kohinoor in th' top iv it—an' me frind
Sargent does him brown an' red. He don't give him th' pitcher iv coorse.
If ye have ye'er porthrait painted be a gr-reat painther, it's ye'er porthrait but 'tis his pitcher, an' he keeps it till ye don't look that way
anny more. So Higbie's porthrait is hung up in a gallery an' th' doctors
bring people to see it that ar-re sufferin' fr'm narvous dyspepsia to cheer
thim up. Th' pa-apers says 'tis fine. 'Number 108 shows Sargent at his
best. There is the same marvellous ticknick that th' great master dis-
played in his cillybrated take-off on Mrs. Maenheimer in last year's gal-

lery. Th' skill an' ease with which th' painther has made a monkey iv his victim are beyond praise. Sargent has torn th' sordid heart out iv th' wretched crather an' exposed it to th' wurruld. Th' wicked, ugly little eyes, th' crooked nose, th' huge graspin' hands, tell th' story iv this miscreant's character as completely as if they were written in so manny wurruds, while th' artist, with wondherful malice, has painted onto th' face a smile iv sickenin' silf-complacency that is positively disgustin'. No artist iv our day has succeeded so well in showin' up th' maneness iv th' people he has mugged. We ondershtand that th' atrocious Higbie paid wan hundherd thousan' dollars f'r this comic valentine. It is worth th' money to ivrybody but him.'

"But Higbie don't see th' pa-aper. He's over in Paris. Th' chimes are rung, bonefires are lighted in th' sthreets an' th' Pannyma Comp'ny declares a dividend whin he enters th' city. They'se such a demand f'r paint that th' supply runs out an' manny gr-reat imprishonist pitcher facthries is foorced to use bluein'. Higbie ordhers paintin's be th' ton, th' runnin' foot, th' foot pound, th' car load. He insthructs th' pitcher facthries to wurruk night an' day till his artistic sowl is satisfied. We follow his coorse in th' pa-apers. 'Th' cillybrated Gainsborough that niver wud be missed has been captured be Misther Higbie, th' American millyionaire. Th' price paid is said to be wan hundherd thousan' dollars. Th' pitcher riprisints a lady in a large hat fondlin' a cow. It is wan iv th' finest Gainsboroughs painted be th' Gainsborough Mannyfacthrin' comp'ny iv Manchester. At th' last public sale, it was sold f'r thirty dollars. Misther Higbie has also purchased th' cillybrated Schmartzmeister Boogooroo, wan iv th' mos' horrible examples iv this delightful painther's style. He is now negotyatin' with th' well-known dealer Moosoo Mortheimer f'r th' intire output iv th' Barabazah School. Yisterdah in a call on th' janial dealer, th' name iv th' cillybrated painther Mooney was mintioned. "How manny pitchers has he painted?" "Four hundherd and forty-three thousan' at ilivin o'clock to-day," says th' dealer. "But four hundherd thousan' iv thim ar-re in America." "Get th' r-rest iv thim f'r me," says th' connysoor. "What did ye say th' gintleman's name was? . . .

"An' whin he comes home, he hangs thim in his house, so that his frinds can't turn around without takin' off a pasthral scene on their coats, an' he pastes th' price on th' frame, an' whin he dies, he laves his pitcher to some definceless art museum. An' there ye ar-re. . . . . .

"Well," said Mr. Hennessy, "perhaps a bum Europeen pitcher is betther thin a good American pitcher."

"Perhaps so," said Mr. Dooley. "I think it is so. Annyhow, no matther how bad a painther he is, annywan that can get money out iv an American millyionaire is an artist an' desarves it. There's th' rale art. I wish it was taught in th' schools. I'd like to see an exhibition at th'

Museum with 'Check iv American Gintleman, dhrawn fr'm life,' hung on th' wall."

X

How to get an appropriation for a new railroad: Mark Twain parodies the corrupt liaison between business and politics.

FROM: *The Gilded Age,* a novel about business and politics, 1873.

WHEN Mark Twain and lawyer-editor Charles Dudley Warner collaborated on the novel *The Gilded Age,* they determined to expose the materialism of American society, and incidentally provided historians with an apt label for the post-Civil War period. Colonel Beriah Sellers, the novel's chief character, epitomizes the perennial business optimism and fever for speculation during the era. Magnificent dreams, enormous private projects, and lush profits seemed very American in their boldness and scope. But the novel also satirized the cynical cooperation of business and politics in a supposedly *laissez-faire* era. Thus, young Harry Brierly, an engineer employed on one of Colonel Seller's vaster speculations (a railroad designed mostly to run a gravy train rather than the conventional kind) discovered that business associations with government could be uncommonly costly.

In what ways did the very rapid industrial and territorial expansion of the postwar years encourage and perhaps necessitate rampant speculation?

Present evidence from the selection charging that the love of money corrupted much of contemporary American society besides government.

HE called, with official importance in his mien, at No. — Wall Street, where a great gilt sign betokened the presence of the headquarters of the "Columbus River Slackwater Navigation Company." He entered and gave a dressy porter his card, and was requested to wait a moment in a sort of anteroom. The porter returned in a minute, and asked whom he would like to see?

"The president of the company, of course."

"He is busy with some gentlemen, sir; says he will be done with them directly."

That a copper-plate card with "Engineer-in-Chief" on it should be received with such tranquillity as this, annoyed Mr. Brierly not a little. But he had to submit. Indeed, his annoyance had time to augment a

Samuel Clemens [Mark Twain] and Charles Dudley Warner, *The Gilded Age: A Tale of Today* (Hartford: American Publishing Company, 1874), pp. 250–257, 260–261.

good deal; for he was allowed to cool his heels a full half-hour in the anteroom before those gentlemen emerged and he was ushered into the presence. He found a stately dignitary occupying a very official chair behind a long green morocco-covered table, in a room sumptuously carpeted and furnished, and well garnished with pictures.

"Good morning, sir; take a seat—take a seat."

"Thank you, sir," said Harry, throwing as much chill into his manner as his ruffled dignity prompted.

"We perceive by your reports and the reports of the chief superintendent, that you have been making gratifying progress with the work. We are all very much pleased."

"Indeed? We did not discover it from your letters—which we have not received; nor by the treatment our drafts have met with—which were not honored; nor by the reception of any part of the appropriation, no part of it having come to hand."

"Why, my dear Mr. Brierly, there must be some mistake. I am sure we wrote you and also Mr. Sellers, recently—when my clerk comes he will show copies—letters informing you of the ten per cent. assessment."

"Oh, certainly, we got *those* letters. But what we wanted was money to carry on the work—money to pay the men."

"Certainly, certainly—true enough—but we credited you both for a large part of your assessments—I am sure that was in our letters."

"Of course that was in—I remember that."

"Ah, very well, then. Now we begin to understand each other."

"Well, I don't see that we do. There's two months' wages due the men, and—"

"How? Haven't you paid the men?"

"Paid them! How are we going to pay them when you don't honor our drafts?"

"Why, my *dear* sir, I cannot see how you can find any fault with us. I am sure we have acted in a perfectly straightforward business way. Now let us look at the thing a moment. You subscribed for one hundred shares of the capital stock, at one thousand dollars a share, I believe?"

"Yes, sir, I did."

"And Mr. Sellers took a like amount?"

"Yes, sir."

"Very well. No concern can get along without money. We levied a ten per cent. assessment. It was the original understanding that you and Mr. Sellers were to have the positions you now hold, with salaries of six hundred dollars a month each, while in active service. You were duly elected to these places, and you accepted them. Am I right?"

"Certainly."

"Very well. You were given your instructions and put to work. By your reports it appears that you have expended the sum of $9,640 upon the said work. Two months' salary to you two officers amounts altogether to $2,400—about one-eighth of your ten per cent. assessment, you see; which leaves you in debt to the company for the other seven-eighths of the assessment—*viz.*, something over $8,000 apiece. Now, instead of requiring you to forward this aggregate of $16,000 or $17,000 to New York, the company voted unanimously to let you pay it over to the contractors, laborers from time to time, and give you credit on the books for it. And they did it without a murmur, too, for they were pleased with the progress you had made, and were glad to pay you that little compliment—and a very neat one it was, too, I am sure. The work you did fell short of $10,000, a trifle. Let me see—$9,640 from $20,000—salary $2,400 added—ah, yes, the balance due the company from yourself and Mr. Sellers is $7,960, which I will take the responsibility of allowing to stand for the present, unless you prefer to draw a check now, and thus—"

"Confound it, do you mean to say that instead of the company owing us $2,400, we owe the company $7,960?"

"Well, yes."

"And that we owe the men and the contractors nearly ten thousand dollars besides?"

"Owe them! Oh bless my soul, you can't mean that you have not paid these people?"

"But I *do* mean it!"

The president rose and walked the floor like a man in bodily pain. His brows contracted, he put his hand up and clasped his forehead, and kept saying, "Oh, it is too bad, too bad, too bad! Oh, it is bound to be found out—nothing can prevent it—nothing!"

Then he threw himself into his chair and said:

"My dear Mr. Bryerson, this is dreadful—perfectly dreadful. It will be found out. It is bound to tarnish the good name of the company; our credit will be seriously, most seriously impaired. How could you be so thoughtless—the men ought to have been paid though it beggered us all!"

"They ought, ought they? Then why the devil—my name is not Bryerson by the way—why the mischief didn't the compa— why what in the nation ever became of the appropriation? Where *is* that appropriation?—if a stockholder may make so bold as to ask."

"The appropriation?—that paltry two hundred thousand dollars, do you mean?"

"Of course—but I didn't know that two hundred thousand dollars was so very paltry. Though I grant, of course, that it is not a large sum, strictly speaking. But where is it?"

"My dear sir, you surprise me. You surely cannot have had a large acquaintance with this sort of thing. Otherwise you would not have expected much of a result from a mere *initial* appropriation like that. It was never intended for anything but a mere nest-egg for the future and *real* appropriations to cluster around."

"Indeed? Well, was it a myth, or was it a reality? Whatever become of it?"

"Why the matter is simple enough. A Congressional appropriation costs money. Just reflect, for instance. A majority of the House committee, say $10,000 apiece—$40,000; a majority of the Senate committee, the same each—say $40,000; a little extra to one or two chairmen of one or two such committees, say $10,000 each—$20,000; and there's $100,000 of the money gone, to begin with. Then, seven male lobbyists, at $3,000 each—$21,000; one female lobbyist, $10,000; a high moral Congressman or Senator here and there—the high moral ones cost more, because they give tone to a measure—say ten of these at $3,000 each, is $30,000; then a lot of small-fry country members who won't vote for anything whatever without pay—say twenty at $500 apiece, is $10,000 altogether; a lot of dinners to members—say $10,000 altogether; lot of jim-cracks for Congressmen's wives and children—those go a long way—you can't spend too much money in that line—well, those things cost in a lump, say $10,000—along there somewhere;—and then comes your printed documents—your maps, your tinted engravings, your pamphlets, your illuminated show-cards, your advertisements in a hundred and fifty papers at ever so much a line—because you've *got* to keep the papers all right or you are gone up, you know. Oh, my dear sir, printing bills are destruction itself. Ours, so far amount to—let me see—10; 52; 22; 13;—and then there's 11; 14; 33—well, never mind the details, the total in clean numbers foots up $118,254.42 thus far!"

"What!"

"Oh, yes indeed. Printing's no bagatelle, I can tell you. And then there's your contributions, as a company, to Chicago fires and Boston fires, and orphan asylums and all that sort of thing—head the list, you see, with the company's full name and a thousand dollars set opposite —great card, sir—one of the finest advertisements in the world—the preachers mention it in the pulpit when it's a religious charity—one of the happiest advertisements in the world is your benevolent donation. Ours have amounted to sixteen thousand dollars and some cents up to this time."

"Good heavens!"

"Oh, yes. Perhaps the biggest thing we've done in the advertising line was to get an officer of the U.S. government, of perfectly Himalayan official altitude, to write up our little internal improvement for a religious paper of enormous circulation—I tell you, that makes our bonds go handsomely among the pious poor. Your religious paper is by far the best vehicle for a thing of this kind, because they'll 'lead' your article and put it right in the midst of the reading-matter; and if it's got a few Scripture quotations in it, and some temperance platitudes, and a bit of gush here and there about Sunday-schools, and a sentimental snuffle now and then about 'God's precious ones, the honest hard-handed poor,' it works the nation like a charm, my dear sir, and never a man suspects that it is an advertisement; but your secular paper sticks you right into the advertising columns and of course you don't take a trick. Gives me a religious paper to advertise in, every time; and if you'll just look at their advertising pages, you'll observe that other people think a good deal as I do—especially people who have got little financial schemes to make everybody rich with. Of course, I mean your great big metropolitan religious papers that know how to serve God and make money at the same time—that's your sort, sir, that's your sort—a religious paper that isn't run to make money is no use to *us,* as an advertising medium—no use to anybody in our line of business. I guess our next best dodge was sending a pleasure trip of newspaper reporters out to Napoleon. Never paid them a cent; just filled them up with champagne and the fat of the land, put pen, ink, and paper before them while they were red-hot, and bless your soul when you come to read their letters you'd have supposed they'd been to heaven. And if a sentimental squeamishness held one or two of them back from taking a less rosy view of Napoleon, our hospitalities tied his tongue, at least, and he said nothing at all and so did us no harm. Let me see—have I stated all the expenses I've been at? No, I was near forgetting one or two items. There's your official salaries—you can't get good men for nothing. Salaries cost pretty lively. And then there's your big high-sounding millionaire names stuck into your advertisements as stockholders—another card, that—and they *are* stockholders, too, but you have to *give* them the stock and non-assessable at that—so they're an expensive lot. Very, very expensive thing, take it all around, is a big internal-improvement concern—but you see that yourself, Mr. Bryerson—you see that, yourself, sir." . . . . .

"Which leaves us in debt some $25,000 at this moment. Salaries of some officers are still going on; also printing and advertising. Next month will show a state of things!"

"And then—burst up, I suppose?"

"By no means. Levy another assessment."

"Oh, I see. That's dismal."

"By no means."

"Why isn't it? What's the road out?"

"Another appropriation, don't you see?"

"Bother the appropriations. They cost more than they come to."

"Not the next one. We'll call for half a million—get it and go for a million the very next month."

The president smiled, and patted his secret letters affectionately. He said:

"All these people are in the next Congress. We shan't have to pay them a cent. And what is more, they will work like beavers for us—perhaps it might be to their advantage."

Harry reflected profoundly a while. Then he said:

"We send many missionaries to lift up the benighted races of other lands. How much cheaper and better it would be if those people could only come here and drink of our civilization at its fountainhead."

"I perfectly agree with you, Mr. Beverly. Must you go? Well, good morning. Look in, when you are passing; and whenever I can give you any information about our affairs and prospects, I shall be glad to do it."

FOR FURTHER THOUGHT

Are the interrelationships between business and American society significantly different today from those characteristic of the Gilded Age? Explain the reasons for any differences.

Why should historians have such varying opinions of the nature of the business society in the half-century following the Civil War? What precautions does this suggest in regard to the character and practice of historical interpretation?

In order fully and fairly to understand the nature of American society during the period 1865–1914 what other factors than the influence of business must be considered?

2. The Maturing of Industry, 1865-1921

WITHIN a generation of Lee's surrender at Appomattox, the United States had become the world's foremost industrial power. But most of the ingredients needed to transform America from a collection of simple, primarily rural, agrarian communities into a complex, urban, industrial society were at hand long before the firing on Fort Sumter. The United States possessed a vast area filled with an immense quantity and variety of natural resources. Its rich soils produced abundant foodstuffs and raw materials. A dominant and prospering middle class, which accepted change and believed in progress, stood ready to back up its faith by investing heavily in promising new production techniques. A rapidly expanding population provided an adequate, if not plentiful, labor supply and constituted a growing market for the products that flowed from the nation's factories.

American industrialization had gone through a lengthy gestation period before the trauma of Civil War—reaching back, some historians would say, at least to the Embargo Act of 1807 (see Volume I, Chapter Ten). During that long period, its basic structure and many of its institutions were laid down. It did not, however, fully take on its modern form or develop its characteristic features—immense scale of operation, concentration of industries into relatively few firms, and increasing managerial control—until after the Civil War.

Several economic forces united to bring about the scale of modern American enterprise. The size and appetite of the market to be served, for example, made ever larger businesses both possible and necessary. That market, in turn, was created by the transportation network of canals, and then railroads, which took shape in the middle decades of the nineteenth century, linking together the nation's many isolated local and regional markets and fashioning them into the world's largest self-contained producing-consuming unit.

That some businesses thrived and grew great in this market while others shriveled and died was usually because the competitive system rewarded efficiency. But as some firms succeeded and expanded their operations the process speeded up. Cost benefits, which economists call "economies of scale," began to accrue to the larger firms. They found that raw materials were cheaper when purchased by wholesale lots, that shipping by the trainload was less expensive than shipping by the box or carload, and that constant, full-time production was less costly per unit than intermittent production. Large-scale operations also made possible experimentation with new, more complex labor-saving machines and mass production techniques, including, eventually, the moving assembly line.

Big business was possible only with large-scale investment to finance it. The characteristic business forms of the pre-industrial era (the single proprietorship and the partnership) were incapable of raising the funds needed for ever bigger businesses. Industrialists gradually turned to another business form, the corporation, whose chief advantage was its ability to draw together capital from widely scattered sources and to place it under the management of a relatively few men. Because of this capability, corporations, although unpopular in early America, had been used to perform a few quasi-public functions such as bridge and turnpike construction and banking. The great need, after 1850, for masses of capital for large-scale industry led to an expanded use of the corporate form for wholly private, profit-seeking ventures.

The evolution of the modern corporation greatly advanced the concentration of managerial control over American big business. An increasing number of stockholders, coupled with the use of proxy voting, shifted actual (as opposed to theoretical) control of many corporations from the stockholders to the boards of directors. By the twentieth century, control shifted to the hired managers in many corporations. The need for technical expertise to reach competent decisions in modern big businesses induced the directors to elect managers to the boards. Corporations dominated by self-perpetuating oligarchies of director-managers tended to operate with a minimum of friction. There was no one to oppose the goals set and approved by the managers who now sat on the boards of directors and who collected and voted the proxies of the stockholders. In the process, corporations became less democratic, and the policies of the technician-directors were no longer subjected to review by laymen representing the shareholding owners. Although the interests of the managers and the owners often coincided, they also frequently clashed—especially with respect to the disposal of company earnings [I].

While the growth of little firms into large ones tended to reduce the number of competitors within a field, it frequently intensified the competition among those remaining. The greater resources of those larger firms made their price wars more protracted and ultimately ruinous than the struggle between small firms. However much economists of that era hailed competition as the fountain of all economic progress, practical businessmen found it chaotic, demoralizing, and wasteful, and sought ways to eliminate it [II].

To bring order from the anarchy of "cut-throat" competition among themselves, industrial leaders experimented with various combinations: pools [III], syndicates, trusts [IV], mergers, holding companies, and interlocking boards of directors. A climax to the movement started about the turn of the century when investment bankers began to promote supermergers among their larger clients. Vigorous competition between two or more of a bank's customers not only posed a threat to the firms involved; it also endangered the bank's investments. To prevent this, financiers urged consolidation. In return for financing these enormous ventures, the bankers asked for a seat on the board of the new combine. This single director, speaking for the combine's source of credit, frequently determined policy. Thus bankers, who often lacked industrial competence and whose chief concern was the safety of their investment, wrested control from the more adventuresome industrialists, ushering in the age of finance capitalism.

As early as the 1880s, the consolidation movement occasionally produced a monopoly (a single firm controlling an entire industry), or, as was more frequent, an oligopoly (a few large firms dominating a whole field). From the point of view of those who combined, the results were beneficial: reduced competition, greater market predictability, output geared to anticipated demand, and more general stability. Consumers frequently enjoyed uniform, more plentiful, and less expensive goods. The nation's standard of living rose.

But big business had many opponents. Small businessmen felt driven to the wall by their giant rivals. Ambitious young men feared that trusts were reducing their opportunities for economic success. Laborers seemed powerless when bargaining with industrial titans who demanded ever more output at the same or lowered wages. Farmers who sold to and bought from the trusts regarded themselves as victimized. Conservationists believed that predatory big businessmen were exploiting and wasting the nation's vital store of natural resources. Students of government sounded the alarm that the trusts were corrupting the democratic process by their frequent use of economic power to buy political favors.

During the late 1880s, these opponents of big business coalesced into the Antitrust Movement. The dominant view at first (which was written into the Sherman Act of 1890) was that all large business combinations were evil and should be outlawed and broken up [V]. Vigorous trust-busting did not follow, however. Apathetic or pro-business Attorneys General failed to prosecute, and the federal courts within a decade had weakened the law by narrowly defining its scope [VI].

President Theodore Roosevelt briefly revived trust-busting during his first administration. But the federal government during the Progressive Era (1901–1917) was less interested in crushing out big business than in bringing it under control for the public benefit. Roosevelt's distinction between "good" and "bad" trusts [VII], the Supreme Court's "rule of reason" [VIII], and the trust legislation of the Woodrow Wilson administration [IX] all represented attempts to live with and to regulate rather than to destroy the modern corporate business structure.

Economic as well as political forces were at work counteracting the trend towards exclusive control of the economy by either big business or by investment banks. Laborers were creating a counterweight to industrial power in the form of unions (see Chapter Three). Meanwhile, industrialists, resentful of banker control, were struggling to wrench free from Wall Street domination [X]. EDITED BY GERALD G. EGGERT

I
_____

*An objecting stockholder sees "conspiracy" in
director-manager control of corporations.*

FROM: An 1863 book on the abuses of corporate management.

BY the 1860s, many eastern corporations (including the Lowell Company discussed here) were already in their third or fourth decade of
operation. The trend away from stockholder control was well-advanced.
This selection catalogues the case against director-domination and at-
tributes it to a conspiracy by the directors to deprive the shareholders of
control of their property. From the perspective of another hundred years,
during which the power of stockholders had eroded much further, the
author appears to have overstressed the role of conspiracy. Modern
scholars tend to see the problem in terms of economic forces which have
outstripped political devices for controlling them.

*Why isn't the town-meeting type of democracy well-suited to the
conduct of modern big business affairs?*

To whom, if anyone, do corporation officials answer for their conduct?

*What uses, other than salaries and bonuses for themselves, might com-
pany officials prefer to make of corporation earnings?*

❧

THE capital and labor employed in Manufacturing Corporations
constitute one of the great interests of the State, which profits by their
prosperity, and suffers with any adversity that befalls them.

These institutions were originally organized by a few men, who
united their capital like co-partners, and obtained such charters as they
desired from the State Government. Under charters thus granted, which
were well suited to their early condition, our manufacturing companies,
so long as that condition continued, were well managed and very prosperous. The small number of owners, by devoting their personal attention, and by bringing all their shrewdness, energy and perseverance to
bear for the welfare of their enterprises, as other partners do in the
management of their property, were so far successful as to afford a
generous employment to industry and a profitable investment to capital.

But a generation has passed away. Time has changed the relations
of owners and managers, until only traces of their original condition
remain. The originators—large stockholders, or principal owners, as they
were called—of the institutions have died . . .; their estates have been

J[ames] C[ook] Ayer, M.D., *Some of the Usages and Abuses in the Management of our
Manufacturing Corporations* (Lowell, Mass.: C. M. Langley & Company, 1863), pp.
3–5, 8, 15–18, 21–22, 24.

distributed to their heirs, and sold out to the public. They subscribed for and held their stock in lots ranging from $25,000 to $100,000 in a corporation. Now the average ownership is about three $1,000 shares to one individual. The present stockholders, instead of having, as the original owners did, a personal and intimate acquaintance, rarely know each other at all. They are scattered all over New England, and even other States. They have bought their shares as an investment, and with the delusive hope that somebody is interested in it who can and will take care of it.

As the charters were granted, and as the laws of the State now stand (charters and laws, be it remembered, made expressly for the condition of things already described, when it was wisely intended to elect the large owners as officers and managers), it is possible, and is the practice, for the officers in possession to re-elect themselves perpetually into the places they hold, in defiance of the stockholders, or any combination of them that can be made. How this has been and continues to be done, and by what appliances, we will explain as follows:—

The law leaves it with the officers to call the annual meeting of the stockholders for their election where and when they please. They call these meetings at the office of the Treasurer in Boston. This is generally a room which can hold from 40 to 80 people, while each corporation has from 350 to 600 individual stockholders. The Treasurer and Directors can, and often do, more than half fill it with their immediate partizans, friends, and retainers, provided with proxy votes. Some stockholders succeed in getting in, but many more come too late, find the room filled, and leave. This secures a hand vote for the officers. Now, as to the method of securing the stock vote: It has long been the practice for the officers to have the clerk at the desk ask the stockholders, as they come into the Treasurer's office for their dividends, to sign one book or paper, which is a receipt, and another, which is a proxy. Sometimes this demand is explained as a necessity to get a quorum, and sometimes no explanation is given, because the stockholder (perhaps a woman) supposes both signatures required for a receipt. By this process a majority of the proxies of any corporation is easily taken, and kept in possession of the officers to be used by them, or their partizans, at the annual meeting, for their own purposes; which, of course, gives them entire control of the franchise of the Corporation. Under these circumstances, it is impossible for the owners to prevent their officers from re-electing themselves again and again, no matter how outrageous their abuse of the properties they govern. It must be remembered that not one quarter of the stockholders are present, *or could gain admission to the room if they came;* and that the officers have virtual possession and control of the meeting, with appliances always at hand to talk down, choke down, or crowd out anything or anybody not in complicity with themselves. With these arrangements in full force, let us see the uses that are made of them. . . . . .

At the last annual meeting of this Corporation [the Lowell Company], called by the Directors at the Treasurer's office in Boston, a room which measures 17 x 32 feet, *twenty-nine* of the four hundred and sixty-two stockholders in the Company, a majority of whom were the immediate associates and friends of the Treasurer, or interested with him as officers in manufacturing corporations, were present. The Treasurer resigned his office. He had devoted but a portion of his time to the service of this Company, and had received a salary of $6,000 a year—more than the Governor or Chief Justice of the State; and yet the meeting, constituted as above stated, voted him a present of $6,000 as a compliment! Of the owners of this Company many are poor, and a large majority are unable and indisposed to give their money for such a purpose. It would seem that they ought to have been present to prevent such a disposition of their money. But they could not have gained admission to the room if they had gone, for it could not hold, with the desk, table and settees in it, fifty people; much less could they have resisted the proxy vote if one hundred men had attended. The Treasurer was a wealthy man, and had received enormous emoluments from other manufacturing corporations, while holding his office. It has never been claimed that he had any uncommon fitness or skill, or had done anything more than his duty for this Company. . . . . .

It is the general belief that the Treasurers and Directors in Corporations are large owners in them, and consequently interested to preserve and foster their own property. This was true formerly, but is not now. It has been asserted, and so far as we are able to verify it, justly, that there are individuals without the slightest voice in the management, who own more stock than all the Treasurers in both Lowell and Lawrence, excepting one, who runs mills that are mainly his own. With few exceptions, they have but little interest in these properties. One of the Treasurers, who has been most prominent in the management of the Corporations, and who has at the present time as much control of them as any other man, was lately found to own just one share in several of them, just enough to give him a right of presence in the annual meetings of stockholders, in order to manage them. He voted on his one share in the Hamilton, and then transferred it to a friend, to serve him at the same meeting.

Other appliances [expedients], besides those already given, are employed to seize and retain the control of these great public properties, in the permanent possession of a few hands. Among these are the selection of officers. From a clique of twelve or fifteen men in Boston, Directors enough are taken to make a majority of each board in most of the great manufacturing corporations of the State. So persistently is this done that it has lately been found one man was a Director in twenty-three Companies and a President in eleven, not all manufacturing. Several men are Directors in from five to eight Corporations. . . . . .

Another expedient sometimes employed to elude the stockholders, where they have become alarmed by some publicity of the abuse of their interests, is to call meetings of two or more Corporations at the same time in different places. This divides the stockholders, but not the proxy vote. Still another is to call them on so short notice that stockholders shall be without opportunity for any considerable consultation together before the meeting. Still another, which has been attempted, if not put into execution, is to call them before the full arrival of the morning trains from the country, thus to gather the Boston members only. Still another is to withhold notice altogether from some owners. . . . . .

The salaries of the officers [in these companies] are much the largest of any paid in the State. We do not say that they are more than would command the services of the very ablest men of the best experience and skill; but the high-salaried offices are rarely filled by such men. They are more generally occupied by men who have failed to be very valuable in any other pursuit—the son, son-in-law, nephew, or relative of some Director, who, in turn, allows the other Directors to put their dependents in good positions, also. This system of nepotism robs the Corporations of the abilities and talents for which they so liberally pay. . . . . .

We do not assert that the individuals who compose these official cliques, and have fattened themselves with such insatiable voracity upon these institutions, were originally worse than other men. But we do maintain that the *system* is thoroughly bad, and that it has demoralized its administrators until they can and do unblushingly perpetrate acts which would anywhere else banish them from the fellowship of honorable men.

II

Economic forces induce businesses to consolidate.

FROM: The report of a federal investigating commission, 1901.

IN June 1898, Congress established an industrial commission made up of five senators, five congressmen, and nine representatives of different industries and authorized it to hire a staff of experts. Congress instructed the commission to study "trusts" and other industrial combinations and from time to time to report to Congress, recommending appropriate legislation. After three years of investigation, during which it questioned more than a hundred business leaders, the commission reported on, among other things, why businesses consolidate.

By what devices do business combines prevent competitive prices?

How does "standardization" of product benefit both the producer and the consumer?

ᴥᶚ

IT is clearly the opinion of most of those associated with industrial combinations that the chief cause of their formation has been excessive competition. Naturally all business men desire to make profits, and they find their profits falling off first through the pressure of lowering prices of their competitors. The desire to lessen too vigorous competition naturally brings them together.

A second way of increasing profits is through the various economies which they think will come by consolidation. . . . . .

THE SAVINGS OF COMBINATION

(a) Among the economies that are generally recognized as resulting from combination is the regulation of production. Where there is no general understanding among producers there is a strong tendency to overproduction, so that markets become demoralized and competition excessive. The combination is able so to fit the supply to the demand that while customers can be fully supplied at reasonable prices there is no danger of overproduction. It is thus a means of preventing panics and periods of depression.

(b) Closely allied with this adaptation of supply to demand is the advantage that comes from the possibility of carrying much smaller stocks of goods. This saves not merely the investment of capital, but also interest on running capital, insurance, storage charges, shop-work charges, etc.

(c) This same control of production enables the combination to keep its factories running full time, thus keeping labor fully employed. . . .

(d) When a large proportion of an industry is under the control of one central management, it becomes essential to success that the various products be standardized. In this way the quality of goods can be made much more uniform than would otherwise be the case, and its

Report of the Industrial Commission, XIII (Washington: Government Printing Office, 1901), v–vii.

excellence can be guaranteed. Furthermore, the number of styles of goods can regularly be very much reduced, thus lessening the cost of manufacture and effecting a saving in the amount of stock that needs to be carried.

(e) The same influence leads to the larger use of special machinery, and to the adaptation of the workmen and the superintendents to the special departments for which they are best suited. In many cases through this specialization more can be saved than through the introduction even of new machines. . . .

(f) The specialization mentioned above saves also materially through a lessening in the cost of superintendence, which is sometimes very large. Likewise the increased efficiency often enables the manufacturer to lessen the number of laborers per unit of product.

(g) There are also noteworthy savings along somewhat similar lines in connection with the cost of selling; for example, the number of traveling men can often be greatly reduced. . . . Substantial economies can be made through direct sales instead of through middlemen; and the cost of advertising can be materially lessened, owing to more intelligent distribution and method of advertising. Advertising in a large way permits also the securing of more favorable rates. The popularity of a trade-mark can be more readily secured when the sales are direct.

(h) There is often through combination a better knowledge and control of credit conditions, so that bad debts may be guarded against. . . .

(i) Of course there is a very material saving in many instances through shipping goods to customers from the nearest plants. In this matter of freight saving also the large combinations can often supply themselves with storage facilities at central points and then ship their goods in large quantities during the seasons of the year when freight rates are lowest, thus often securing the advantages of water transportation which otherwise would not be available.

III

Pools operate as "gentlemen's agreements."

FROM: (A) The minutes of a meeting of the Anthracite Coal Pool.
(B) A magazine editorial on railroad pooling.

POOLS were among the oldest devices of businessmen for escaping from the disadvantages of rigorous competition. The common law in both England and the United States regarded them as illegal conspiracies. Consequently, they operated as "gentlemen's agreements" outside the law. If a "gentleman" broke the agreement, the others could not appeal to the law to enforce it. Despite the difficulty of enforcement, pools were popular, especially among the railroads, in the 1870s. They fell into disuse after the Interstate Commerce Act of 1887 specifically outlawed the practice on railways. Meanwhile, stronger forms of consolidation were devised and substituted for pools.

In a pool, what happens to the supply and demand mechanism for setting the price of a service or commodity?

Why did the editor in the second selection have qualms about the pool which ended the "mischievous" competition among railroads?

What alternatives to pooling does he suggest?

(A) FROM THE MINUTES OF THE ANTHRACITE POOL MEETING[1]

A NUMBER of gentlemen, representatives of the anthracite interests, met by invitation of J. Pierrpont [*sic*] Morgan at his house, No. 219 Madison Avenue, on Monday evening, March 22d, 1886. Mr. Morgan stated that the object in asking the gentlemen to assemble was that they might take counsel as to the possibility of preventing further injury to the interests they represented by some concerted action looking to an arrest of the demoralization of business which resulted from the existing want of harmony.

[A chairman and secretary were selected and a roll call taken of the ten interests represented at the meeting.]

After a very general discussion of all the interests involved and the best result that it was desired to attain, it was moved by Mr. Sloan as follows:

The representatives of the anthracite interests agree upon a pool of the anthracite to be mined between March 31st, 1886, and March 31st, 1887. The output for the year just named is, for the purposes of this agreement estimated at 33,500,000 tons. The percentage of each interest is to be determined hereafter. Any party shipping over its percentage shall account to the pool for the amount by which it may be found on the 31st of March, 1887, to have exceeded its percentage at the rate of fifty cents per ton. This motion, being seconded by Mr. Olyphant, was agreed to by a unanimous vote. On motion the meeting estimated that the market would require for the month of April, 2,000,000 tons of anthracite. On motion the meeting resolved that the price of coal should be immediately advanced twenty-five cents per ton f.o.b. at New York.

---

[1] United States Congress, House of Representatives, Select Committee on Labor Troubles in the Anthracite Regions of Pennsylvania, 1887–1888. 50th Congress, 2d Session, *House Report No. 4141* (Washington: Government Printing Office, 1889), pp. 648–649.

On motion the meeting adjourned to meet at the office of the Pennsylvania Coal Company in New York on Monday, March 29, 1886, at 12 o'clock noon.

(B) FROM *THE NATION'S* EDITORIAL, "THE 'POOLING' OF RAILROAD RECEIPTS"[2]

"WE learn that the three lines which carry passengers between Chicago and Council Bluffs have made an agreement to pool the earnings on through business between these two places, and divide them equally." This modest little announcement, taken from a contemporary devoted to railway interests, is deserving of more than a passing notice. It marks, indeed, the entrance upon a new stage of railroad development; whether for better or worse, remains to be seen. . . .

The last summer witnessed probably the most severe railroad "war" ever maintained between the leading trunk lines of this continent. . . . The "war" broke out early in the season, and, as all business men know, rates between competing points tumbled down lower and lower, until they absolutely touched the zero point. For weeks cattle were drawn over the Erie and Central roads at a dollar a car on one line, in competition with a cent a head on the other. Fares and freights fell 50, 60, and 70 per cent, while the corporations seemed sternly bent on ruining each other. . . . One day in August it was intimated that the officials of the three great trunk lines were in conference, and on the next day competition ceased. A new tariff was then announced, the increased rates of which ranged between one hundred per cent. on first-class freights in general and fifteen thousand per cent (the rise being from $1 to $150 per car) on live stock in particular. The conferring managers, however, did not stop here. . . . Long experience had demonstrated both the folly of "cutting rates" and the certainty that rates under the existing system were sure periodically to be cut. The moment there is not a glut of business for all the lines, that one which is least busy attempts to underbid its competitors, and thus begins a "war." Some radical measure only could put a stop to this. "Pooling" receipts, as it is called, naturally suggested itself. This certainly went to the root of the difficulty. By virtue of this arrangement, all money received for business done by any road between points of competition was to be paid into a common fund, or "pool;" this sum was then subsequently to be divided in fixed proportions among the parties to the agreement. Such a plan certainly held out small inducements to "cutting." Any road indulging in the practice would have the privilege of doing all the work

[2] Editorial, "The 'Pooling' of Railroad Receipts," *The Nation,* 11 (November 10, 1870), 309–310.

in order to divide the receipts. . . . The arrangement involved, in fact a practical consolidation of all the great East and West trunk lines, and the creation of a united interest which was to control in close alliance some 10,000 miles of track, and in the neighborhood of $600,000,000 of capital.

This certainly has an alarming sound. At the same time, we are not clear that, even for the public, the arrangement would not possess decided advantages. It would, in the first place, effectually dispose of the existing system of railroad competition, than which few things can be more mischievous. Stability—something which eliminates the gambling element and renders calculation possible—is the first essential of a sound business condition. . . . it is not easy to see how any legitimate business has been conducted in this country during the last ten years; there have been about as many elements of chance in trade as would naturally be encountered at the faro table. . . . Anything, therefore, which replaced this wretched attempt at a law of supply and demand by an equable, regulated, and permanent system, could not be wholly bad. The combination suggested would at least establish a certain sort of responsibility—not the best, perhaps, but still better than nothing. Under the present system, no one can be held to any account; one line "cuts," or extorts, because another does it; a locality is ruined to-day and enriched to-morrow, simply because two or three men, over whom it has no real control, see fit to quarrel or be friends. No one controls; there is no defined objective against which public opinion can be directed—no one, in a word, is responsible. . . . Not improbably, then, it would prove far easier to produce beneficial results when acting on a recognized and responsible railroad combination, no matter how powerful or widely ramified, than on the disconnected members of an unorganized system, each one of whom disavows responsibility, and, indeed, disputes its existence.

While all this is true, it must at the same time be conceded that the power held by such a combination would be a very dangerous one; it would, in fact, have its fingers around the throat of our whole system of internal communication. It could exercise an influence over trade, and levy taxes in a manner scarcely within the power of the Government itself. The character of the individuals in whose hands such a control over our fortune seems likely soon to centre, becomes, therefore, a matter of some interest. This aspect of the case, it must be confessed, is most uninviting. We do not like to resort to strong language, yet none other does justice to the occasion. Cornelius Vanderbilt, Jay Gould, and J. Edgar Thompson—here is, indeed, a trio in whose hands an enlightened people are invited to confide most delicate interests! The contemplation of them in this new capacity certainly puts a heavy strain on the confidence one entertains in the future. These men, however, actually do, and long have absolutely controlled all our great trunk lines. . . . Here they are, . . . avaricious, unscrupulous, often dishonest, always unreliable—as discreditable a triumvirate as ever domineered over Rome; and the question is simply whether they can best be dealt with together or separately. We now incline to the opinion that the public could, on the whole, take them best together. . . .

. . . One thing may safely be predicted. This, at last, must inevitably carry the railroad and transportation problem to Washington. Congress must regulate commerce between the States, or it must go unregulated. A body more utterly unqualified for such a delicate task could hardly be conceived; but upon it the work must perforce devolve. The inevitable may not be avoided; but a future, big with the result of an attempt on the part of the United States Congress to regulate and control our railroad triumvirs, is to the philosophic mind the reverse of assuring.

IV

An industrialist explains why trusts appear and why they fail.

FROM: A magazine article by Andrew Carnegie, 1889.

TRUSTS were a form of business consolidation that presented no enforcement problems. A group of firms would agree to end competition by subjecting themselves completely to centralized direction. A trustee or board of trustees was named. The value of each member firm was determined and trust certificates were issued and exchanged for all voting stock of the participating companies. These certificates entitled the holders to a share of the trust's profits, but gave them no voice whatever in policy determination. Since they held all stock, the trustees under this system answered to no one. The device came under attack in the courts in the late 1880s and was specifically outlawed by the Sherman Act of 1890.

What possible impediments were there to the rise of more and more competitors who would have to be absorbed into the trust?

What determines the "legitimate" or "normal" return on invested capital? Is it also subject to control?

◦◦

IT is worth while to inquire into the appearance and growth of Trusts and learn what environments produce them. Their genesis is as

Andrew Carnegie, "The Bugaboo of Trusts," *North American Review*, 148 (February, 1889), 141–142, 144–146.

follows: a demand exists for a certain article, beyond the capacity of existing works to supply it. Prices are high, and profits tempting. Every manufacturer of that article immediately proceeds to enlarge his works and increase their producing power. In addition to this the unusual profits attract . . . attention. . . . New partnerships are formed, and new works are erected, and before long the demand for the article is fully satisfied, and prices do not advance. In a short time the supply becomes greater than the demand, there are a few tons or yards more in the market for sale than required, and prices begin to fall. They continue falling until the article is sold at cost to the less favorably situated or less ably managed factory; and even until the best managed and best equipped factory is not able to produce the article at the prices at which it can be sold. Political economy says that here the trouble will end. Goods will not be produced at less than cost. This was true when Adam Smith wrote, but it is not quite true to-day. When an article was produced by a small manufacturer, employing, probably at his own home, two or three journeymen and an apprentice or two, it was an easy matter for him to limit or even to stop production. As manufacturing is carried on to-day, in enormous establishments with five or ten millions of dollars of capital invested, and with thousands of workers, it costs the manufacturer much less to run at a loss per ton or per yard than to check his production. Stoppage would be serious indeed. The condition of cheap manufacturing is running full. Twenty sources of expense are *fixed charges*, many of which stoppage would only increase. Therefore the article is produced for months, and in some cases that I have known for years, not only without profit or without interest upon capital, but to the impairment of the capital invested. . . . While continuing to produce may be costly, the manufacturer knows too well that stoppage would be ruin. His brother manufacturers are of course in the same situation. They see the savings of many years, as well perhaps as the capital they have succeeded in borrowing, becoming less and less, with no hope of a change in the situation. It is in soil thus prepared that anything promising relief is gladly welcomed. The manufacturers are in the position of patients that have tried in vain every doctor of the regular school for years, and are now liable to become the victims of any quack that appears. Combinations—syndicates—trusts—they are willing to try anything. A meeting is called, and in the presence of immediate danger they decide to take united action and form a trust. Each factory is rated as worth a certain amount. Officers are chosen, and through these the entire product of the article in question is to be distributed to the public, at remunerative prices.

Such is the genesis of "Trusts" in manufactured articles. . . . . .
. . . The question is, Do they menace the permanent interest of

the nation? Are they a source of serious danger? Or are they to prove, as many other similar forms have proved, mere passing phases of unrest and transition? To answer this question let us follow the operation of the manufacturing trust. . . . The sugar refiners, let us say, have formed a Trust after competing one with another through years of disastrous business, and all the sugar manufactured in the country in existing factories is sold through one channel at advanced prices. Profits begin to grow. Dividends are paid, and those who before saw their property vanishing before their eyes are now made happy. The dividends from that part of a man's capital invested in the sugar business yield him profit far above the capital he has invested in various other affairs. The prices of sugar are such that the capital invested in a new factory would yield enormously. He is perhaps bound not to enlarge his factory or to enter into a new factory, but his relatives and acquaintances soon discover the fresh opportunity for gain. He can advise them to push the completion of a small factory, which, of course, must be taken into the Trust. Or, even if he does not give his friends this intimation, capital is always upon the alert, especially when it is bruited about that a Trust has been formed, as in the case of sugar, and immediately new sugar manufactories spring up, as if by magic. The more successful the Trust, the surer these off-shoots are to sprout. Every victory is a defeat. Every factory that the Trust buys is the sure creator of another, and so on, *ad infinitum,* until the bubble bursts. The sugar refiners have tried to get more from capital in a special case than capital yields in general. They have endeavored to raise a part of the ocean of capital above the level of the surrounding waters, and over their bulwarks the floods have burst, and capital, like water, has again found its level. It is true that to regain this level a longer or a shorter period may be required, during which the article affected may be sold to the consumer in limited quantities at a higher rate than before existed. But for this the consumer is amply recompensed in the years that follow, during which the struggle between the discordant and competitive factories becomes severer than it ever was before, and lasts till the great law of the survival of the fittest vindicates itself. Those factories and managers that can produce to the best advantage eventually close the less competent. Capital wisely managed yields its legitimate profit. After a time, the growth of demand enables capital to receive an unusual profit. This in turn attracts fresh capital to the manufacture, and we have a renewal of the old struggle, the consumer reaping the benefit.

Such is the law, such has been the law, and such promises to be the law for the future; for, so far, no device has yet been devised that has permanently thwarted its operation. Given freedom of competition, and all combinations or trusts that attempt to exact from the consumer more than a legitimate return upon capital and services, write the charter of their own defeat.

V

An enemy of trusts urges that they be broken up.

FROM: A magazine article of 1888.

THE demand for governmental action against the trusts reached a peak in 1888. Articles debating the merits and demerits of trusts appeared in the nation's leading magazines, and that summer both major political parties pledged in their national platforms to enact a federal antitrust law. The following selection gives the flavor of the attack on trusts.

How does this article differ from the Report of the Industrial Commission and from Andrew Carnegie's explanation of the origin of trusts?

Why does the author of this article propose legislation against trusts rather than simply relying on competition to eliminate them?

◄§

WE have entered upon a dangerous epoch in the evolution of our civilization, and hardly a fortnight passes now without developing some new combination of gigantic "trusts" of some corporate, industrial, or commercial interest, to fix the price to consumers of all sorts of things and commodities, independent of the economic operations of the law of supply and demand. One of the first, as well as one of the greatest combinations ever formed was the Standard Oil Company, and it has thus far been so eminently successful in absolutely controlling the market price of oil, regardless of consumers or producers, and in defiance of supposed well settled principles of political economy, that it has inevitably bred an ugly brood of imitators. . . . . .

Perhaps one clear and concise statute forbidding corporations or aggregated capital to do business except as a unit would break up these pernicious trusts, which have been so serious a menace to commercial progress and to our future national prosperity. The introduction of such an enactment is imperatively demanded by the requirements of the situation. Otherwise all competition, the life of all trade, will be eventually crushed out. . . . . .

. . . Let us just for a moment look at things as they really are. Practically, all the great necessities of life in this country, excepting only the air—and that would be monopolized if it had solidity, like the earth —are now controlled by soulless and mercenary combinations. Are these

W. M. Rapsher, "Dangerous 'Trusts'," *North American Review*, 146 (May, 1888), 509–514.

things inevitable? Are they the legitimate product of our civilization? If they are, we had better begin anew. But they are not the outgrowth of progress. They are rather fungous growths—horrible excrescences. They are the fruits of bad legislation; and bad judicial construction of already bad laws. Laws enacted by professional politicians have erected monopolies that have already absorbed more than one-half of the wealth of the country and like vampires are sucking the life-blood of the people. The unorganized masses of consumers and producers can protect themselves against these "trusts" in but one way, and that is through laws which will utterly overthrow and prevent such giant growths. The primary object and justification of government is to protect the weak and prevent a powerful few from wronging the many. But if we cannot bring the Standard Oil Trust into subjection to the law, how will we ever cope with all those other "trusts" organized for the express purpose of evading all laws Congress may pass, and to violate with impunity every State law that can be enacted. But these combinations have at present such a powerful grip upon Congresses and Legislatures, that they will not permit efficient laws to restrain them to be enacted. Think of it! It is estimated by reliable authority that much more of the wealth of the United States is now owned and controlled by corporations and monopolistic trusts, than by private persons. Fifty years ago corporations were nothing; now they are everything. They dominate all channels of activity; they control governors, judges and legislatures; they make hewers of wood and drawers of water of all who are outside of their charmed circles. . . . . .

. . . the work of creating new gigantic and dangerous "trusts" or combinations, seems to be increasing and going steadily on. The plain truth is that gigantic corporations . . . are beyond and above the control of municipal ordinances or State laws. It is even doubted by many, whether the vast powers of the General Government will prove to be sufficiently potential against such an aggregation of capital and brains. Exercising functions that are largely public in their character they nevertheless enjoy all the rights and all the advantages of private enterprises. As absolutely essential agencies for the transaction of business they are protected by the business interests of the country from the operation of laws enacted for the purpose of bringing them into subjection to authority.

There is nothing democratic about such vast monopolies for controlling those channels through which intelligence and traffic are effected. Competition is crushed by its very weight, holding business men by the throat, and forcing them to deliver. They are despotic in spirit, tyrannical in method, openly hostile to liberty and free institutions, and threatening menaces to the pursuit of happiness, and to equality and equal opportunities under the law. When the people of this country once get their eyes wide open they will hardly permit such dangerous excrescences to fasten their deathlike grip upon our liberties and our laws. . . .

. . . The only salvation for republican institutions is the utter abolition of our present system of tolerating unequal opportunities, whether they be natural or the creatures of law.

Harshly as the system grates on the true interests and the sense of justice of the people, they are but slowly provoked to aggressive action; but when they once plainly see these great so-called trusts reaching out to control arbitrarily the cost of necessaries of business or of life, there will be a speedy popular combination against the combines, and it will be revolutionary if revolutionary action shall be needed to overthrow this assault upon the natural and economic laws of production and consumption, and of supply and demand.

VI

Attorney General Richard Olney gives the Antitrust Law a narrow construction.

FROM: The annual report of the Attorney General for 1893.

ON July 2, 1890, the Sherman Antitrust Act became the law of the land. It declared "every contract, combination in the form of trust or otherwise, or conspiracy, in restraint of trade or commerce among the several states, or with foreign nations" to be illegal. "Every person," it continued, "who shall monopolize, or attempt to monopolize, or combine or conspire with any other person or persons, to monopolize any part" of the same trade was to be "deemed guilty of a misdemeanor." During President Benjamin Harrison's administration, seven antitrust cases were launched. Only three were completed by the end of that administration: two were lost and only a small pool of coal dealers in Tennessee was broken up.

Grover Cleveland's Attorney General, Richard Olney, in private life had been a leading corporation and railroad lawyer. Just prior to his appointment he had successfully defended the Whisky Trust against charges of having violated the Sherman Act. As Attorney General, Olney pushed the Sugar Trust Case (*U.S.* v. *E. C. Knight*) to final decision before the Supreme Court. On the eve of the decision in that case, Olney interpreted the current standing of the law in his annual report.

What major segments of the economy did Olney interpret as beyond the scope of the act?

Under what circumstances did Olney later authorize the institution of criminal suits under the Sherman Act?

⊷⟨

THERE has been and probably still is a widespread impression that the aim and effect of [the Sherman Act] are to prohibit and prevent those aggregations of capital which are so common at the present day and which are sometimes on so large a scale as to control practically all the branches of an extensive industry. It would not be useful, even if it were possible, to ascertain the precise purposes of the framers of the statute. It is sufficient to point out what small basis there is for the popular impression referred to.

In the first place, the subject-matter upon which the statute operates and alone can operate is "any part of the trade or commerce among the several States or with foreign nations." There is, therefore, necessarily exempt from its provisions all that immense mass of contracts, dealings, and transactions which arise and are carried on wholly within State lines and are wholly within the jurisdiction of a State. On another ground, namely, that special and exclusive legislation has been enacted respecting them, railroad companies engaged in interstate transportation have been held not to be within the purview of the statute.

In the next place, the subject-matter of the statute as thus limited is to be protected from (1) monopolies, (2) attempts to monopolize, (3) combinations or conspiracies to monopolize, and (4) contracts, combinations, or conspiracies, in form of trusts or otherwise, in restraint of trade or commerce. But as all ownership of property is of itself a monopoly, and as every business contract or transaction may be viewed as a combination which more or less restrains some part or kind of trade or commerce, any literal application of the provisions of the statute is out of the question. It is not surprising, therefore, that different judges who have been called upon to put a legal meaning upon the statute have found the task difficult and have generally contented themselves with deciding the case in hand without undertaking to construe the statute as a whole. To this there is but one notable exception in a judgment given in the circuit court of the United States for the southern district of Ohio, which deals with the statute thoroughly and comprehensively and, coming from a judge who is now associate justice of the Supreme Court, must be regarded as entitled to the highest consideration. His conclusions, as briefly summarized, are: (1) That Congress can not limit the right of State corporations or of citizens in the acquisition, accumulation, and control of property; (2) that Congress can not prescribe the prices at which such property shall be sold by the owner, whether a corporation or individual; (3) that Congress·can not make criminal the intents and purposes of persons in the acquisition and

Annual Report of the Attorney General of the United States for the Year 1893 (Washington: Government Printing Office, 1893), pp. xxvi–xxviii.

control of property which the States of their residence or creation sanction; (4) that "monopoly," as prohibited by the statute, means an exclusive right in one party, coupled with a legal restriction or restraint upon some other party which prevents the latter from exercising or enjoying the same right; (5) and that contracts in restraint of trade and commerce as prohibited are contracts in general restraint thereof and such as would be void at common law independently of any statute.

This exposition of the statute has not so far been questioned in any court and is to be accepted and acted upon until disapproved by a tribunal of last resort. In view of it the cases popularly supposed to be covered by the statute are almost without exception obviously not within its provisions, since to make them applicable not merely must capital be brought together and applied in large masses, but the accumulation must be made by means which impose a legal disability upon others from engaging in the same trade or industry. Numerous suits under the statute, however, have already been brought—others may be—and it is manifest that questions of such gravity, both in themselves and in respect of the pecuniary interests involved, ought not to rest for their final determination upon the decision of a single judge, however forcible and weighty. I have, therefore, deemed it my duty to push for immediate hearing a case involving those questions, and unless prevented by some unforeseen obstacle, shall endeavor to have it advanced for argument at the present term of the Supreme Court.

It should, perhaps, be added, in this connection—as strikingly illustrating the perversion of a law from the real purpose of its authors—that in one case the combination of laborers known as a "strike" was held to be within the prohibition of the statute, and that in another, rule 12 of the Brotherhood of Locomotive Engineers [authorizing boycotts] was declared to be in violation thereof.

[When the Supreme Court ruled against the government in the Sugar Trust case, Olney wrote to his private secretary: "You will have observed that the govt. has been defeated in the Supreme Court on the trust question. I always supposed it would be & have taken the responsibility of not prosecuting under a law I believed to be no good. . . ." Olney to Miss Antoinette Straw, January 22, 1895, Olney Papers, Library of Congress.]

VII

Theodore Roosevelt distinguishes "good" trusts from "bad" trusts.

FROM: Roosevelt's autobiography.

PRESIDENT Theodore Roosevelt earned the title of "trust-buster" for his administration's successful prosecution of the Northern Securities

Case. Roosevelt, however, believed that big businesses were inevitable and that they could be either beneficial or harmful. In messages to Congress and in public addresses he repeatedly urged that a distinction be made between "good" and "bad" trusts and that only the latter be prosecuted. Nowhere did he define what he meant more succinctly than in his autobiography, written after he left office.

Did the Sherman Act itself make any distinction between good and bad trusts?

Which of Roosevelt's definitions were ambiguous and in need of further clarification?

৺§

. . . I HOLD that a corporation does ill if it seeks profit in restricting production and then by extorting high prices from the community by reason of the scarcity of the product; through adulterating, lyingly advertising, or overdriving the help; or replacing men workers with children; or by rebates; or in any illegal or improper manner driving competitors out of its way; or seeking to achieve monopoly by illegal or unethical treatment of its competitors, or in any shape or way offending against the moral law either in connection with the public or with its employees or with its rivals. Any corporation which seeks its profit in such fashion is acting badly. It is, in fact, a conspiracy against the public welfare which the Government should use all its powers to suppress. If, on the other hand, a corporation seeks profit solely by increasing its products through eliminating waste, improving its processes, utilizing its by-products, installing better machines, raising wages in the effort to secure more efficient help, introducing the principle of cooperation and mutual benefit, dealing fairly with labor unions, setting its face against the underpayment of women and the employment of children; in a word, treating the public fairly and its rivals fairly: then such a corporation is behaving well. It is an instrumentality of civilization operating to promote abundance by cheapening the cost of living so as to improve conditions everywhere throughout the whole community.

Theodore Roosevelt: An Autobiography (New York: Charles Scribner's Sons, 1913), p. 577.

VIII

A constitutional lawyer finds that the Supreme Court's statement of the "rule of reason" leaves fundamental issues unresolved.

FROM: An analysis of the ruling in a magazine article of 1911.

THE Supreme Court found in 1911 that both the Standard Oil and the American Tobacco companies had violated the Sherman Act and ordered their dissolution. More important than breaking up these two giants—which did not cripple either firm permanently—was the high court's acceptance of the "rule of reason." In legal terminology, the court in effect accepted President Theodore Roosevelt's proposition that all business combines were not evil or illegal. Only "unreasonable" combinations were prohibited by the Sherman Act, the court ruled.

James M. Beck, a prominent author and constitutional lawyer of the era, like many businessmen and attorneys, had mixed emotions about the court's new position.

Why did Beck and others object to the flexibility of the court's new ruling?

Through the years, would you say that the court has been able to avoid making the hard choices outlined by Beck?

&

. . . BEYOND defining the attitude of the Court as one of reasonableness, the [Standard Oil and American Tobacco] decisions, however voluminous, suggest little that is tangible in the solution of the vexed problem of reconciling the liberty to combine with the industrial independence of the individual. We are little wiser than before as to what a restraint of trade is under the Sherman Law, or what restraints will be hereafter regarded as unreasonable. While we are admonished that the "normal" growth of business expansion is permissible and the abnormal inhibited, little light is shed by the judicial lamp of reason upon the social or legal principles which shall hereafter distinguish the "normal" from the "abnormal." Still less do we know when the instinct for expansion becomes "unduly restrictive" of competition. . . . . .

. . . What are the limits of permissible growth? What proportion of a given trade may any competitor by his energy and resources secure? . . . . .

I do not criticise the Court. It could only enforce as best it could a cryptic law. It faced a crisis in the administration of law of extraordinary difficulty. It had given in the Trans-Missouri and Joint Traffic cases a literal interpretation to the Sherman Law, which, if impartially enforced by the Executive Department against all combinations within the spirit of the decisions, would have resulted in business chaos. At least twelve hundred industrial corporations, with capital and resources easily exceeding $10,000,000,000, had been formed by the voluntary combination of individuals, theretofore competitors, and each of these combinations had necessarily resulted in a technical restraint of trade. . . . This interpretation of the law, as . . . Justice Holmes [has said], "would make eternal the *bellum omnium contra omnes* and disintegrate society, so far as it could, into individual atoms. . . . *It would be an attempt to reconstruct society.*"

Such a law was impossible of enforcement. To avoid committing a great, practical industrial nation to a policy of hari-kari, successive Attorneys-General necessarily ignored its impartial enforcement and as a sop to a supposed public sentiment brought suit only against a few of the larger and more unpopular combinations. A government of caprice was thus substituted for a government of law. . . . . .

The unhappy position of the business man was intensified by the fact that not only had the administration of law ceased to be impartial, but neither bench nor bar had any clear idea what was legal or illegal. Business could probably have adjusted itself to almost any economic theory, however archaic, provided that the rules of the game were clearly defined and impartially enforced. . . .

The Supreme Court has [now] interpreted the cryptic characters of the Sherman Law as announcing the "rule of reason." Wall Street acclaims this as a solution in the hope that a temporary sentiment of enthusiasm may push the wheels of industry through the slough of despond. But hard-headed business men either recognize or will soon recognize that presidents, attorneys-general, district attorneys, grand juries, petit juries, and courts will soon differ as to what the "rule of reason" is. . . . . .

. . . a real crisis . . . confronted the Supreme Court when it considered the Standard Oil and Tobacco cases. It could do little to save a dangerous situation unless it was prepared to disregard its own precedents and conform the interpretation of the statute to the reasonable necessities of the American people and the obvious tendencies of an age pre-eminently of combination. . . .

. . . It gave a new and more reasonable interpretation to the statute. While it has not solved a vexed question, it has at least made its ultimate solution a possibility. In doing so, the court simply applied a well-recognized and elementary rule of interpretation. . . . whether in a contract, a statute or a constitution, a court always subordinates the mere letter to its obvious purpose and reasonable spirit. . . . . .

To the student of our institutions the . . . interesting question suggests itself whether the practical application of the "rule of reasonableness" will not involve an extraordinary assumption by the judiciary of essentially legislative powers. This is emphasized by the decree of the Supreme Court in the Tobacco case, which requires the lower court to recreate by "disintegration" a new condition in "honest harmony" with the law. Having determined that Congress intended to forbid any combination which is injurious to the public welfare, the Supreme Court now assumes, as a judicial duty, the determination of what forms of business activity are thus injurious and what are the limits of permissible growth. This requires it to lay down principles of public policy, which seem to me essentially legislative in their character. Had Congress inserted the word "unreasonable" in the statute and left it to the judiciary to interpret and apply, the judiciary might well have declined to do so on the ground that it was a virtual delegation by Congress of its duty to legislate. This is even more true when it is the Supreme Court, and not Congress, that has inserted in the statute the qualifying adjective "unreasonable." . . . . .

The Supreme Court . . . has assumed a crushing burden. The Federal Courts in applying the rule of reasonableness must now determine the limits of combination, the lawful and unlawful forms thereof, the economic necessities of a people, the degree to which competition may be restricted, the ethical character of commercial methods, the invalidity of different forms of competition, the degree to which the telegraph, the railroad, and the steamship may be utilized in consolidating different and competing units into a more efficient and non-competing unit, the proportion of a given trade or industry that a given individual may enjoy, how far prices may be regulated to prevent loss and how far production can be restricted to prevent waste. In other words, they must now be arbiters of conflicting schools of philosophy and economic ideals. Which was right, Jefferson and Adam Smith, or Hamilton and Karl Marx, the individualism of Herbert Spencer or the socialism of John Ruskin? I cannot envy them their self-imposed burden.

IX

President Woodrow Wilson praises Congress for passing laws supporting his trust program.

FROM: A letter from the President to a member of Congress.

THE desire to plug loopholes in the Sherman Act and to clarify for businessmen those practices which were unreasonable led Congress to enact the Federal Trade Commission Act and the Clayton Antitrust Act early in the Wilson administration. Those two laws, added to the Underwood Tariff of 1913 and to the Federal Reserve Banking Act, constituted the heart of Wilson's so-called "New Freedom." Unlike Theodore Roosevelt, Wilson did not accept big business as inevitable and sought by his legislative program to reform it by restoring competition.

What are the advantages and the disadvantages of spelling out very precisely which acts of businessmen are illegal?

Are there any ambiguous statements in the new laws which might provide enforcement problems in the future?

✑

I CAN not let this session of Congress close without expressing my warm admiration for the fidelity and intelligence with which the program outlined in April and December of last year has been carried out, and my feeling that the people of the country have been served by the members of this Congress as they have seldom, if ever, been served before. The program was a great one, and it is a matter of deep satisfaction to think of the way in which it has been handled.

It had several distinct parts and many items, but, after all, a single purpose, namely, to destroy private control and set business free. That purpose was manifest enough in the case of the tariff and in the legislation affecting trusts; but, though perhaps less evident upon the surface there, it lay at the very heart of the currency bill, too. . . .

Private control had shown its sinister face on every hand in America, had shown it for a long time, and sometimes very brazenly, in the trusts and in a virtual domination of credit by small groups of men. The safest hiding place and covert of such control was in the tariff. There it for a long time hid very shrewdly. The tariff was a very complicated matter; none but experts thoroughly understood its schedules. Many of the schedules were framed to afford particular advantages to special groups of manufacturers and investors. That was the soil in which trade combinations and combinations of manufacturers most readily grew, and most rankly. High prices did not spring directly out of the tariff. They sprang out of the suppression of domestic, no less than of foreign, competition by means of combinations and trade agreements which could be much more easily contrived and maintained under the protection of a high tariff than without it. . . . . .

. . . the Congress has sought, in the Trade-Commission bill and in the Clayton bill, to make men in a small way of business as free to succeed as men in a big way, and to kill monopoly in the seed. Before these bills were passed the law was already clear enough that monopolies once formed were illegal and could be dissolved by direct process of law and those who had created them punished as for crime. But there was no law to check the process by which monopoly was built up until the tree was full grown and its fruit developed, or, at any rate, until the full opportunity for monopoly had been created. With this new legislation there is clear and sufficient law to check and destroy the noxious growth in its infancy. Monopolies are built up by unfair methods of competition, and the new Trade Commission has power to forbid and prevent unfair competition, whether upon a big scale or upon a little;

Woodrow Wilson to Congressman Oscar W. Underwood, October 17, 1914, *Supplement to the Messages and Papers of the Presidents* (n.p.: Bureau of National Literature [Inc.], 1917), pp. 8000–8002.

whether just begun or grown old and formidable. Monopoly is created also by putting the same men in charge of a variety of business enterprises, whether apparently related or unrelated to one another, by means of interlocking directorates. That the Clayton bill now in large measure prevents. Each enterprise must depend upon its own initiative and effectiveness for success, and upon the intelligence and business energy of the men who officer it. And so all along the line: Monopoly is to be cut off at the roots. . . . . .

The accomplishment of this legislation seems to me a singularly significant thing. If our party were to be called upon to name the particular point of principle in which it differs from its opponents most sharply and in which it feels itself most definitely sustained by experience, we should no doubt say that it was this: That we would have no dealings with monopoly, but reject it altogether; while our opponents were ready to adopt it into the realm of law, and seek merely to regulate it and moderate it in its operation. It is our purpose to destroy monopoly and maintain competition as the only effectual instrument of business liberty.

We have seen the nature of the power of monopoly exhibited. We know that it is more apt to control government than to be controlled by it; for we have seen it control government, dictate legislation, and dominate Executives and courts. We feel that our people are safe only in the fields of free individual endeavor where American genius and initiative are not guided by a few men as in recent years, but made rich by the activities of a multitude, as in days now almost forgotten. We will not consent that an ungovernable giant should be reared to full stature in the very household of the Government itself.

X

An industrialist explains how he kept his business out of the hands of bankers.

FROM: The memoirs of Henry Ford.

THE growth of banker domination over large sectors of the economy during and after the Panic of 1893 was not welcomed by industrialists. Many had no choice but to yield, since they faced either bankruptcy or a revival of cut-throat competition. Henry Ford, during the brief depression of 1920–1921, refused to surrender and resolved his problem in another way.

Why did the bankers offer to furnish Ford with a new treasurer rather than an engineer or an efficiency expert?

Where, other than from banks, do present-day businessmen secure funds needed for plant expansion?

❧

IN December, 1920, business the country over was marking time. More automobile plants were closed than were open and quite a number of those which were closed were completely in the charge of bankers. Rumours of bad financial condition were afloat concerning nearly every industrial company, and I became interested when the reports persisted that the Ford Motor Company not only needed money but could not get it. . . . I learned that I had overcome my prejudice against borrowing and that I might be found almost any day down in Wall Street, hat in hand, asking for money. And rumour went even further and said that no one would give me money and that I might have to break up and go out of business.

It is true that we did have a problem. In 1919 we had borrowed $70,000,000 on notes to buy the full stock interest in the Ford Motor Company. On this we had $33,000,000 left to pay. We had $18,000,000 in income taxes due or shortly to become due to the Government, and also we intended to pay our usual bonus for the year to the workmen, which amounted to $7,000,000. Altogether, between January 1st and April 18, 1921, we had payments ahead totalling $58,000,000. We had only $20,000,000 in the bank. Our balance sheet was more or less common knowledge and I suppose it was taken for granted that we could not raise the $38,000,000 needed without borrowing. For that is quite a large sum of money. Without the aid of Wall Street such a sum could not easily and quickly be raised. We were perfectly good for the money. Two years before we had borrowed $70,000,000. And since our whole property was unencumbered and we had no commercial debts, the matter of lending a large sum to us would not ordinarily have been a matter of moment. In fact, it would have been good banking business.

However, I began to see that our need for money was being industriously circulated as an evidence of impending failure. Then I began to suspect that, although the rumours came in news dispatches from all over the country, they might perhaps be traced to a single source. This belief was further strengthened when we were informed that a very fat financial editor was at Battle Creek sending out bulletins concerning the acuteness of our financial condition. Therefore, I took care not to deny a single rumour. We had made our financial plans and they did not include borrowing money.

I cannot too greatly emphasize that the very worst time to borrow money is when the banking people think that you need money. . . . [Instead] we planned a thorough house-cleaning. . . . . .

. . . We knew that we would have to shut down in order to take an

Henry Ford, *My Life and Work*, in collaboration with Samuel Crowther (New York: Doubleday, Page & Company, 1926), pp. 169–170, 172–176. Reprinted by permission of Mrs. Mary Owens Crowther.

inventory and clean house. We wanted to open with [a big price cut] and to have cars on hand to supply the demand. Then the new cars could be built out of material bought at lower prices. We determined that we were going to get lower prices.

We shut down in December with the intention of opening again in about two weeks. We found so much to do that actually we did not open for nearly six weeks. The moment that we shut down the rumours concerning our financial condition became more and more active. I know that a great many people hoped that we should have to go out after money—for, were we seeking money, then we should have to come to terms. We did not ask for money. We did not want money. We had one offer of money. An officer of a New York bank called on me with a financial plan which included a large loan and in which also was an arrangement by which a representative of the bankers would act as treasurer and take charge of the finance of the company. Those people meant well enough, I am quite sure. We did not want to borrow money but it so happened that at the moment we were without a treasurer. To that extent the bankers had envisaged our condition correctly. I asked my son Edsel to be treasurer as well as president of the company. That fixed us up as to a treasurer, so there was really nothing at all that the bankers could do for us.

Then we began our house-cleaning. During the war we had gone into many kinds of war work and had thus been forced to depart from our principle of a single product. This had caused many new departments to be added. The office force had expanded and much of the wastefulness of scattered production had crept in. War work is rush work and is wasteful work. We began throwing out everything that did not contribute to the production of cars. . . . . .

. . . The house-cleaning swept out the waste that had both made the prices high and absorbed the profit. We sold off the useless stuff. Before we had employed fifteen men per car per day. Afterward we employed nine per car per day. This did not mean that six out of fifteen men lost their jobs. They only ceased being unproductive. We made that cut by applying the rule that everything and everybody must produce or get out.

We cut our office forces in halves and offered the office workers better jobs in the shops. Most of them took the jobs. We abolished every order blank and every form of statistics that did not directly aid in the production of a car. We had been collecting tons of statistics because they were interesting. But statistics will not construct automobiles—so out they went.

We took out 60 per cent. of our telephone extensions. Only a comparatively few men in any organization need telephones. We formerly had a foreman for every five men; now we have a foreman for every twenty men. The other foremen are working on machines.

We cut the overhead charge from $146 a car to $93 a car, and when you realize what this means on more than four thousand cars a day you will have an idea how, not by economy, not by wage-cutting, but by the elimination of waste, it is possible to make an "impossible" price.

Most important of all, we found out how to use less money in our business by speeding up the turnover. . . .

We discovered, after a little experimenting that freight service could be improved sufficiently to reduce the cycle of manufacture from twenty-two to fourteen days. That is, raw material could be bought, manufactured, and the finished product put into the hands of the distributor in (roughly) 33 per cent. less time than before. We had been carrying an inventory of around $60,000,000 to insure uninterrupted production. Cutting down the time one third released $20,000,000, or $1,200,000 a year in interest. Counting the finished inventory, we saved approximately $8,000,000 more—that is, we were able to release $28,000,-000 in capital and save the interest on that sum.

On January 1st we had $20,000,000. On April 1st we had $87,300,000, or $27,300,000 more than we needed to wipe out all our indebtedness. That is what boring into the business did for us! . . .

Now I have told about all this not in the way of an exploit, but to point out how a business may find resources within itself instead of borrowing, and also to start a little thinking as to whether the form of our money may not put a premium on borrowing and thus give far too great a place in life to the bankers.

We could have borrowed $40,000,000—more had we wanted to. Suppose we had borrowed, what would have happened? Should we have been better fitted to go on with our business? Or worse fitted? If we had borrowed we should not have been under the necessity of finding methods to cheapen production. Had we been able to obtain the money at 6 per cent. flat—and we should in commissions and the like have had to pay more than that—the interest charge alone on a yearly production of 500,000 cars would have amounted to about four dollars a car. Therefore we should now be without the benefit of better production and loaded with a heavy debt. Our cars would probably cost about one hundred dollars more than they do; hence we should have a smaller production, for we could not have so many buyers; we should employ fewer men, and in short, should not be able to serve to the utmost. You will note that the financiers proposed to cure by lending money and not by bettering methods. They did not suggest putting in an engineer; they wanted to put in a treasurer.

And that is the danger of having bankers in business. They think solely in terms of money. They think of a factory as making money, not goods. They want to watch the money, not the efficiency of production. They cannot comprehend that a business never stands still, it must go forward or go back. They regard a reduction in prices as a throwing away of profit instead of as a building of business. . . . . .

. . . The banker is, as I have noted, by training and because of his position, totally unsuited to the conduct of industry.

FOR FURTHER THOUGHT

What impact did big business and the consolidation movement have on the highly competitive marketplace? Did public understanding of these new economic institutions keep pace with their growing power?

What was the relationship between the "American Dream" that every man could hope to be self-employed or go into business for himself and the Antitrust Movement? How has that "American Dream" changed through the years?

How is the Antitrust Movement apt to be affected as increasing numbers of Americans invest in large corporations or are employed by big businesses?

3. Workingmen and Unions, 1865-1921

INDUSTRIALIZATION and the rise of big business did not affect all laboring people alike. Depending on where they lived, conditions in their trade, and their own talents and good fortunes, many skilled craftsmen such as carpenters, masons, and plumbers, benefited from the new order. If their wages did not rise significantly—and few did between 1870 and 1896—the steady decline in the cost of living tended to improve their lot. For other skilled workers such as cobblers, machinists, and printers, new labor-saving machines took over much of their work, displaced many men, and converted others into mere machine-tenders.

The vast majority of workers, semi-skilled or unskilled, who made up the labor force in the giant new factories and in the mines, suffered more severely. A flood of immigrants from abroad and a stream of farmers moving to the cities added constantly to their number and frequently created oversupplies of labor of which employers hastened to take advantage. Lacking prestige or status, and possessing little individual bargaining power compared to that of their corporate employers, such workmen found their wages low, their hours long, their working conditions intolerable. They enjoyed no job security. Under the law, a workman had no claim whatever to his employment and might be discharged arbitrarily. Neither employers nor the state offered workmen protection when injured, sick, unemployed, or too old to work.

Laborers were obliged to conform to the demands of the costly machines they tended. When owners found it more profitable to operate their machines twenty-four hours a day, part of the work force learned to work at night and sleep by day. In the steel mills, where operations had to be continuous, two shifts of workmen labored twelve hours a day, seven days a week. When machines overproduced and drove down prices, wages tumbled; if demand did not warrant more production, workmen were laid off.

It is not surprising that labor unions eventually arose among American workmen. They were essential to establish some balance in labor's bargaining position; they were needed to protect workers' wages and to improve working conditions, and they alone could defend workmen against arbitrary treatment by either giant corporations or petty foremen.

More difficult to explain, given conditions at the time, was the long delay in the rise of strong labor unions. It was due in part, certainly, to the strength of employers and to the tenacity with which they clung to their established position. Also, the public attitude, shaped by America's individualistic, agrarian tradition, frowned on collective action by workmen. Another significant retarding influence was the anti-union stance of local, state and even federal governments.

However important these outside forces were in retarding unionization, powerful factors within the ranks of labor also worked to slow down the movement. Many workmen brought with them to the factories the same individualistic attitudes that prevailed among the public at large. They accepted as part of the natural order the harsh doctrines of Social Darwinism. They believed in the success myth and dreamed of someday becoming self-employed (see Chapter One). A part of the labor force, especially women, children, immigrants, and later Negroes, proved difficult to organize when approached by unions. More often, unions ignored or discriminated against these workers. Labor leaders, too, often unintentionally hindered successful organization. They differed sharply over the objectives and goals of the labor movement, the best patterns of organization, and the tactics and weapons to be used against employers.

Many nineteenth century unions, including the briefly powerful Knights of Labor, never fully accepted modern industrial capitalism. Union leaders sought to end "wage-slavery" by elevating the workers into the self-employed classes. They proposed cooperatively owned factories so that workmen would be self-employed rather than hired employees of others. The leaders also preached that land reform and temperance were among the chief reforms needed by workers. The leadership and the rank and file of the Knights disagreed bitterly over means. The national officers disapproved of strikes and boycotts, urging their men instead to negotiate with employers and to rely on persuasion, education, and some legislation to achieve their goals. The membership found that employers denied their right to organize, refused to negotiate, to be persuaded or educated, and lobbied successfully against labor legislation. Consequently, the membership frequently resorted to strikes and boycotts.

Another current in the labor movement was revolutionary. It accepted industrialization, but rejected capitalism. Various socialistic and other Marxist-oriented unions called for an end to the exploitation of labor by capital and demanded that the means of production be turned over to the workers themselves, directly or through government. Although small in membership, the radical doctrines of these unions and their willingness to use violence, excited considerable alarm among employers. In the end, radical unionism probably hastened the acceptance by employers of more conservative labor unions.

The mainstream of the American labor movement accepted both industrialization and capitalism, but fought for a greater share of capitalism's benefits for labor. Such unions as those making up the American Federation of Labor and the railway brotherhoods aimed chiefly at "bread and butter" issues—higher wages, shorter working hours, and improved working conditions. Their principal weapon was organization into strong craft unions with which employers would have to deal. Strikes and boycotts were used when necessary to force concessions. These unions eschewed radicalism and direct political actions, preferring to rely on their economic power as organized skilled craftsmen.

The selections which follow illustrate different aspects of the labor problem as seen by public officials, writers, employers, and labor leaders. The first three items show the reactions of a prominent clergyman [I], a President [II], and a federal judge [III] to the "labor question" as it appeared to them during labor crises. The specific problem of wage-setting in the late nineteenth century is next considered, theoretically by a scholar [IV] and more practically by an industrialist [V]. The strike as a labor weapon is defended by a labor leader [VI] and denounced by a federal judge [VII]. There follow illustrations of three obstacles to improved labor conditions—the impact of immigration on unionization [VIII], the refusal of employers to recognize unions [IX], and the refusal of courts to accept labor reforms brought about by legislation [X].

By the turn of the century, the industrial order was firmly established. The depression of the 'nineties was over, and Progressive reformers were beginning their push for social justice. A host of labor and other reform measures issued from state houses and from Congress—some even survived tests before the courts. A number of influential business leaders began to reassess organized labor. The National Civic Federation (made up of businessmen, public figures, and labor leaders) undertook, for example, the substitution of arbitration for strikes. Many employers granted tacit, if not explicit, recognition to conservative labor unions. In the final two selections a steel executive urges acceptance of the right of workmen to bargain collectively [XI], while an automobile manufacturer defends paying his men wages that were considerably higher than the going rate [XII].

A more general acceptance of organized labor became evident during World War I: labor leaders served on war boards, the government protected unions in war plants, and union membership swelled to over five million by 1920. Symbolic of labor's new status was Woodrow Wilson's appearance—the first by a President of the United States—before the 1917 convention of the American Federation of Labor. EDITED BY GERALD G. EGGERT

I
───
The Reverend Mr. Henry Ward Beecher discusses the strike problem.

FROM: Newspaper reports of two sermons, 1877.

AMERICANS first became acutely aware that the nation had a "labor problem" during the Panic of 1873. Depressed business conditions during the next four years led to widespread unemployment and labor disorders. Men who kept their jobs faced frequent lay-offs and wage reductions. When the eastern railroad lines ordered wage cuts in

July 1877, railway workmen revolted. The strikes, unplanned and directed only by impromptu leaders, spread from one rail center to another. Rioting, mob violence, and looting followed. State guards and the United States Army suppressed the strikes and finally restored law and order.

Thoughtful Americans began to ask themselves what had caused the strikes. What did labor want? What could be done to prevent such disorders in the future? Henry Ward Beecher, popular pastor of the fashionable Plymouth Church in New York City, spoke out forcefully on the labor question while the strikes were in progress.

What did Beecher see as the fundamental cause of the strikes? What could be done about the problem?

What answer could be given to his argument that trades-unions destroy the individuality and the liberty of the worker?

FROM A REPORT OF BEECHER'S SERMON OF JULY 22, 1877[1]

PLYMOUTH Church was crowded last evening by a large audience, and Mr. Beecher in the course of his discourse alluded to the great railroad strike. He said that disorder had broken out all along the great roads of several portions of the country, and riots of an unusual magnitude had taken place.

This Sabbath day was not, he said, one of stillness, for there were military movements throughout the land, and from their city soldiers were being dispatched to quell the riots. In a few days peace would be restored. Such outbreaks were but transient bubbles, which burst almost as soon as they were formed. They sprang from ignorance and passion. Such riots arose because their promoters and those who abetted them were ignorant of political economy. . . . He proceeded to eulogize the working classes, and dwelt particularly on the industry, sobriety, and heroism of the railroad employees, and pointed out the necessity for harmonious working together of the laborer and the capitalist. He explained at great length the elementary principles of political economy, and dwelt particularly on the causes which gave rise to the long depression of trade in this country. . . . He then said: "What right had the working men . . . to say to any one, 'You shall not work for wages which we refuse.' They had a perfect right to say to the employers, 'We shall not work for you,' but they had no right to tyrannize over their fellow-men. . . . The necessities of the great railroad companies demanded that there should be a reduction of wages. There must be con-

[1] *The New York Times,* Monday, July 23, 1877.

tinual shrinkage until things come back to the gold standard, and wages, as well as . . . provisions, and property, must share in it. It was true that $1 a day was not enough to support a man and five children, if a man would insist on smoking and drinking beer. Was not a dollar a day enough to buy bread? Water costs nothing. [Laughter.] Man cannot live by bread, it is true, but the man who cannot live on bread and water is not fit to live. [Laughter.] When a man is educated away from the power of self-denial, he is falsely educated. A family may live on good bread and water in the morning, water and bread at midday, and good water and bread at night. [Continued laughter.] Such may be called the bread of affliction, but it was fit that man should eat of the bread of affliction. Thousands would be very glad of a dollar a day, and it added to the sin of the men on strike for them to turn round and say to those men, 'You can do so, but you shall not.' There might be special cases of hardship, but the great laws of political economy could not be set at defiance." He concluded by declaring that, in the end, the men on strike would be defeated, trade resumed, and prosperity once more reign throughout the land. [Applause.]

FROM BEECHER'S SERMON DENOUNCING "COMMUNISM"[2]

SO much discussion has been had, and so much ill will disseminated against Rev. Henry Ward Beecher at communistic meetings during the last week, on account of a misconstruction of the words of his sermon on the 22d inst., that it was shrewdly guessed that Mr. Beecher would take an early opportunity of more clearly defining his position on the question of the rights of laboring men. . . . The Police authorities, in anticipation of any trouble which might have arisen, sent about 30 policemen in citizens' clothes, who were distributed among the congregation, and a squad of detectives were placed in the immediate neighborhood of the church. . . .

Mr. Beecher . . . said that . . . he desired to make a few remarks upon the events which have occurred since Sunday last. He said he had been grossly misrepresented—not willfully or intentionally, but by careless reporting—as saying what he did not say and does not believe. The reports had had the effect of bringing to him score [*sic*] of letters, some of them obscene, others expressing indignation, some threatening, many from cowardly men ashamed of their own names, besides others pleading for the cause of humanity and for the working man. . . .

[2] *The New York Times,* Monday, July 30, 1877.

. . . Is the great working class oppressed? asked the speaker. Yes, undoubtedly it is, he answered, both by the Governments and the rich men, and by the educated classes. This is not because the Governments, the rich men, or the educated forces desire to oppress them, but because it must be so. . . . When men are ignorant and poor and weak, they can't help being oppressed. That is so by a great natural law. . . . It is to say that intelligence gets ahead of ignorance. It is to say that a ton outweighs a half-ton. It can't be said this is so by reason of selfishness or injustice. . . . They reap the misfortunes of inferiority, not because men desire to oppress them, but because it must be so.

. . . The theories of Europe in regard to the community of property we reject because they are against natural law and will never be practicable. God has intended the great to be great and the little to be little. No equalization process can ever take place until men are made equal as to productive forces. It is a wild vision, not a practicable theory. The European theories of combinations between workmen and trades-unions and communes destroy the individuality of the person, and there is no possible way of preserving the liberty of the people except by the maintenance of individual liberty, intact from Government and intact from individual meddling. Persons have the right to work when or where they please, as long as they please, and for what they please. . . . . .

. . . Every man should stand on his own level, be that what it might. It is sometimes said that the world owes a man a living. Certainly, if he earns it. It is also said that every man is entitled to be taken care of, certainly—by himself, unless he depends on the support of his mother, or in later years of his wife. [Laughter.] Mr. Beecher here introduced the instances of the fly, the sparrow, and the eagle, which fill different spheres. He said that a person doing the work of a fly should take the position of one; the one doing that of a sparrow should take its position, while the one who filled the eagle's part should go aloft like the eagle and soar through the upper air. Every man has the right to be where he can put himself by his proper acquisitions, labor, and productiveness. . . . . .

. . . He said the workmen should call on God and stop using tobacco and beer, subdue their passions, and try by self-denial to make homes for themselves and families. Men who have been cast down from affluence to poverty should not grunt and grumble, but bear matters unflinchingly. They should never forget they are men, even though they die of hunger. . . . The manly way to meet misfortune is to go down boldly to poverty. In losing everything else a man should not lose his manliness. I don't say that $1 per day is enough to support a working man, but it is enough to support a man. He is going through a transition, and a man should be superior to his circumstances.

II

President Hayes ponders the labor problem.

FROM: A diary entry of 1877 and a letter of 1886.

PRESIDENT Rutherford B. Hayes, who authorized the use of federal troops to suppress rioting, kept matters in perspective throughout the disorders of 1877. Many labeled the strikers anarchists or communists and regarded the strikes as rebellion. Hayes, however, noted that the workers' attacks were against railroad property—not against the government—and he declared them but manifestations of labor unrest. At the close of the 1877 strikes, Hayes weighed the causes of, and possible solutions to, the labor question. Again during the railroad strikes of 1886, after leaving the Presidency, Hayes discussed the same issues in a letter to a life-long friend. Unfortunately, Hayes never converted his ideas into actions.

Given Hayes' views of striking, how could laboring men improve their conditions?

Where do Beecher (in the previous selection) and Hayes disagree as to the ultimate solution to the strike problem?

DIARY ENTRY FOR AUGUST 5, 1877[1]

✎

. . . THE strikes have been put down by *force,* but now for the *real* remedy. Cant [*sic*] something [be] done by education of the strikers, by judicious control of the capitalists, by wise general policy to end or diminish the evil? The R.R. strikers, as a rule are good men sober intelligent and industrious. The mischiefs are

1. Strikers prevent men willing to work from doing so.
2. They seize and hold the property of their employers.
3. The consequent excitement furnishes an opportunity for the dangerous criminal classes to destroy life and property.

Now, "every man has a right if he sees fit to quarrel with his own bread and butter, but he has no right to quarrel with the bread and butter of other people." Every man has a right to determine for himself the value of his own labor, but he has no right to determine for other men the value of their labor. . . .

Every man has the right to refuse to work if the wages dont [*sic*]

---

[1] Diary entry, August 5, 1877, Diary and Letters of Rutherford Birchard Hayes, The Rutherford B. Hayes Library, Fremont, Ohio. Used with permission.

suit him, but he has no right to prevent others from working if they
are suited with the wages. . . . . .

HAYES' LETTER TO GUY M. BRYAN, MAY 12, 1886[2]

. . . ON the labor question. My position is: —1. The previous
question always must be in any popular excitement *the supremacy of
law.* All lawless violence must be suppressed *instantly, with overwhelming force* and *at all hazards.* To hesitate or tamper with it is a fatal
mistake. *Justice, humanity,* and *safety* all require this.

2. I agree that Labor does not get its fair share of the wealth it
creates. The Sermon on the Mount, the golden rule, the Declaration of
Independence all require extensive reforms to the end that labor may be
so rewarded that the working man can with temperance, industry & thrift
own a home, educate his children, & lay up a support for old age.

3. *The United States* must begin to deal with the whole subject.

[2] Rutherford B. Hayes to Guy M. Bryan, May 12, 1886, *ibid.* Used with permission.

III

A federal judge discusses labor reform.

FROM: Judge Peter S. Grosscup's charge to a grand jury in 1894.

MUCH discussion of the labor question in the late nineteenth century
occurred in periods of crisis, especially during the railroad strikes of
1877, 1886, and 1894. Federal Circuit Court Judge Grosscup played a
major role in suppressing the last of these strikes, the Chicago Railway
Boycott and Strike of 1894. When a minor strike at the Pullman sleeping-
car company near Chicago escalated into a general tie-up of all railroads
in the Chicago area, Grosscup was one of the judges who issued the
famous "blanket injunction," which forbade any interference with the
operation of any railroad carrying the mail or interstate commerce. In a
subsequent charge to a grand jury during the crisis, Grosscup discussed
the methods of bringing about reforms.

> *What arguments can be made against Grosscup's method of reform?*
> *What good, if any, came from strikes which became violent?*

ᴇᔓ

YOU have been summoned here to inquire whether any of the laws
of the United States within the judicial district have been violated. You

In Re Charge To Grand Jury, 62 Federal Reporter 829 (1894).

have come in an atmosphere and amid occurrences that may well cause reasonable men to question whether the government and laws of the United States are yet supreme. Thanks to resolute manhood, and to that enlightened intelligence which perceives the necessity of a vindication of law before any other adjustments are possible, the government of the United States is still supreme.

You doubtless feel, as I do, that the opportunities of life, under present conditions, are not entirely equal, and that changes are needed to forestall some of the dangerous tendencies of current industrial tendencies. But neither the torch of the incendiary, nor the weapon of the insurrectionist, nor the inflamed tongue of him who incites to fire and sword is the instrument to bring about reforms. To the mind of the American people; to the calm, dispassionate sympathetic judgment of a race that is not afraid to face deep changes and responsibilities, there has, as yet, been no appeal. Men who appear as the champions of great changes must first submit them to discussion, discussion that reaches not simply the parties interested, but the outer circles of society, and must be patient as well as persevering until the public intelligence has been reached, and a public judgment made up. An appeal to force before that hour is a crime, not only against government of existing laws, but against the cause itself; for what man of any intelligence supposes that any settlement will abide which is induced under the light of the torch or the shadow of an overpowering threat?

IV

A nineteenth century scholar explains the wage-fund theory.

FROM: An 1886 magazine article.

THE advent of the labor problem during the post-Civil War era gave rise to much discussion of how workers' wages were determined and how they should be determined. Social reformers suggested, as President Hayes did (p. 76), that in calculating labor's share of the returns of production, employers should consider what the worker needed to support himself and his family decently. Most economists and businessmen, on the other hand, subscribed to the hard-headed wage-fund theory described here by a political economist.

Modern theorists see the wage-fund formula as a much too simplistic explanation of wages. While they recognize supply and demand as the broad determinants of wages, other factors such as costs, productivity, efficiency, prices and interest rates are all relevant.

If the wage-fund theory was correct, what impact could unions have on wages?

By what means could laborers hope to raise their wages under the wage-fund theory?

⳵

IT may very much simplify the discussion . . . if . . . we state two or three pretty well established conclusions of economic science, viz.:

1. Labor, like flour or cotton cloth, should always be bought in the cheapest market and sold in the dearest.

2. The sole legitimate condition that regulates wages is the demand for service and the supply of workers. If the demand diminishes, wages decrease; if the supply diminishes, wages increase.

3. The wage ordinarily paid is determined by the automatic division of the whole amount which a community is willing to pay for the specified sort of work, by the whole number of persons willing and able to do it.

The first and second of these propositions come so near being economic axioms that they will be allowed to stand for the present without support. If they are sound, every laborer ought to sell his services for the most he can get, and every employer ought to pay the market price of labor and no more. If they are sound, every laborer has a right to strike; that is, A has a right to refuse to work for B, either because B exacts too much service or offers too little pay, or because his manners are arrogant, or his place of business unventilated, or even because his language is ungrammatical or his hair curly; and B has an equal right to discharge A for reasons of his own. But A has no right to prevent other workmen from hiring to B in his stead, at any wages or hours they may choose to accept; and whenever he does so, either by violence on his own part or conspiracy with others, it is the duty of all right-thinking men to suppress and punish him, as they would punish any other law-breaker—any invader of property-rights or personal liberty.

The law of wages is stated in proposition three.

To illustrate it: Why is Patti paid $5,000 a night for singing? Managers do not offer that price because they are sentimental or sympathetic—because she has a large family, or unusual expenses. No; they pay it because the best opera-singing is widely demanded, and cannot be had for less. The world gives $20,000 a night for music by the queens of song. If there were a thousand of them, many might get only $20 apiece. But such minstrelsy is a very difficult acquirement, and results from a most infrequent combination: great physical strength, beauty, vivacity, dramatic instinct, the requisite formation of the larynx and

W. A. Croffut, "What Rights Have Laborers?" *Forum,* I (May 1886), 294–296.

other organs of song, persistent application, the right teacher, the wealthy backer, and the melodious *je ne sais quoi* behind them all. These are indispensable, and their happy concurrence is so rare that when society looks about for entertainment it discovers that there are only twenty prima donnas on the planet to divide the $20,000 daily, and only one is Patti. So her $5,000 a night is the result of the competitive bidding of those who can hear her on no other terms.

Again, the world pays a certain sum per day, say a million dollars, for plain sewing. It is not a difficult accomplishment, requiring long training and a rare blending of qualities. So, instead of there being twenty women to respond to the demand, there are twenty million women. Therefore, instead of commanding $1,000 or $5,000 a day each, they can command only fifty or thirty or twenty cents a day.

There are hundreds of men in the United States who get salaries of $25,000 to $50,000 a year each, and abundantly earn them by bringing to bear unusual skill, courage, integrity, knowledge, experience, and, above all, business prescience, in the increase and protection of extensive properties; but a man of humble intellect, and without special training, who knows just enough to wheel a barrow along a plank, gets only his daily dollar.

"But," says an objector, "the wheelbarrow-man ought to have more than $1 a day; it is not fair wages." The reply is that any wages are "fair" which are as high as that sort of work commands in the open market; and to say that a laborer "ought" to have more than the sum which results from a division of the demand by the supply, is just as reasonable as it would be to say that a farmer "ought" to get more than the market price for his wool or his potatoes.

I admit, nay, I assert, the demands of charity on every human being; but charity and business are and ought to be perpetually divorced. An employer is under no more financial obligation to his workman after he has paid them current wages, than they are to him or to a passer-by on the street whom they never saw.

V

An industrialist explains his wage policy.

FROM: The testimony of George M. Pullman before the United States Strike Commission, 1894.

AT the close of the Chicago Railway Strike of 1894, President Grover Cleveland appointed a commission to investigate the causes of the great strike and to recommend legislation. Among the many men questioned was George M. Pullman, the sleeping-car magnate, at whose plant the strike had its origins. The commissioners, among other things, closely examined how the Pullman Company determined wages.

How do Pullman's answers to specific questions square with the views he expressed in his opening statement?

What arguments can be made for and against the Pullman Company officers using the $25 million undivided profits fund to maintain wages?

[FROM PULLMAN'S PRELIMINARY STATEMENT]

THE object in building Pullman [the company town] was the establishment of a great manufacturing business on the most substantial basis possible, recognizing, as we did, and do now, that the working people are the most important element which enters into the successful operation of any manufacturing enterprise. We decided to build, in close proximity to the shops, homes for workingmen of such character and surroundings as would prove so attractive as to cause the best class of mechanics to seek that place for employment in preference to others. We also desired to establish the place on such a basis as would exclude all baneful influences, believing that such a policy would result in the greatest measure of success, both from a commercial point of view, and also, what was equally important, or perhaps of greater importance, in a tendency toward continued elevation and improvement of the conditions not only of the working people themselves, but of their children growing up about them. . . . . .

[FROM THE INTERROGATION OF PULLMAN]

. . . . . Q.—Do you know what the total, amount of dividends paid out by the company since its organization amounts to; have you ever figured that? A.—I couldn't tell you from memory. . . .

Q.—The first two years, I understood you to say, that it paid about 3 per cent? A.—Three per cent, quarterly, for the first two years.

Q.—That would be 12 per cent a year? A.—Yes, sir.

Q.—And for the next few years it paid about 9½ per cent annually? A.—My impression is it was about three years.

Q.—And for the rest of the time about 2 per cent, quarterly, or 8 per cent per year? A.—Yes, sir; 8 per cent has been the regular dividend from that time, and there has been no change in it.

Report on the Chicago Strike of June-July, 1894 (Washington: Government Printing Office, 1895), pp. 529, 543–544, 554–555, 556–557, 564, 567.

Q.—Now, in addition to those dividends, you have accumulated from sixteen to eighteen millions of undivided profits? A.—The undivided profits are something like twenty five millions; that is my impression. . . .

Q.—Then in addition to the annual dividend that you have mentioned, there has also been accumulated about $25,000,000 of undivided profit? A.—Yes, sir; from the date of the organization of the company. We have never made any extra dividends. There has been no stock watering and no extra dividends. The surplus earnings during what we call prosperous years, the company has put aside to meet the bad times, practically guaranteeing the investors in the stock of the company their permanent dividends. . . . . .

Q.—Did the Pullman company during its years of prosperity ever voluntarily increase the wages of any class or of all classes of its employees? A.—Not specially on account of prosperous business. It has always paid its employees liberal wages. . . . I think that it has never had a strike, with the exception of the strike in 1886 and some little strikes in departments—unimportant ones—it has had none in all these years.

Q.—But it has never increased the wages of its employees voluntarily? A.—Certainly it has not increased them any other way.

Q.—It has never divided any of its profits with them in any shape or form? A.—The Pullman company divides its profits with the people who own the property. It would not have a right to take the profits belonging to the people who own that property—

Q.—Well, we will not discuss that question. . . . Now, when the first year of losses comes, it makes a reduction of 20 or 25 per cent on its employees. A.—In that particular branch. It was a question whether we could get cars to build or whether we should shut up our shops.

Q.—Was this reduction upon one class of your employees or upon all classes? . . . . . A.—No; when we reduced the wages in one part of the manufacturing plant we would reduce the wages in all parts of it. You can not be paying one set of men higher wages than you are paying others. Our repair men are paid the same rate of wages in Pullman that they are in Wilmington, and they pay the same rate all around. The wages of car builders and car repairers generally have been reduced. . . . . .

Q.—Suppose a board of arbitration had examined into the matter and had said: "Yes, we accept your statement that you are losing money on these jobs and that the times are hard, and you are not receiving as much money on car mileage as heretofore; but with a body of workmen who had been with you some time—and a person would imagine it would be a good thing to do that under all the circumstances—you ought to divide with them a little, give them at least enough to make

a good living"—wouldn't that have been a fair matter to be considered?
A.—I think not. How long a time should a man be with a company
before he would be entitled to a gift of money? For that is what this
would mean. The wage question is settled by the law of supply and
demand. We were obliged to reduce wages in order to get these cars—
to compete with other people in the same business, that were doing
the same thing. . . . . .

Q.—Who has the power to reduce rents at Pullman? A.—Any question
of that kind would come to me. . . .

Q.—Was the question of reducing rents [on company houses] when
wages were reduced one that came under discussion at all? A.—No, sir;
the question of reducing rents did not come under discussion between
the officers of the company. The income from the rent was so low that
there was no room for reducing the rent and bringing any income from
it; and, as I explained to the men, there was no necessary connection
between the employment of men and the renting of homes; that they
had the privilege of living where they chose. . . . . .

Q.—When this reduction of wages was made was your salary reduced
and what of the other officers? A.—No, sir.

Q.—Were the salaries of the superintendents and foremen reduced? A.—
No, sir.

Q.—Now, let me ask you why, in this general reduction, that was not
done? A.—Because it is not easy for the manager of a corporation to
find men to fill the positions. Men that have been with a corporation
for twenty-five years, it don't lie with me to go to him and say to him,
"I am going to reduce your salary $1,000," because he will say, "Very
well; you will find somebody else to take my place." And there are very
few officers of a corporation, comparatively, to the number of employees,
and they are able to command their salaries. It would be a matter of
agreement whether they would take less, and it is a matter, then, whether
a corporation could afford to dispense with their services.

Q.—In other words, a corporation could not afford to make a reduction
of their salaries? A.—It would be impossible for me, as the president
of a corporation, to reduce the salaries of my officers arbitrarily, because
I would find myself possibly without them.

Q.—You might reduce your own, perhaps, but not theirs. A.—I might, if
I chose, but the difference that it would make on the cost of a car would
be so infinitesimal and fractional that it would not be worth considering. . . .

Q.—Under the circumstances, don't you think that you ought to have,
fairly and in justice to the other classes, attempted to reduce those
salaries? A.—That might come; we can not do everything at once, and
we can not tell how long this depression is going to last.

VI

A labor leader justifies strikes.

FROM: The testimony of Samuel Gompers before the United States Strike Commission, 1894.

SAMUEL GOMPERS, president of the American Federation of Labor, believed that labor could best accomplish its goals by organizing into craft unions and making use of its economic power to win concessions from employers. Collective bargaining was the chief weapon of unions, he believed. Strikes and boycotts were to be used sparingly and only when they offered a likelihood of success. Nonetheless, Gompers defended the strike as a legitimate and useful device for supporting demands from recalcitrant employers.

Why, according to Gompers, were lost strikes really labor victories?

Do you feel that present day strikes tend to win support for labor's demands? Do you think they serve the same purposes as in the 1890s?

◄§

I DO not join this general hue and cry against strikes. I believe in diminishing the number as much as possible, and I have worked and contributed, I think, as much as any other one living man to the diminution in the number of strikes; but in the denunciation of strikes I will not join. I regard the strikes as the sign that the people are not yet willing to surrender every spark of their manhood and their honor and their independence. It is the protest of the worker against unjust conditions; and the strike has commanded the attention of the employing class, the capitalist class, and the thinkers throughout the world to the problem of labor, who would otherwise not have given the laborer a second's consideration. . . .

A strike is the movement of one of the forces in the industrial life and the commercial life, and gives evidence that we shall not go down further in the social and economic scale, and it is a warning that labor has more rights than it now enjoys, and a determination that it is going to secure them, if not today, some other day.

Strikes are not the failures that they are usually written down to be. Speaking of the strikes gained, the various bureaus of labor statistics, both of the General Government and the various State governments, demonstrate that a vast majority of them are gained. . . . [T]he reports of the bureau of labor statistics of the State of New York show that more than two-thirds of the strikes undertaken are victories for the workers,

Report on the Chicago Strike of June-July, 1894 (Washington: Government Printing Office, 1895), pp. 195–197.

and that they involved the largest number of employees; that they are not, as a rule, against reduction of wages, but for an increase of wages or for a diminution of the hours of labor, or for improved conditions. Some four years ago I sent out a blank to our affiliated organizations, and obtained from them reports of the strikes they had had within a year, officially recognized, and the costs and results, how many involved, etc. There were more than 80 per cent of them victories, about 4 per cent compromised, and about 16 per cent which were lost.

Now, apart from the question of strikes which are won, strikes which are lost—that is, which do not succeed in obtaining the conditions which the workers started out to achieve— . . . there are few if any instances where some advantage has not been gained. First, the immediate advantage, the warning to the employing class generally that the workingman will not go down further, and that any attempt to force them down will be very expensive if nothing else—very expensive, and that it would be dearer to them, even if they succeeded in enforcing a reduction, than to concede the wages or hours then paid or allowed. It can scarcely be accepted to be or to mean a diminution of production either. There are few workingmen in the entire country who do not lose from one week to three months of employment throughout the year, and I refer to those who are employed. . . .

I have thought this matter of strikes over very carefully, and there is another conclusion that I have come to, and that I have not seen dealt with largely or at all, and that is, whether defeated strikes do not . . . raise the economic condition of the people. Let me give an illustration of what I refer to. Say a railroad company whose employees are on a strike . . . against a reduction of wages . . . gets other workers to take the place of their former employees. As a rule . . . these new employees . . . have been much lower in the economic scale than the position that they are about to occupy—in other words, economically they are raised—and I think that is undisputed, otherwise men would not change as a rule from equal employments to take the place of their brothers who were on a strike. . . . Now, as to those who go on the strike, would they change places relatively to those who have been recruited? My experience and my inquiries demonstrate that that is not so, that a few may suffer and suffer quite a time, but that as a whole they do not go down in the social scale. I refer to the employees who went on strikes; there are a few who suffered, but the whole number, as a class, have either remained where they were before the strike or are pushed higher in the social and economic scale. And thus, though the defeated strike loses the immediate object of the men who went out on the strike, yet on the whole it has benefited the whole people socially and economically. That is the result of my observation and inquiry.

I think I have already spoken of the influence on the public mind of strikes. The fact that this honorable commission was appointed to investigate the strike of the American Railway Union is an evidence of the beneficial results of the strike. . . .

VII

A federal judge defines a strike.

FROM: Judge James G. Jenkins' decision to uphold an injunction against striking, 1894.

RAILWAY strikes in the late nineteenth century resembled present day national emergency strikes in that they often tied up large segments of the nation's transportation network. During the 1890s, a number of federal judges vehemently lashed out against strikers. In the case in question, Circuit Court Judge Jenkins of Milwaukee, in justifying an injunction forbidding a strike, virtually outlawed strikes by definition. Though extreme, his view was not unique on the bench at that time.

What factors tended to make strikes violent in the 1890s?

Why do present day strikes tend to be less frequently violent?

. . . A STRIKE is this: A combined effort among workmen to compel the master to the concession of a certain demand, by preventing the conduct of his business until compliance with the demand. The concerted cessation of work is but one of, and the least effective of, the means to the end; the intimidation of others from engaging in the service, the interference with, and the disabling and destruction of, property, and resort to actual force and violence, when requisite to the accomplishment of the end, being the other, and more effective, means employed. It is idle to talk of a peaceable strike. None such ever occurred. The suggestion is impeachment of intelligence. From first to last, from the earliest recorded strike to . . . [the present], force and turbulence, violence and outrage, arson and murder, have been associated with the strike as its natural and inevitable concomitants. No strike can be effective without compulsion and force. . . . The moment that violence becomes an essential part of a scheme, or a necessary means of effecting the purpose of the combination, that moment the combination, otherwise lawful, becomes illegal. All combinations to interfere with perfect freedom in the proper management and control of one's lawful business, to dictate the terms upon which such business shall be conducted, by

Farmers' Loan & Trust Co. v. *Northern Pacific Railway Co.,* 60 Federal Reporter 821–822 (April 6, 1894).

means of threats or by interference with property or traffic or with the
lawful employment of others, are within the condemnation of the law
It has well been said that the wit of man could not devise a legal strike
because compulsion is the leading idea of it. A strike is essentially a
conspiracy to extort by violence; the means employed to effect the end
being not only the cessation of labor by the conspirators, but the neces
sary prevention of labor by those who are willing to assume their places
and, as a last resort, and in many instances an essential element of
success, the disabling and destruction of the property of the master. . .
I know of no peaceable strike. I think no strike was ever heard of that
was or could be successful unaccompanied by intimidation and violence

VIII

*A young immigrant changes his mind about join-
ing a labor union.*

FROM: *The Jungle*, a popular novel of 1906.

THE immigrant was a constant, dependable source of cheap labor in
America well into the twentieth century. Indeed, between 1900 and
1914, over thirteen million persons from abroad poured into "the land of
opportunity." Most were uneducated, untrained, and rural in background
They crowded into the nation's industrial centers seeking work as un
skilled laborers. There they competed with one another and with un
skilled, native-born workmen; their abundance tended to drive down the
wages of all. Most immigrants at first accepted their lot without complaint. By the time that they came to understand the value of unions
floods of green new immigrants stood ready to take their places.

Upton Sinclair's novel, *The Jungle*, from which this selection was
taken, was most famous for its exposure of unwholesome conditions in
the meat-packing industry. The book was directly responsible for the
adoption, in 1906, of the Federal Beef Inspection Act. In the passage
which follows, Sinclair relates how Jurgis, Lithuanian immigrant and
hero of the story, comes to change his view of labor unions.

*Given their rural origins, why did not most of the immigrants settle on
farms?*

*What factors other than their failure to understand the purposes of
unions tended to keep immigrants from becoming union members?*

◄§

JURGIS talked lightly about work, because he was young. They
told him stories about the breaking down of men, there in the stockyards

Upton Sinclair, *The Jungle* (New York: Doubleday, Page & Company, 1906), pp. 23–
24, 68, 102–105, 107. All rights reserved. Reprinted by permission of The Viking
Press, Inc.

of Chicago, and of what had happened to them afterwards—stories to make your flesh creep, but Jurgis would only laugh. He had only been there four months, and he was young, and a giant besides. There was too much health in him. He could not even imagine how it would feel to be beaten. "That is well enough for men like you," he would say, "*silpnas,* puny fellows—but my back is broad."

Jurgis was like a boy, a boy from the country. He was the sort of man the bosses like to get hold of, the sort they make it a grievance they cannot get hold of. When he was told to go to a certain place, he would go there on the run. When he had nothing to do for the moment, he would stand round fidgeting, dancing, with the overflow of energy that was in him. If he were working in a line of men, the line always moved too slowly for him, and you could pick him out by his impatience and restlessness. That was why he had been picked out on one important occasion; for Jurgis had stood outside of Brown and Company's "Central Time Station" not more than half an hour, the second day of his arrival in Chicago, before he had been beckoned by one of the bosses. Of this he was very proud, and it made him more disposed than ever to laugh at the pessimists. In vain would they all tell him that there were men in that crowd from which he had been chosen who had stood there a month—yes, many months—and not been chosen yet. "Yes," he would say, "but what sort of men? Broken-down tramps and good-for-nothings, fellows who have spent all their money drinking, and want to get more for it. Do you want me to believe that with these arms"—and he would clench his fists and hold them up in the air, so that you might see the rolling muscles—"that with these arms people will ever let me starve?"

. . . . .

One of the first problems that Jurgis ran upon was that of the unions. He had had no experience with unions, and he had to have it explained to him that the men were banded together for the purpose of fighting for their rights. Jurgis asked them what they meant by their rights, a question in which he was quite sincere, for he had not any idea of any rights that he had, except the right to hunt for a job, and do as he was told when he got it. Generally, however, this harmless question would only make his fellow-workingmen lose their tempers and call him a fool. There was a delegate of the butcher-helpers' union who came to see Jurgis to enroll him; and when Jurgis found that this meant that he would have to part with some of his money, he froze up directly, and the delegate, who was an Irishman and only knew a few words of Lithuanian, lost his temper and began to threaten him. In the end Jurgis got into a fine rage and made it sufficiently plain that it would take more than one Irishman to scare him into a union. Little by little he gathered that the main thing the men wanted was to put a stop to the habit of "speeding-up"; they were trying their best to force a lessening of the pace, for there were some, they said, who could not keep up with it, whom it was killing. But Jurgis had no sympathy with such ideas as this—he could do the work himself, and so could the rest of them, he declared, if they were good for anything. If they couldn't do it, let them go somewhere else. Jurgis had not studied the books, and he would not have known how to pronounce "laissez-faire"; but he had been round the world enough to know that a man has to shift for himself in it, and that if he gets the worst of it, there is nobody to listen to him holler. . . . . .

The men upon the killing-beds felt also the effects of the slump . . . in . . . a way which made Jurgis understand at last all their bitterness. The big packers did not turn their hands off and close down, like the canning factories; but they began to run for shorter and shorter hours. They had always required the men to be on the killing-beds and ready for work at seven o'clock, although there was almost never any work to be done till the buyers out in the yards had gotten to work, and some cattle had come over the chutes. That would often be ten or eleven o'clock, which was bad enough, in all conscience; but now, in the slack season, they would perhaps not have a thing for their men to do till late in the afternoon. And so they would have to loaf around, in a place where the thermometer might be twenty degrees below zero! At first one would see them running about, or skylarking with each other, trying to keep warm; but before the day was over they would become quite chilled through and exhausted, and, when the cattle finally came, so near frozen that to move was an agony. And then suddenly the place would spring into activity, and the merciless "speeding-up" would begin!

There were weeks at a time when Jurgis went home after such a day as this with not more than two hours' work to his credit—which meant about thirty-five cents. There were many days when the total was less than half an hour, and others when there was none at all. The general average was six hours a day, which meant for Jurgis about six dollars a week; and this six hours of work would be done after standing on the killing-bed till one o'clock, or perhaps even three or four o'clock in the afternoon. Like as not there would come a rush of cattle at the very end of the day, which the men would have to dispose of before they went home, often working by electric light till nine or ten, or even twelve or one o'clock, and without a single instant for a bite of supper. The men were at the mercy of the cattle. . . . There was no use kicking about this—there had been one delegation after another to see the packers about it, only to be told that it was the rule, and that there was not the slightest chance of its ever being altered. . . .

All this was bad; and yet it was not the worst. For after all the hard work a man did, he was paid for only part of it. Jurgis had once been among those who scoffed at the idea of these huge concerns cheating; and so now he could appreciate the bitter irony of the fact that it was precisely their size which enabled them to do it with impunity. One of the rules on the killing-beds was that a man who was one minute late was docked an hour; and this was economical, for he was made to work the balance of the hour—he was not allowed to stand round and wait. And on the other hand if he came ahead of time he got no pay for that—though often the bosses would start up the gang ten or fifteen minutes before the whistle. And this same custom they carried over to the end of the day; they did not pay for any fraction of an hour— for "broken time." A man might work full fifty minutes, but if there was no work to fill out the hour, there was no pay for him. Thus the end of every day was a sort of lottery—a struggle, all but breaking into open war between the bosses and the men, the former trying to rush a job through and the latter trying to stretch it out. . . .

One of the consequences of all these things was that Jurgis was no longer perplexed when he heard men talk of fighting for their rights. He felt like fighting now himself; and when the Irish delegate of the butcher-helpers' union came to him a second time, he received him in a far different spirit. A wonderful idea it now seemed to Jurgis, this of the men—that by combining they might be able to make a stand and conquer the packers! Jurgis wondered who had first thought of it; and when he was told that it was a common thing for men to do in America, he got the first inkling of a meaning in the phrase "a free country." The delegate explained to him how it depended upon their being able to get every man to join and stand by the organization, and so Jurgis signified that he was willing to do his share. Before another month was by, all the working members of his family had union cards, and wore their union buttons conspicuously and with pride. . . . . . .

. . . Since the time of his disillusionment, Jurgis had sworn to trust no man, except in his own family; but here he discovered that he had brothers in affliction, and allies. Their one chance for life was in union, and so the struggle became a kind of crusade. Jurgis had always been a member of the church, because it was the right thing to be, but the church had never touched him, he left all that for the women. Here, however, was a new religion—one that did touch him, that took hold of every fibre of him; and with all the zeal and fury of a convert he went out as a missionary. There were many non-union men among the Lithuanians, and with these he would labor and wrestle in prayer, trying to show them the right. Sometimes they would be obstinate and refuse to see it, and Jurgis, alas, was not always patient! He forgot how he himself had been blind, a short time ago—after the fashion of all crusaders since the original ones, who set out to spread the gospel of Brotherhood by force of arms.

IX
―――――――――――――――――――――――

An employer refuses to recognize unions.

FROM: The testimony of Thomas H. Wickes, Second Vice President of
the Pullman Company, before the United States Strike Commission, 1894.

MODERN collective bargaining between unionized workingmen and
their employers obviously could not begin until employers recognized
and dealt with unions. Until well into the present century most employers
denied the right of any organization to speak for their men. Wickes,
speaking in 1894, expressed views typical among employers at the time.

*Has the recognition of unions resulted in unions forcing employers to
pay "any wages which they saw fit," as Wickes predicted?*

*How do Wickes' views differ from those of present day champions of
"Right to Work" laws?*

ᴥᶳ

Q.—HAS the company had any policy with reference to labor unions
among its help? A.—No; we have never objected to unions except in one
instance. I presume that there are quite a number of unions in our
shops now.

Q.—What are they? A.—I couldn't tell you, but I have heard of some of
them. I suppose the cabinetmakers have a union, and I suppose the car
builders have a union, and the carvers and the painters and other classes
of men. We do not inquire into that at all.

Q.—That is, unions among themselves in the works? A.—Members of the
craft, belonging to other unions; that is, the cabinet union might have
its headquarters in Chicago and our men would be members of it; but
we did not object to anything of that kind.

Q.—The only objection you ever made was to the American Railway
Union, wasn't it? A.—Yes, sir.

Q.—What is the basis of your objection to that union? A.—Our objection
to that was that we would not treat with our men as members of the
American Railway Union, and we would not treat with them as members of any union. We treat with them as individuals and as men.

Q.—That is, each man as an individual, do you mean that? A.—Yes, sir.

Q.—Don't you think, Mr. Wickes, that would give the corporation a very
great advantage over those men if it could take them up one at a time
and discuss the question with him. With the ability that you have got,
for instance, where do you think the man would stand in such a discussion? A.—The man has got probably more ability than I have.

Q.—You think that it would be fair to your men for each one of them

Report on the Chicago Strike of June-July, 1894 (Washington: Government Printing
Office, 1895), pp. 621–622.

to come before you and take up the question of his grievances and attempt to maintain his end of the discussion, do you? A.—I think so; yes. If he is not able to do that that is his misfortune.

Q.—Don't you think that the fact that you represent a vast concentration of capital, and are selected for that because of your ability to represent it, entitles him if he pleases to unite with all of the men of his craft and select the ablest one they have got to represent the cause? A.—As a union?

Q.—As a union. A.—They have the right; yes, sir. We have the right to say whether we will receive them or not.

Q.—Do you think you have any right to refuse to recognize that right in treating with the men? A.—Yes, sir; if we chose to.

Q.—If you chose to. Is it your policy to do that? A.—Yes, sir.

Q.—Then you think that you have the right to refuse to recognize a union of the men designed for the purpose of presenting, through the ablest of their members, to your company the grievances which all complain of or which any complain of? A.—That is the policy of the company; yes, sir. If we were to receive these men as representatives of the unions they could probably force us to pay any wages which they saw fit, and get the Pullman company in the same shape that some of the railroads are by making concessions which ought not to be made.

Q.—Don't you think that the opposite policy, to wit, that all your dealings with the men, as individuals, in case you were one who sought to abuse your power, might enable you to pay to the men, on the other hand, just what you saw fit? A.—Well, of course a man in an official position, if he is arbitrary and unfair, could work a great deal of injustice to the men; no doubt about that. But then it is a man's privilege to go to work somewhere else.

Q.—Don't you recognize as to many men, after they had become settled in a place at work of that kind, that really that privilege does not amount to much? A.—We find that the best men usually come to the front; the best of our men don't give us any trouble with unions or anything else. It is only the inferior men—that is, the least competent—that give us the trouble as a general thing.

X ──

The Supreme Court invokes "liberty of contract."

FROM: A decision invalidating a New York State law which fixed maximum hours for bakers, 1904.

STATE legislatures and Congress from time to time enacted laws to improve the conditions of working people. These enactments included health and safety measures, laws requiring the regular payment of wages in cash, and acts which fixed maximum hours and minimum wages for workers. A good many of these laws were struck down in the state and federal courts on the grounds that they interfered with "liberty of contract"—the right of free, competent persons (including corporations) to agree on the terms of employment among themselves. In the Lochner case, the United States Supreme Court explains why it has invalidated a New York State "health measure" which set maximum hours for bakers.

Why, according to the court, should the state not step in to protect bakers from excessive hours of labor?

Why did liberty of contract, as interpreted by the courts, tend to operate against workers?

THE question whether this act is valid as a labor law, pure and simple, may be dismissed in a few words. There is no reasonable ground for interfering with the liberty of person or the right of free contract, by determining the hours of labor, in the occupation of a baker. There is no contention that bakers as a class are not equal in intelligence and capacity to men in other trades or manual occupations, or that they are not able to assert their rights and care for themselves without the protecting arm of the State, interfering with their independence of judgment and of action. They are in no sense wards of the State. Viewed in the light of a purely labor law, with no reference whatever to the question of health, we think that a law like the one before us involves neither the safety, the morals nor the welfare of the public, and that the interest of the public is not in the slightest degree affected by such an act. The law must be upheld, if at all, as a law pertaining to the health of the individual engaged in the occupation of a baker. It does not affect any other portion of the public than those who are engaged in that occupation. Clean and wholesome bread does not depend upon whether the baker works but ten hours per day or only sixty hours a week. The limitation of the hours of labor does not come within the police power on that ground. . . . . .

. . . It is unfortunately true that labor, even in any department, may possibly carry with it the seeds of unhealthiness. But are we all, on that account, at the mercy of legislative majorities? A printer, a tinsmith, a locksmith, a carpenter, a cabinetmaker, a dry goods clerk, a bank's, a lawyer's or a physician's clerk, or a clerk in almost any kind of business, would all come under the power of the legislature, on this assumption. No trade, no occupation, no mode of earning one's living, could escape this all-pervading power, and the acts of the legislature in limiting the hours of labor in all employments would be valid, although such limitation might seriously cripple the ability of the laborer to support himself and his family. . . . . .

Lochner v. *New York,* 198 United States Reports 57, 59, 64 (1904).

. . . It seems to us that the real object and purpose were simply to regulate the hours of labor between the master and his employees . . . in a private business, not dangerous in any degree to morals or in any real and substantial degree, to the health of the employees. Under such circumstances the freedom of master and employee to contract with each other in relation to their employment, and in defining the same, cannot be prohibited or interfered with, without violating the Federal Constitution.

XI

A steel executive urges acceptance of collective bargaining.

FROM: A magazine article of 1919.

ABOUT the time of World War I, some employers began to adopt a position less hostile towards labor unions. William B. Dickson, who began work in the steel mills as a boy, resolved to do something someday about working conditions. He rose through the ranks and by age 32 was assistant to the president of Carnegie Steel. When that company merged into United States Steel, Dickson became first vice president of the new company. From that position he led a fight against both the twelve-hour work day and the seven-day work week. Losing that battle, he resigned in 1911. Later, Dickson became a vice president and treasurer of the Midvale Steel & Ordnance Company, where he championed the cause of collective bargaining.

For what practical business reasons did Dickson favor granting labor a voice in company management?

What significant event in the steel industry in 1919 counteracted Dickson's program?

OUR past history is full of instances where men in control of large aggregations of capital have been guilty of grave abuses against the public welfare and against the most elementary morality. These autocrats of capital have been partly balanced (whether as an effect, or a cause, might depend upon the point of view) by equally autocratic and irresponsible labor leaders, who have not hesitated to use force in order to win their ends. . . .

The only way out of this senseless conflict between capital and labor is for employers to realize that the day of industrial democracy

William B. Dickson, "Getting Our Men To Help Us Manage," *System, The Magazine of Business*, 35 (June, 1919), 1043–1044. Copyright 1919. Used by permission of McGraw-Hill Book Company and Charles K. Dickson, Susan Dickson Taylor, Helen Dickson Ware, Emma Dickson Carswell and Eleanor Dickson Redfield.

has dawned, and that "the establishment of wage rates and other conditions of employment without representation is tyranny" also.

Much has been done by benevolent employers to improve working conditions, but however conditions may be improved, the right of the workmen to collective bargaining must be recognized as a legitimate outgrowth of American ideals. The individual workman, dependent on his own strength and resources, cannot hope to bargain on equal terms with the corporation. If he cannot do so, and is debarred from association with his fellow-workmen, he is no longer a freeman but a serf; and the serf has no place in the future of America. . . . . .

The companies with which I am connected have recently established a system of collective bargaining which is as democratic as any of which I have any knowledge. . . . . .

To us in the management the plan seems not merely a reasonable concession to the workers but a step forward for the whole business. It gives the workmen more power, but also, we believe, sobers them—gives them a better understanding of the problems of the business, and, therefore, gives them a better attitude toward it.

The typical workman now has only the haziest ideas as to the nature and function of the business he is in. Often he thinks of its resources as a kind of inexhaustible reservoir, from which the employer can raise wages as much as he likes by simply opening the spigot wider. Look into almost any workman's thought on the subject, and you will find something like that. Small wonder the demands of labor are often unreasonable!

The workman needs to know more about the actual problems of management. He needs to learn something about overhead, about marketing difficulties, about the dependence of production and production conditions upon marketing and the dependence of marketing upon economical production, about the numberless hazards and chances of loss which his employer must face. He needs, in short, more of the manager's point of view. And the obvious way to give it to him is to let him have some part in handling management problems.

That is what we have tried to do.

XII
───
A manufacturer introduces the five-dollar-a-day wage.

FROM: Henry Ford's memoirs.

THE Ford Motor Company was the first to adopt the assembly line for automobile production, and it pioneered in selling many cars cheaply rather than a few at high prices. Ford also was among the first to view employees not simply as a cost of production, but also as potential consumers of automobiles. In this selection, Henry Ford discusses his company's inauguration of the five-dollar-a-day wage.

Why does Ford reject both "supply and demand" and "cost of living" as bases for fixing wage rates?

What possible areas of disagreement between Ford and his employees can you see under the new system?

⤐

IT ought to be the employer's ambition, as leader, to pay better wages than any similar line of business, and it ought to be the workman's ambition to make this possible. Of course there are men in all shops who seem to believe that if they do their best, it will be only for the employer's benefit—and not at all for their own. It is a pity that such a feeling should exist. But it does exist and perhaps it has some justification. If an employer urges men to do their best, and the men learn after a while that their best does not bring any reward, then they naturally drop back into "getting by." But if they see the fruits of hard work in their pay envelope—proof that harder work means higher pay—then also they begin to learn that they are a part of the business, and that its success depends on them and their success depends on it. . . . . .

. . . The employer can gain nothing by looking over the employees and asking himself, "How little can I get them to take?" Nor the employee by glaring back and asking, "How much can I force him to give?" Eventually both will have to turn to the business and ask, "How can this industry be made safe and profitable, so that it will be able to provide a sure and comfortable living for all of us?" . . . . .

When can a wage be considered adequate? How much of a living is reasonably to be expected from work? . . . To say that it should pay the cost of living is to say almost nothing. The cost of living depends largely upon the efficiency of production and transportation; and the efficiency of these is the sum of the efficiencies of the management and the workers. Good work, well managed, ought to result in high wages and low living costs. . . . When we try to regulate wages according to the cost of living, we are imitating a dog chasing his tail. And, anyhow, who is competent to say just what kind of living we shall base the costs on? Let us broaden our view and see what a wage is to the workmen— and what it ought to be.

The wage carries all the worker's obligations outside the shop; it

Henry Ford, *My Life and Work*, in collaboration with Samuel Crowther (New York: Doubleday, Page & Company, 1926), pp. 117–119, 121–123, 124, 125–127, 128, 129–130. Reprinted by permission of Mrs. Mary Owens Crowther.

carries all that is necessary in the way of service and management inside the shop. . . . Certainly it ought to bear not less than all the worker's outside obligations. And certainly it ought to be made to take care of the worker's sunset days when labour is no longer possible to him—and should be no longer necessary. . . . . .

If only the man himself were concerned, the cost of his maintenance and the profit he ought to have would be a simple matter. But he is not just an individual. He is a citizen, contributing to the welfare of the nation. He is a householder. He is perhaps a father with children who must be reared to usefulness on what he is able to earn. We must reckon with all these facts. How are you going to figure the contribution of the home to the day's work? You pay the man for his work, but how much does that work owe to his home? How much to his position as a citizen? How much to his position as a father? The man does the work in the shop, but his wife does the work in the home. The shop must pay them both. On what system of figuring is the home going to find its place on the cost sheets of the day's work? . . . [A]fter having supported himself and family, clothed them, housed them, educated them, given them the privileges incident to their standard of living, ought there to be provision made for still something more in the way of savings profit? And are all properly chargeable to the day's work? I think they are. Otherwise, we have the hideous prospect of little children and their mothers being forced out to work. . . . . .

I have learned through the years a good deal about wages. I believe in the first place that, all other considerations aside, our own sales depend in a measure upon the wages we pay. If we can distribute high wages, then that money is going to be spent and it will serve to make storekeepers and distributors and manufacturers and workers in other lines more prosperous and their prosperity will be reflected in our sales. . . . . .

. . . starting about 1913 we had time studies made of all the thousands of operations in the shops. By a time study it is possible theoretically to determine what a man's output should be. Then, making large allowances, it is further possible to get at a satisfactory standard output for a day, and, taking into consideration the skill, to arrive at a rate which will express with fair accuracy the amount of skill and exertion that goes into a job—and how much is to be expected from the man in the job in return for the wage. Without scientific study the employer does not know why he is paying a wage and the worker does not know why he is getting it. . . .

We do not have piece work. Some of the men are paid by the day and some are paid by the hour, but in practically every case there is a required standard output below which a man is not expected to fall.

Were it otherwise, neither the workman nor ourselves would know whether or not wages were being earned. . . .

Having these facts in hand we announced and put into operation in January, 1914, a kind of profit-sharing plan in which the minimum wage for any class of work and under certain conditions was five dollars a day. At the same time we reduced the working day to eight hours— it had been nine—and the week to forty-eight hours. This was entirely a voluntary act. . . . It was to our way of thinking an act of social justice, and in the last analysis we did it for our own satisfaction of mind. . . .

There was, however, no charity in any way involved. That was not generally understood. Many employers thought we were just making the announcement because we were prosperous and wanted advertising and they condemned us because we were upsetting standards—violating the custom of paying a man the smallest amount he would take. There is nothing to such standards and customs. They have to be wiped out. Some day they will be. Otherwise, we cannot abolish poverty. We made the change not merely because we wanted to pay higher wages and thought we could pay them. We wanted to pay these wages so that the business would be on a lasting foundation. We were not distributing anything—we were building for the future. A low wage business is always insecure.

. . . Workmen quite generally believed that they were going to get five dollars a day, regardless of what work they did.

The facts were somewhat different from the general impression.

. . . . .

. . . The man and his home had to come up to certain standards of cleanliness and citizenship. Nothing paternal was intended!—a certain amount of paternalism did develop, and that is one reason why the whole plan and the social welfare department were readjusted. But in the beginning the idea was that there should be a very definite incentive to better living and that the very best incentive was a money premium on proper living. A man who is living aright will do his work aright. . . . . .

. . . It was expected that in order to receive the bonus married men should live with and take proper care of their families. We had to break up the evil custom among many of the foreign workers of taking in boarders—of regarding their homes as something to make money out of rather than as a place to live in. Boys under eighteen received a bonus if they supported the next of kin. Single men who lived wholesomely shared. The best evidence that the plan was essentially beneficial is the record. When the plan went into effect, 60 per cent. of the workers immediately qualified to share. . . . Within a year and one half only a fraction of one per cent. failed to share.

The large wage had other results. In 1914, when the first plan went into effect, we had 14,000 employees and it had been necessary to hire at the rate of about 53,000 a year in order to keep a constant force of 14,000. In 1915 we had to hire only 6,508 men and the majority of these new men were taken on because of the growth of the business. With the old turnover of labour and our present force we should have to hire at the rate of nearly 200,000 men a year—which would be pretty nearly an impossible proposition. Even with the minimum of instruction that is required to master almost any job in our place, we cannot take on a new staff each morning, or each week, or each month. . . . The matter of labour turnover has not since bothered us. . . .

We have made changes in the system, but we have never deviated from this principle:

If you expect a man to give his time and energy, fix his wages so that he will have no financial worries. It pays. Our profits, after paying good wages and a bonus . . . show that paying good wages is the most profitable way of doing business.

FOR FURTHER THOUGHT

How might capital-labor relations have been different had labor unions developed as equals, side by side with big business, rather than after the rise of big business?

In what ways were labor unions aggressive in the era 1865–1921? In what ways were they defensive?

What has been the role of violence in social change in America? How does the Civil Rights Movement resemble the early labor movement? How do the two movements differ?

4. The Farmer in Depression and Prosperity, 1865-1921

FOR a full generation following the Civil War, American farmers were in distress. Superficially, conditions appeared to favor agricultural prosperity: a burgeoning urban population each year consumed more farm-produced food-stuffs, rapidly developing industries demanded increased amounts of agricultural raw materials, railroads connected the remotest farms with the markets of the world, and the portion of the population engaged in agriculture fell from 61 per cent in 1860 to 37 per cent in 1900. Far from gaining under these circumstances, however, the farmer at best only held his own. Between 1860 and 1900 his share of the gross national income dropped from 30 to 21 per cent, and his share of the nation's aggregate wealth from 40 to 16 per cent. Except for the army of unskilled immigrant laborers, city-dwellers were out-pacing the farmer.

To a substantial degree, the "farm problem" during the final third of the nineteenth century was sectional. Farmers of New England and the Middle Atlantic states, for example, were losing out in the race for survival. Their rough and rocky acres could not compete successfully against the larger, abundantly rich, and level farms of the Midwest, particularly in the production of corn, wheat, and other grains. Northeastern farmers faced the choices of abandoning agriculture altogether or migrating to the West (as many did), or adopting specialized crops suited to the needs of the great cities in their region: fruits, vegetables, poultry, and dairy products.

Farmers in the defeated South lived in more desperate straits. Gone was the plantation system based on slavery. Postwar land owners lacked money for hiring laborers, white or black, to work their fields, and the laborers, who needed land to work, were too poor to buy or rent it. Out of these conditions arose sharecropping, which required little cash. For the next two generations—indeed, until the Great Depression—Southern agriculture was burdened and held back by this vicious system of land tenure. Sharecropping fixed on the South the single crop culture that rapidly exhausted its soil. Falling cotton and tobacco prices drove the 'croppers permanently into debt to the storekeepers who supplied them with food and clothing on credit. In the end, the debt-ridden and dispirited tenant farmers found themselves hopelessly trapped in a "new slavery."

Out on the agricultural frontier—for the most part west of the one hundredth meridian—the farmers' lot was generally harsh. Much of the region was unsuited for the types of farming that settlers had known farther east. Here the land was dry, flat, and treeless. High winds lashed them in season and out. Summers were short, hot, and rainless. Crops were plagued by grasshoppers, chinch bugs, tornadoes, dust and hail storms, and drought. Winters were long, severe, and cold. Ice and snow frequently stranded the farmers and destroyed their livestock. By the 1890s, a combination of dashed hopes, isolation, and growing mortgages had embittered the Western farmer.

Only in the Midwest were farmers relatively well off, endowed as they were with fertile soil, excellent growing conditions, and ready access to markets. But even in that favored region farmers complained that they did not receive a fair return for their labors.

Beyond these particular regional troubles lay the complex general farm problem. In the broadest sense, that problem can be summed up in the word "overproduction." Much of the time between 1865 and 1900 farmers produced more than their markets could absorb at prices profitable to them. One consequence was the attempt of statesmen to develop foreign markets for American produce (see Chapter Six, selection III). Certainly a maldistribution of domestic incomes prevented city workers from consuming more; but, even so, agriculture had expanded faster than the demand for its products. More than 430 million acres of new land were brought under cultivation between 1860 and 1900, and 46 million persons were added to the total farm population. Agricultural colleges, experimental stations, and farm magazines were teaching farmers how to increase their yield per acre. Mechanization both expanded the scale of agriculture and its productivity.

The shift from subsistence to commercial agriculture, while economically more profitable to farmers, was psychologically less satisfying. Rewards did not correspond directly to effort, but were determined by a remote "world market price" over which individual farmers had little control. Moreover, farming for cash promised more benefits than it delivered and raised expectations faster than it satisfied them [I]. Nothing disturbed the farmers' peace of mind more than the mute vote of "no confidence" registered by the steady flow of their sons and daughters to the city [II].

Farmers had some understanding of the deep-seated causes of their problems, but being unable to do anything about them, attacked their more im-

ediate tormentors. Their first target was the railroads. Freight rates were
ever as low as farmers believed they should be. Farmers were convinced that
ailroads manipulated rates to drain all profits from agriculture [III]. This
as often the case because in most rural areas railroad companies operated
ithout competition [IV]. Farmers also accused railroads of controlling state
olitics by the wholesale distribution of favors, free passes, and, if needed,
ribes. Many farmers joined the Granger Movement in the 1870s and under-
ok state legislation to bring railway rates under control. In this drive they
ere aided by small town shippers and businessmen who shared the farmers'
iew of railroad abuses [V]. Initially successful, within a decade state regula-
on of interstate railways was invalidated by the United States Supreme Court.
Whether or not regulated rates would have much benefited the farmer is open
o question [VI].

A second target of the farmers was the middleman [VII]. The Grangers
ought to eliminate this ancient enemy of farmers by substituting coöperative
arketing [VIII]. For a variety of reasons, coöps were of little help in solving
he farm problem [IX].

The deflationary trend of the economy for thirty years following the Civil
War was especially hard on rural debtors, because it made repayment of debts
ncreasingly difficult [X]. A growing number of farmers advocated federal
egislation to restore prosperity by increasing the currency supply [XI]. In the
870s, inflationists favored "greenbacks" or paper money, but once silver
egan to flood the market after 1874, they called for the unlimited coinage of
ilver dollars. Conservatives denied that legislation could in any way help
he farmer [XII].

The climax of the various farm movements came with the Populist political
arty in the 1890s. (For more detailed information on the political impact of
he farmers' movements, see Chapter Five.) In its national platform of 1892,
he new party summed up the demands of the earlier farm movements (gov-
rnmental ownership and operation of the railroads, inflation of the currency,
nd free coinage of silver, among others), and advanced a number of new
eforms (including the eight-hour day for labor, a graduated income tax, the
irect election of senators, a single six-year term for President and Vice Presi-
ent, adoption of the secret ballot and of the initiative, the referendum, and
he recall, and the restriction of immigration). Populism made some advances,
specially in the West and South, but destroyed itself in 1896 by fusing with
he Democrats in support of the candidacy of William Jennings Bryan for the
residency on a free silver platform.

The term of President William McKinley (the Republican candidate who
efeated Bryan in 1896) marked an end of depression and the beginning of a
ew era of prosperity. Good times for the farmer continued until the outbreak
f World War I [XIII]. Agricultural prosperity was not due—as Republican
rators claimed—to the Gold Standard Act or to the Dingley Tariff which they
nacted, but to more fundamental changes in the economic structure [XIV].

As World War I created new markets and unprecedented incomes fc farmers, prices rose dramatically until 1919. Then suddenly, the Europea markets for American farm products evaporated and in 1920 farmers wer plunged back into depression. They were not to enjoy good times again unt the coming of World War II. EDITED BY GERALD G. EGGERT

I

The Nation *criticizes the rising expectations c pioneer-farmers.*

FROM: "Another Aspect of the Farmers' Movement," a magazine articl of 1873.

The Nation magazine was one of the leading shapers of opinion in bot business and intellectual circles in post-Civil War America. It led th fight against all the agrarian movements from the Grangers in the 187(to the Populists in the 1890s. Its editorials repeatedly drove home th message that measures favored by farmer groups were fraudulent, im practical, dishonest, and communistic. In the following selection, *Th Nation's* editor attempts to explain away the farmers' complaints again: high railroad rates.

How might a pioneer-farmer have answered The Nation's *editorial?*

To what would you attribute the growing demands of the farme: pioneers of the late 1870s?

THERE is another important element in . . . discussing the con ditions of agricultural life in the United States. The early frontiersme of the ante-railroad period were, like the European peasantry, a hard simple-minded, rough breed of men, with very rude tastes and very fev wants. When they went out into the wilderness they did it well know ing that they left civilization behind, and neither desiring nor expectin a market for their products. They dressed in leather or homespun, an ate what they raised or killed. If they had more corn than they needec they burnt it or threw it away without qualms or regrets, or considerin what it would bring in New York. They were, too, tolerably ignoran of book-learning, and cared nothing about music, except that of th dancing-fiddle. Their lives, if coarse and laborious and full of hardship were, on the whole, tolerably contented. They swore, and drank, an fought, but they were not troubled with problems of political economy Our modern frontiersman, who clings to the railroads out along th prairies, is a very different person. He insists on being followed up b all the modern conveniences. Not only must he have a church and school, but he must have the newspapers and magazines, and his wife and daughters must have a piano and silk dresses, and the new novels, and their minds, instead of being intent on the homely joys of the forest and the prairie, are vexed by the social and religious discussions of the far East. They want to hear Froude lecture, wonder what Plymouth Church is going to do with Bowen, would like a chance of listening to Lucca, are eager to try the newest thing in stoves, and wonder what the Emperor of Austria will think of the Illinois school-house at the Vienna Exhibition. Now, no railroad that pays interest on its cost will ever satisfy a population of this sort by its rates, as long as this population is dependent on agricultural products, raised two thousand miles from the Atlantic seaboard, for the gratification of its multifarious and growing wants.

II

A *"practical farmer" gives advice on how to keep children on the farm.*

FROM: An 1881 handbook of advice for farmers.

NINETEENTH century Americans generally believed that farm life was infinitely superior to city living. The work of farmers, although hard, was honest, healthful, and in keeping with man's true nature. City dwellers, on the other hand, lived crowded together in small houses or tenements, worked indoors under unhealthful conditions, and were beset by temptations to extravagance and sin (see Chapter Seven, selection V). There was, nevertheless, a steady migration of farm youths to the cities. John E. Read, writer for farm publications, who described himself as a "practical farmer," offered tips to his readers on how to keep their sons and daughters interested in agriculture. In the course of his defense of rural living, he inadvertently revealed many of the reasons why young people were flocking to the cities.

From what Read says, where did many young people get the idea that farming was not a satisfactory way of life?

Why was Read's argument that many boys soon repented of leaving the farm not wholly convincing?

HOW to keep the boys on the farm and induce them cheerfully to choose farming as their occupation for life is a question of deep interest to many parents. The stampede of young men from the country to cities

John E. Read, *Farming For Profit: A Handbook For The American Farmer* (Philadelphia: J. C. McCurdy & Co., 1881), pp. 848–850.

and large towns is not an evil which finds its limit in the domestic circles which they leave, but is one which extends through society and makes its depressing influence felt everywhere. How to check this evil is a question of great importance and is well worthy of consideration.

In order to induce the boys to stay on the farm they must be informed of the true relation which exists between the city and the country. They must be shown that the expenses of living are so high that the city clerk, whom they envy because of his large salary, can hardly keep out of debt. And the fact that the man in the city is tied to his business a great deal more closely than the farmer is to his work should be set before them. Many of the boys who have left the farm have done so because they were allowed so few pleasures and so little time at home. . . .

Boys should be taught that farming is an *honorable occupation.* It is very true that the calling does not make the man, and that a man should not be respected because he follows one honest occupation or despised because he follows another. Character is what a man *is,* and cannot always be determined by reference to the kind of work which he performs. The farmer may be a gentleman or he can be a boor, he may build up a noble character or he may be a villain. He makes his own choice in these respects. Merely being a farmer will make him neither a good man nor a bad one. Still, farming is a business which does not open to its followers so many evil influences, and expose them to as many temptations, as some lines of business. It is the kind of labor which GOD directly marked out for man, and upon the cultivation of the soil the civilization and happiness of mankind must, in a great measure, depend. As far as occupation is concerned, the farmer has no occasion to "look up to" the merchant, manufacturer, or professional man. Clergymen and teachers are doing a work the value of which is beyond all price, and many boys will be called from the farm to fill the ranks of these professions. . . . But before a boy leaves the farm to become a merchant, or to go to a city as a laborer, or to engage in business of any kind, he should very carefully consider the question whether there is any good prospect that he can do better than the thousands of those who have preceded him, and who have soon been led to repent that they ever left the farm. . . . . .

The girls must be taught to respect farming as an occupation, and be required to help their mothers in the work of the house and the dairy. When farmers educate their girls in a manner which will fit them to become farmers' wives, and teach them that farming is one of the most honorable of all occupations, and that the girl who marries a farmer does fully as well as one who marries a merchant or a lawyer, they will thereby do a great deal towards keeping their boys on the farm. The idea that because a young lady has married a farmer she has "thrown herself away" is one of the most preposterous ones which ever found expression in civilized society. The girl who will reject a man simply because he is a farmer shows that she has a very shallow or else a sadly uncultivated mind and a heart which is incapable of deep affection. And the farmer who will advise his daughters to reject honest and intelligent farmers in the hope of securing clerks, business or professional men, thereby shows his own lack of good judgment as well as proves that he has no genuine respect for the calling by means of which he obtains his bread. The mother who advises her daughter to "look higher" than the young men who are farmers is thereby doing a great wrong. There may be reasons why certain farmers' boys are not suitable companions for certain farmers' girls, but the mere fact that the men are farmers should weigh in their favor rather than against them.

We are well aware that many farmers' wives have been terribly overworked, and we can sympathize with the mother who desires an easier lot for her child. But we know that this excessive labor is not an absolute necessity, and that with the aid of the labor-saving implements of the present day a farmer's wife can live as easily as the wives of men engaged in many other pursuits. . . . The wife of the farmer ought to be willing to work in order to help him, and if the man is what he should be he will see to it that she does not go beyond her strength. And any and every girl may rest fully assured of the fact that a man who would make her his slave if he were a farmer would also require her to work extremely hard if he engaged in another occupation.

III

A railroad squeezes the profits out of farming.

FROM: *The Octopus*, an anti-railroad novel, 1901.

FRANK NORRIS, in this turn-of-the-century novel, *The Octopus*, dramatized the bitter conflict between the railroad and agricultural interests in California. The "octopus," was, of course, the railroad company whose steel tentacles caught up the farmers and sucked their life blood by taxing away all their profits. The novel exposed not only the manipulation of rates as portrayed in this selection, but many other railroad abuses as well. The novel's point of view is strictly that of the exploited farmers.

How might farmers generally protect themselves against arbitrary freight rates?

In what way could Dyke have avoided higher freight rates?

ᴥⒺ

"I'LL be wanting some cars of you people before the summer is out," observed Dyke to the clerk as he folded up and put away the order that the other had handed him. He remembered perfectly well that he had arranged the matter of transporting his crop some months before, but his role of proprietor amused him and he liked to busy himself again and again with the details of his undertaking.

"I suppose," he added, "you'll be able to give 'em to me. There'll be a big wheat crop to move this year and I don't want to be caught in any car famine."

"Oh, you'll get your cars," murmured the other.

"I'll be the means of bringing business your way," Dyke went on; "I've done so well with my hops that there are a lot of others going into the business next season. Suppose," he continued, struck with an idea, "suppose we went into some sort of pool, a sort of shippers' organization, could you give us special rates, cheaper rates—say a cent and a half?"

The other looked up.

"A cent and a half! Say *four* cents and a half and maybe I'll talk business with you."

"Four cents and a half," returned Dyke, "I don't see it. Why, the regular rate is only two cents."

"No, it isn't," answered the clerk, looking him gravely in the eye, "it's five cents."

"Well, there's where you are wrong, m'son," Dyke retorted, genially. "You look it up. You'll find the freight on hops from Bonneville to 'Frisco is two cents a pound for carload lots. You told me that yourself last fall."

"That was last fall," observed the clerk. There was a silence. Dyke shot a glance of suspicion at the other. Then, reassured, he remarked:

"You look it up. You'll see I'm right."

S. Behrman came forward and shook hands politely with the ex-engineer.

"Anything I can do for you, Mr. Dyke?"

Dyke explained. When he had done speaking, the clerk turned to S. Behrman and observed respectfully:

"Our regular rate on hops is five cents."

"Yes," answered S. Behrman, pausing to reflect; "yes, Mr. Dyke, that's right—five cents."

The clerk brought forward a folder˙ of yellow paper and handed it to Dyke. It was inscribed at the top "Tariff Schedule No. 8," and underneath these words, in brackets, was a smaller inscription, "*Supersedes No. 7 of Aug. 1.*"

Frank Norris, *The Octopus—A Story of California* (New York: Doubleday, Page & Co., 1901), pp. 346–350.

"See for yourself," said S. Behrman. . . .

In the list that was printed below, Dyke saw that the rate for hops between Bonneville or Guadalajara and San Francisco was five cents.

For a moment Dyke was confused. Then swiftly the matter became clear in his mind. The Railroad had raised the freight on hops from two cents to five.

All his calculations as to a profit on his little investment he had based on a freight rate of two cents a pound. He was under contract to deliver his crop. He could not draw back. The new rate ate up every cent of his gains. He stood there ruined.

"Why, what do you mean?" he burst out. "You promised me a rate of two cents and I went ahead with my business with that understanding. What do you mean?"

S. Behrman and the clerk watched him from the other side of the counter.

"The rate is five cents," declared the clerk doggedly.

"Well, that ruins me," shouted Dyke. "Do you understand? I won't make fifty cents. *Make!* Why, I will *owe*,—I'll be—be— That ruins me, do you understand?"

The other raised a shoulder.

"We don't force you to ship. You can do as you like. The rate is five cents."

"Well—but—damn you, I'm under contract to deliver. What am I going to do? Why, you told me—you promised me a two-cent rate."

"I don't remember it," said the clerk. "I don't know anything about that. But I know this; I know that hops have gone up. I know the German crop was a failure and that the crop in New York wasn't worth the hauling. Hops have gone up to nearly a dollar. You don't suppose we don't know that, do you, Mr. Dyke?"

"What's the price of hops got to do with you?"

"It's got *this* to do with us," returned the other with a sudden aggressiveness, "that the freight rate has gone up to meet the price. We're not doing business for our health. My orders are to raise your rate to five cents, and I think you are getting off easy."

Dyke stared in blank astonishment. For the moment, the audacity of the affair was what most appealed to him. He forgot its personal application.

"Good Lord," he murmured, "good Lord! What will you people do next? Look here. What's your basis of applying freight rates anyhow?" he suddenly vociferated with furious sarcasm. "What's your rule? What are you guided by?"

But at the words, S. Behrman, who had kept silent during the heat of the discussion, leaned abruptly forward. For the only time in his knowledge, Dyke saw his face inflamed with anger and with the enmity and contempt of all this farming element with whom he was contending.

"Yes, what's your rule? What's your basis?" demanded Dyke, turning swiftly to him.

S. Behrman emphasized each word of his reply with a tap of one forefinger on the counter before him:

"All—the—traffic—will—bear."

The ex-engineer stepped back a pace, his fingers on the ledge of the counter, to steady himself. He felt himself grow pale, his heart became a mere leaden weight in his chest, inert, refusing to beat.

In a second the whole affair, in all its bearings, went speeding before the eye of his imagination like the rapid unrolling of a panorama. Every cent of his earnings was sunk in this hop business of his. More than that, he had borrowed money to carry it on, certain of success—borrowed of S. Behrman, offering his crop and his little home as security. Once he failed to meet his obligations, S. Behrman would foreclose. Not only would the Railroad devour every morsel of his profits, but also it would take from him his home; at a blow he would be left penniless and without a home. What would then become of his mother—and what would become of the little tad? She, whom he had been planning to educate like a veritable lady. For all that year he had talked of his ambition for his little daughter to every one he met. All Bonneville knew of it. What a mark for gibes he had made of himself. The workingman turned farmer! What a target for jeers—he who had fancied he could elude the Railroad! He remembered he had once said the great Trust had overlooked his little enterprise, disdaining to plunder such small fry. He should have known better than that. How had he ever imagined the Road would permit him to make any money?

IV

The Nation *describes the long-haul, short-haul differential.*

FROM: "The 'Farmers' Clubs' And The Railroads," an article of 1873.

AMONG the chief complaints of farmers against railroad rates was the long-haul, short-haul differential. In the course of an editorial denouncing state regulation of railroads, *The Nation's* editor explained the practice. Several state legislatures and eventually the United States Congress outlawed charging more for a short haul than for a long haul over the same line when the short haul was between points contained within the long haul.

For what sound economic reasons might a railroad be justified in charging as much (if not more) for short hauls than for long hauls over the same tracks?

How would Western farmers have been seriously injured rather than helped by the setting of a nation-wide, uniform, freight rate per mile?

૭δ

UNDER our system of railroad ownership, an excessive competition exists for the business of all competing points, while the local business of the various competing lines is an absolute monopoly. This has naturally resulted in compelling the corporations to do through business at rates often ruinously unremunerative, which again has compelled these companies to recoup themselves for their losses and secure their profits by excessive charges on the local traffic, of which they hold undisturbed possession. A case of merchandise, for instance, would be carried on through-rates a thousand miles, from New York to Chicago, for $5; but the Illinois road which took it a hundred miles out of Chicago to its point of destination, would make a further charge on it of perhaps $5.50; and this, too, though that same road would probably have completed the carriage from New York to St. Louis, another competing point, for a mere trifle more than the rate to Chicago. The local business, in fact, had to pay all.

As long as the times were good and prices high, as long as the farmers found ready markets and cash sales, this evident abuse, though noticed, excited little clamor. During the last few years, however, enormous areas of new country have been brought under cultivation, harvests have proved abundant, and prices have fallen, until now at last freights to market consume the entire margin of profit. It has ceased to be profitable to raise food. As this unpleasant fact has gradually forced itself upon the notice of the farmers, they have more and more turned their attention upon the question of railroad charges, and two years ago the present agitation began to take shape. Of course, the first resort was to legislation. A law would easily regulate the whole difficulty. Was it not notorious that a usury law always established the rates of interest? Why, then, should not a similar one settle the question of freights? Unfortunately, in granting charters to their railroads, the Legislatures of the Western States had never reserved the power either to amend or repeal those charters, or to regulate the fares and freights which the corporations might charge under them. These charters, therefore, under the famous decision in the Dartmouth College case, amounted to contracts between the States and the corporations, and, as such, came within the scope of the constitutional inhibition of laws impairing the obligation of contracts.

The Nation, 16 (April 10, 1873), 249.

V

Farmers resolve to bring railroads under public control.

FROM: Resolutions adopted by the Illinois State Farmers' Association, Springfield Convention, April 2, 1873.

THE Grange Society (or Patrons of Husbandry) and other farmers' associations in the Midwest began to agitate in the early 1870s for state regulation of railroads. In this drive, they were assisted by small-town shippers and merchants who complained of the same high railway rates. The "granger" point of view and the farmers' proposed remedies are embodied in the following selection. In short order, several states enacted laws setting up state railway commissions, outlawing railroad abuses, and fixing maximum freight rates.

Were railroads really "public highways," subject to public regulation, as the Grangers charged, or were they "private property," free from governmental interference, as the companies insisted?

When, and under what circumstances, did the railroad companies call themselves "public highways"?

❧

[1] *Resolved, By the Farmers of Illinois in Mass Meeting Assembled,* That all chartered monopolies, not regulated and controlled by law, have proved in that respect detrimental to the public prosperity, corrupting in their management, and dangerous to republican institutions.

[2] *Resolved,* That the railways of the world, except in those countries where they have been held under the strict regulation and supervision of the government, have proved themselves arbitrary, extortionate, and as opposed to free institutions and free commerce between States as were the feudal barons of the middle ages.

[3] *Resolved,* That we hold, declare, and resolve that this despotism which defies our laws, plunders our shippers, impoverishes our people, and corrupts our government, shall be subdued and made to subserve the public interest at whatever cost. . . . . .

[6] *Resolved,* That we regard it as the undoubted power, and the imperative duty of the legislature, to pass laws fixing reasonable maximum rates for freight and passengers, without classification of roads, and that we urge upon our General Assembly the passage of such laws. . . . . .

Jonathan Periam, *The Groundswell: A History of the Origin, Aims, and Progress of the Farmers' Movement* . . . (Cincinnati: E. Hannaford & Company; Chicago: Hannaford & Thompson, 1874), pp. 286–288.

[9] *Resolved,* That we urge the passage of a bill enforcing the principle that railroads are public highways, and requiring railroads to make connections with all roads whose tracks meet or cross their own, and to receive and transmit cars and trains offered over their roads at reasonable maximum rates, whether offered at such crossings, or at stations along their roads, and empowering the making of connections by municipal corporations for that purpose, and for the public use. . . . . .

[13] *Resolved,* That the presentation of railroad passes to our legislators, whatever may be the spirit and intent with which they are accepted, are demoralizing in their influence; and we look to our legislature, now in session, to rise above personal considerations of pecuniary interest or convenience, and to pass a law making it a misdemeanor for any Senator, or other state or county officers, to accept any railroad pass, knowing, as we do, that the people look upon the acceptance of these passes with decided and almost universal disapprobation.

VI

The farmers attacked the right target, but for the wrong reason.

FROM: An 1875 magazine article by Charles Francis Adams, Jr., chairman of the Massachusetts Board of Railroad Commissioners.

THE invalidation of the Granger laws by the Supreme Court led to the passage of the Interstate Commerce Act of 1887, which created the Interstate Commerce Commission. Although the Commission was charged with preventing unreasonable railroad rates, the federal courts repeatedly overruled its findings. By 1900, the ICC had been reduced to little more than a statistics-gathering agency, and its impact on railroad rates was negligible. Modern scholars tend to agree with Charles Francis Adams, Jr., who, writing in 1875, blamed the farm problem more on the excessively *low* rather than on high railroad rates. Had state or federal legislation resulted in even lower freight rates, the farm problem might well have been aggravated.

Following Adams' argument, how might higher freight rates have helped the farmer? Who, if anyone, would higher rates harm?

If there were already too many people engaged in farming in the Far West, why were railroad companies of the region such active promoters of immigration to the West from abroad?

❧

. . . THE real cause of complaint, the true source of the evils under which they suffer, has as yet received but little mention among Western

Charles Francis Adams, Jr., "The Granger Movement," *North American Review,* 120 (April 1875), 421–423.

men; in fact, the subject is one the discussion of which they instinctively avoid, for there are no votes in ugly truths. Though the source of all their woes is not apparent on the surface, it may be described in very few words,—*they have gone too far West.* For this they are themselves chiefly, though not wholly, responsible. . . . For years the ruling idea of the Western mind has been the bringing of remote acres, and ever acres more remote, under cultivation. There was thought to be some occult virtue in expediting this process,—a service to God and one's country. Every artificial appliance and inducement was thus set to work to force population out in advance of the steady and healthy growth of civilization into regions beyond the reach of the world's centres and outside the pale of social influence. It was this hurtful forcing process which brought about that condition of affairs which had to culminate in the Granger movement, and in the organized assault on property in railroads. The people were paying the penalty of too rapid growth. . . .

The result brought about by the unnatural diffusion of population, so far as the agricultural interests of the West were concerned, was exactly what any thinking and observing man should have anticipated, —over-production at remote points. This difficulty no increased cheapness of transportation can alleviate; it can only transfer the locality of the difficulty to a point somewhat more remote. The darling vision of the Granger's dreams, the Utopia of his waking fancies, and the constant theme of his noisy rhetoric, is a double-track, steel-rail, government-built, exclusively freight railroad from every farmer's barn-door straight to the city of New York. Paradoxical as it may seem, there is not the slightest room for doubt that even the full realization of this fanciful impossibility would not at all benefit the individual farmer of the West. It would fail to benefit him for a very simple and obvious reason. The difficulty he is now laboring under is over-production; the West grows more of the fruits of the soil than the world will consume at present prices. Meanwhile the area from which production is possible is not only not fully occupied, but is for all practical purposes unlimited. A reduction of the present cost of carriage, therefore, only serves by so much to extend the area from which the supply can be drawn, brings so many additional acres and so many more farmers into the field of competition. The whole benefit of the reduction inures, therefore, not to the producer, but to the consumer. The new-comers glut the market before it can be relieved. Any reduction in the cost of the carriage of agricultural products is, therefore, of enormous importance to us on the Atlantic seaboard, and of yet more importance to the swarming population of the British isles,—to the competing agriculturists of Eastern Europe it involves also most serious consequences,—but to the farmers of the West, as a class, it amounts to nothing more than one additional step in continuance of that same progress which has steadily been going on for over thirty years, and which they now claim has brought them to their present hard and desperate pass. Ever since 1830 the cost of transportation has been growing cheaper and cheaper, until it has now touched points which would once have been considered incredible; yet the standing complaint of the farmer is still that the cost of carriage consumes the whole value of his product; just as much so to-day, when the limit of its carriage is sixteen hundred miles, as fifty years ago when it was but one hundred and sixty miles.

The Granger movement touches, then, the real cause of the evil under which the West is suffering only so far as it tends to supplement the disasters of the recent financial crisis and put a complete stop to all further immediate railroad construction. In this way it may help to hold in check the existing tendency of population to diffuse itself prematurely, and restore the country to a healthy, because more measured process of development.

VII

An alert farmer out-bargains a scheming middle-man.

FROM: A popular book on farm subjects.

NINETEENTH century farmers often underrated the services performed by middlemen—the men who bought up, transported, processed, packaged, advertised, sold, and delivered the product of the farm to the ultimate consumer. Inasmuch as these handlers each added a charge to the raw product, its final selling price was usually much higher than what the farmer originally received. To farmers, it seemed that somehow the handlers received a greater share for less time and effort than they did. The antipathy towards middlemen long antedated the farm depressions of the 1870s and the 1890s. George Brackett's little book of homilies for farmers illustrates the scorn farmers felt for middlemen.

Why isn't the cattle buyer in this selection a fair representative of middlemen generally?

Why wasn't the farmer "taken in" by the cattle buyer's line? Why was he able to hold out and get the price he wanted? Would farmers always be in this farmer's position?

৺

THERE is a large class of persons in this country called *middle-men*, who operate in all communities, and who are of no benefit what-

George E. Brackett, *Farm Talk: A Series of Articles in the Colloquial Style, Illustrating Various Common Farm Topics* (Boston: Lee & Shepard, 1868), pp. 61–65.

ever. They are non-producers, deriving their sustenance from the labor of others, like a parasitic plant. They buy from the producer, and sell to the consumer, thus directly injuring both parties,—the one paying too high for his necessities, the other being obliged to sell his products under price. These drones in the social hive are numerous, and are particularly inimical to the farmers' interests. From various causes we are in a condition to be more easily preyed upon by these cormorants than any other profession. If the producers and consumers could be brought more directly together, so as to save the large profits of the middle-men, it would be greatly for the interests of both, and there would be less reason for bewailing the small profits of the one, and the high prices of products by the other.

These middle-men comprise several minor classes, some stationary and others itinerant. These latter are found perambulating the producing regions wherever their keen visions scent the possibility of a "trade." One of these gentry, whose specialty is cattle buying, called upon me yesterday, while I was in the field, ploughing.

"Mornin', Captin."

"Good morning, sir."

"Heerd ye had some cattle to sell."

"I have a yoke of beeves. Are you buying stock?"

"Wall, a leetle; kinder off an' on like. Where's your oxen, Captin?"

"Over yonder in the pasture. You can go down and look at them. I am very busy today. Drive on, John."

He goes off to the pasture, and returns in about fifteen minutes. I ask him,—

"What do you think of them? fat, ain't they?"

"Middlin', Captin; only middlin'."

"How much do you make their girth?"

" 'Bout seven foot; rawny-boned too."

"Why, I make them girth seven feet two, strong."

"Kinder flabby; they'll dress away a good deal."

"They'd ought to be pretty solid. I fed them corn meal all last winter and this spring."

"What's yer price, Captin?"

"Two hundred dollars."

"Two hundred! Can't go that, no how."

"Very well. Start up the team, John."

Buyer looks rather disappointed, but follows me round till we reach the next headland, when he breaks out,—

"Say, Captin, ain't that rather steep? Beef's a-goin' down. My brother come from Brighton t'other day, and says you can't hardly give it away there."

"When did he leave Brighton?"

"One day last week."

"Well, I've yesterday's cattle market report, and beef is tending upward. What makes you so anxious to buy if it is falling?"

"Fact is, Captin, I like the looks of them oxen. I'll split the difference betwixt that and a hundred and seventy-five."

"My price is two hundred."

"Let's go down and look at 'em agin."

"Can't spend the time."

"A feller couldn't make his salt to pay two hundred for 'em."

"You're not obliged to take them."

"That off one ain't in near so good order as the nigh one. Think he is?"

"How did you know which was the off one?"

"Say, I'll go a five better."

"You have heard my price."

We have reached the end of the bout. Buyer makes a motion as if to leave. I make no remark, but set the plough in the next furrow, when he suddenly wheels with—

"Here's your money. Dang it! I'll take the oxen."

"All right. John, drive them up into the yard. Let the team 'blow' a few minutes."

"Hain't got an old yoke, or halter, or somethin' that you'll throw in, to fasten 'em with, have ye?"

"Give him a halter, John."

"Good day, Captin. Looks as if we might have a spell o' weather soon."

As he goes down the road, he meets Smith, to whom he says, "The Captin is a 'hard cud' to trade with: couldn't beat him down a cent."

VIII

The National Grange resolves to sponsor coöperatives.

FROM: The proceedings of the seventh session of the National Grange of the Patrons of Husbandry, St. Louis, Missouri, February 4, 1874.

CONVINCED that they were being robbed by parasitic middlemen, many farmers became interested in coöperative buying, selling, and even producing. Since it was an article of faith among farmers that middlemen did little, it was assumed that farmer-operated coöp stores would be easily run and would produce large savings for farmers. The Grange Society, among other farm groups, promoted coöps, most of which were short-lived. Many of them, such as coöperative insurance and telephone companies, though useful, had little impact on total farm incomes.

According to the Grange resolutions, which specific middlemen did the farmers hope to avoid? Which ones would they be forced to deal with?

What problems would you expect farmer coöp stores to encounter?

🔊

. . . YOUR committee would take this occasion to impress upon the members of the Order, that taking the matter in their own hands and organizing effective coöperation between themselves as producers and the transportation companies as legitimately engaged in a necessary function of the business of exchange, is one of the most practical means for producing immediate results.

Your committee were also enjoined to take into consideration the subject of business coöperation. Under this head, we feel the imperative necessity of some definite action, to the end that there may be an exchange of products between producers in the different sections of country. The cotton and sugar-growing States, the manufacturing and mining districts of the Eastern and Middle States and the bread and meat-producing States of the West, are all united by a common bond of interest, an interest which the Order of Patrons will bring together and utilize.

It should be our purpose to arrange a business system by which an exchange of products may be made direct between the producer and consumer without the intervention of an unnecessary number of middle men. It is of but little satisfaction to our brothers of the South to know that corn in Iowa is selling at thirty cents per bushel while they pay eighty, or that meat in Illinois is four cents per pound, while it costs them eight. It is a questionable consolation to the manufacturer of New-England to know that in the valley of the Mississippi a yard of his cloth will buy three loaves of bread, when but one of them ever reaches his family.

Your committee recognize fully that these differences are not caused by a fair and equitable system of transportation or business needs, but by an unhealthy system of watered stock and an unnecessary number of middle men, which together eat up too large a share of the products of labor. In view of these facts, we respectfully submit the following resolution:

Resolved, That the Executive Committee of the National Grange

Proceedings of the Seventh Session of the National Grange of the Patrons of Husbandry [1874] (New York: S. W. Green, Printer, 1874), pp. 79–80.

be instructed to give especial attention to furnishing Patrons with tools and implements for the cultivation of our farms, and all family and farm supplies, at as low a price as a legitimate business profit will permit, and also to make arrangements by which a mutual exchange of products between different sections of the country may be made; and they are hereby authorized to employ, if in their judgment it may be necessary, competent agents to aid them in the work.

That they be also instructed to devise some safe plan for coöperative stores, for the information of members of the Order, and transmit the same to the Executive Committees of the several State granges.

IX

A coöp manager discusses why coöps often failed.

FROM: "Coöperation Among Farmers," an 1895 magazine article by Edward F. Adams.

MANY coöperative stores were unable to survive in competition with established businesses. Merchants worked hard to undersell and to drive the coöps into bankruptcy. They were often assisted by their suppliers, who had no desire to see coöps flourish. About the time that coöp stores appeared, another rival, the Chicago mail-order houses, began to offer farmers quality goods at low prices.

Edward F. Adams, the author of this selection, was a California fruit grower and the manager of a fruit-marketing coöp, who became disillusioned and cynical about coöperatives. In this selection he discusses some of the shortcomings of such enterprises.

Why, according to Adams, did coöps have difficulty in hiring competent managers?

Why were internal politics of coöps so much more disruptive generally than the internal politics of corporations?

᠊ᥱᢃ

. . . THE cost of coöperative selling is equal to that of selling through commission houses. This is partly due to inexperience and the lack of executive vigor, which must always be a feature of coöperation, but mainly to a vicious duplication of expense, or to the omission of expense which is essential to proper management. For example, the operation of selling fruit is simple enough if you only know what price to set so as to move your product when you wish to, and yet secure the highest price which conditions warrant. But to learn the facts upon which sound judgment as to these transactions can be based is a labor of infinite detail, requiring decided ability; for in a coöperative marketing society, in which all products of the same grade are mingled and sold together, and the same net proceeds paid to all, the management is compelled so to frame its policy from the beginning of the season to the end as to ensure the best results to all its members. This requires a fund of information, a touch with the market, and a breadth of view not attainable by a small society of farmers; nor have our strongest deciduous-fruit societies ever yet spent enough money in securing the necessary information to enable them to become as good judges of the probable course of the market as our best commission men or the great merchants. . . . In the same way the advertising of our common product, the opening of new markets, the testing of new methods, the securing of uniform and the best methods of grading and packing, are all essential to the profitable management of our crops, and should be done by a common agency maintained at the common expense. It is also doubtless true that, loudly as we farmers denounce trusts and declaim in favor of coöperation, as a matter of fact that form of coöperation which comes nearest to doing for us what is accomplished by the most successful trusts is the form which will best suit us, and what we really seek; but to obtain any such result requires control of the output, which can be gained only by organization. It is therefore to the interest of those growers who are organized, to induce others to join them in efforts for the common benefit. . . . [Footnote: It is amusing to observe the unwillingness of farmers to acknowledge that the principle of our organizations is identical with that of the great commercial trusts. Of course, the fact is that such coöperation as we are engaged in is simply the organization of one class to compete more effectively with others. The reason why the great commercial trusts are objectionable, in spite of the economic saving involved in their methods, is that they are strong, and, being strong, will probably abuse their power just as we would could we attain a like strength. Our societies are not thus objectionable, because, with human nature as it is, we can never be strong enough to be dangerous; the most we can expect is to protect ourselves against the better organized classes. We are no better than the commercial classes; we simply have less ability and less strength.] . . . . .

. . . Coöperation outside the wine and orange interests does not yet command the support of the largest growers; to a man, they desire to see it go on, but they will not aid the movement except by talk. Their reasons are various. Some are so involved by indebtedness to commission houses that they are not really at liberty to coöperate; others are of the opinion that in the struggle for existence they will survive and be better off if they do not help others to survive with them. And so it results that our deciduous-fruit organizations represent mostly small growers not very firmly held together, and controlling possibly one-fifth of the total output. . . . . .

For the present I believe that we must confine coöperative effort to very simple matters, which are familiar to most of those coöperating. Coöperative stores, coöperative mills, coöperative canning companies, I constantly warn farmers against touching. They are almost always promoted by some one desiring a place for which he is not fit, and usually come to grief. I draw the line at all coöperative enterprises involving the purchase of material or merchandise to be sold again. These are unsafe for farmers in their present state of development. The objects of our societies are very simple: they are, first, to inform ourselves, before selling, of the condition of the market,—remembering that our market is thousands of miles away; second, to increase our market by proper advertising at the general expense, and by ensuring honest and uniform packing; third, to ensure the sale of our own labor to as great an extent as possible, by doing for ourselves whatever we do not find it more profitable to hire others to do; fourth, to obtain for our product in each year whatever the conditions of the market warrant; fifth, to eliminate from the process of marketing all unnecessary labor; and sixth, to prevent speculation by refusing to sell until our product is ready, and then selling at the market price, keeping our goods in our own possession until sold. This is all that we try to do, and we find even this sufficiently complex for farmers to deal with.

It is evident that if one capable person owned all the orchards in California, the above are in the main the lines upon which he would work. The question to be solved is whether some thousands of growers can so organize as to attain these ends. It is plain that our product will be more wisely marketed under a single direction, provided that direction be competent; and this raises the crucial question . . . of coöperation. . . . Can a community so organize as to bestow the management of its larger industrial affairs on the fittest? . . .

I am holding a position for which I am incompetent, and which I do not desire. Hundreds of orchardists are looking to me for advice which I am incompetent to give, for the lack of such knowledge and experience as will support strong convictions. I am supposed to be as competent as any one available, or we should secure a better man; we need the service of one trained not only in commercial life, but in our special line, and although we know many who could do what we need done, we know no one who is not now better situated than he would be in any employment we could give. The farmer has no conception of the labor and expense required to obtain the knowledge wisely to direct large affairs, nor any notion of the strain of business. He does not know— and will not believe—that it is far more exhausting to dictate letters and decide business questions all day than to split rails for the same length of time; nor that those to whom large affairs are entrusted must mingle, out of business hours, with others doing business in a large way, and that this involves serious expense. We could get a capable man in my place in a week if we could pay him and ensure him permanence in office; but at the annual meeting a party would be quite sure to develop in favor of "economy" and against "fat salaries," and our capable man, if he were not displaced, would be made very uncomfortable and very uncertain of his future.

. . . The good of the community requires that important affairs be managed by able men. The management of a coöperative society is hampered from the start by difficulties never encountered by the managers of ordinary commercial houses. It must not only transact the business entrusted to it, but must hold its constituency together to get the business. In competitive society the agent is at least sure of the support of his employers; in coöperation his employers are quite likely to desert him at any minute, and then hold him responsible for the consequences of their own desertion.

. . . The farmer knows almost nothing of the facts or routine of commercial life, and, being ignorant, is easily deceived; being often deceived, he becomes suspicious; and, being more often deceived by those who profess to serve him than by others, he is especially suspicious of that class. This renders it very difficult to hold them together in coöperative work. The enthusiasm of a public meeting may easily cement them, but they are prone to fall asunder while the mortar is still green. Those who prey upon popular ignorance and weakness must necessarily dislike the progress of coöperation, which they invariably seek to defeat, not by attacking its principles, but by impugning the motives of those actively promoting it,—and to such insinuations or open charges farmers lend very ready ears. It is not unreasonable that they should, for there is now no commercial reason why capable men should take charge of coöperative affairs; and those who can be moved to do so by sentimental reasons are not at all sure to be commercially competent. In fact, as matters now stand, I think the chances two to one that if a coöperative leader is capable, he is dishonest, and that, if he is honest, he is incapable. In a blind sort of way farmers feel this, and the great infirmities of human nature—lack of exact knowledge and firm will—make them easy to deceive and then easy to lead.

These are some of the fundamental difficulties with which we have to deal in coöperation, as they appear to one who is earnestly trying to surmount them. There are troubles of detail, of course, with which this paper has no concern. We are dealing with these difficulties . . . to the best of our ability, and the aggregate of encouragement is very large;

but so, alas, is the aggregate of discouragement. What the outcome may be, of course we know not, but we who have hope and courage expect to succeed.

X

A farmer expresses his views on currency to President Grover Cleveland.

FROM: A letter of W. Chas. Maben, Prattsville, New York, to President Cleveland, December 7, 1895.

DURING the depression from 1893 to 1896, President Cleveland received many letters on the money question. Those from bankers and businessmen almost unanimously urged him to protect the gold standard at all costs to maintain "sound" and "honest" dollars. Debtor groups, on the other hand, complained that there was too little money in circulation. They believed that gold, like any other commodity, was governed by the law of supply and demand, and had been rising in value because there was not enough in circulation. This meant that each gold dollar commanded more and more goods, or to put it the other way around, goods commanded fewer and fewer dollars. Hence farm prices, for example, were falling, while debts remained unchanged. Farmer Maben's letter clearly expressed the debtor's view of the currency problem.

Why did not creditors reduce the principal and interest on debts owed them when they saw that it took twice as much produce in 1895 to repay each dollar as it had in 1885?

Suppose that the value of currency had inflated rather than deflated between 1885 and 1895: why would farmers have objected to paying their creditors sums equal in value to the amounts they had borrowed?

᛫ᣥ

MOST Esteemed Friend:—

Like Millions of other men to night I have been reading your Message to Congress to get your view of the money question. I am a farmer. When gold was worth half its present value ten years ago I had $4,000.00. I bought a $12,000.00 farm and gave a mortgage for $8,000.00 paying in my $4,000.00. For 4 years I paid my interest and $500.00 principal annually since which time I have barely paid my interest. During this time hundreds of mortgages have been foreclosed and hard working men have lost their all. Hundreds of others in this vicinity and all over New York State and New England are struggling like me to save their homes.

The Grover Cleveland Papers, Manuscripts Division, The Library of Congress, Washington, D. C.

They are honest men. They do not wish to "debase" the currency nor to "repudiate their debts," but they find themselves confronted with a condition of things just the reverse of repudiation. In order to pay each dollar of interest or principal we must sell double the amount of produce required in former times and our farms have depreciated in value, one half, or to tell the truth as it is the standard of value, *gold* has been doubled thus obliging us to pay two dollars actual value for each dollar of our indebtedness as well as 12% interest instead of 6%.

To use your own words of former days regarding the McKinly [*sic*] Tariff. This is a condition and not a theory and millions of honest men who have no silver mines and who never read a Free Silver Coinage article in their lives but whose eyes have been opened by "Sound" money literature to the *cause* of their trouble see it.

Volumes could be written of heartrending scenes of families sold out and driven from their homes by mortagees [*sic*] who have no idea of being cruel, and who do not know *why* the farm won't bring more than half it sold for a dozen years ago. The truth is real estate is worth as much now as then but the *standard dollar is doubled in value.*

Until that value is restored to its original place as compared with all commodities, it is a libel on the debtors of this country to accuse them of a desire to repudiate and the debtor class of today has been the debtor class for many years.

> An Old Admiror [*sic*], truly,
> W. Chas. Maben

XI

A Populist Senator argues for legislative control of the money supply.

FROM: Editor Albert Shaw's interview with William V. Allen, 1894.

THOSE advocating expansion of the nation's currency supply resented the charge that they favored runaway inflation, debt repudiation, or dishonest money. Farmer Maben in the previous selection rejected any such notions. So did a spokesman for Western farmers, William V. Allen. Originally a successful Republican lawyer in Nebraska, he left his party and became a Populist. Allen won an elected judgeship as a Populist in 1891, and two years later the Nebraska legislature elected him to the United States Senate. Unlike many of the Populist leaders, Allen was neither colorful nor eccentric; but he was intelligent, competent, and reasonable.

In the 1890s most economists and businessmen regarded proposals such as Allen's as unworkable and misguided. How would present-day economists regard his proposals?

What arguments might be advanced against having Congress under-take to regulate in detail the nation's money supply?

❧

. . . THE Western men do not want a period of wild inflation either now or in the future, and we would regulate the volume of money upon some sound principles which would recognize the growth of population, the assessed wealth of the country and the volume of production and of commercial transactions. What we want to accomplish is very simple and easily explained. We believe it possible by legislation so to regulate the issue of money as to make it of approximately the same value at all times. The value of money ought to bear as nearly as possible a fixed relation to the value of commodities. If a man should borrow a thousand dollars on five years' time to-day, when it would take two bushels of wheat to pay each dollar, it is clear that it ought not to take any more wheat to pay that debt at the time of its maturity, except for the accrued interest. In other words, a dollar ought to have the same command, and no greater command, over the products of the farm and the factory at one time than at another. In the little town where I live, in 1892 wheat just after the harvest was selling for fifty-two cents per bushel. In 1893 it was selling at forty-two cents. This year it is selling, I believe, at from thirty-five to thirty-seven cents. Now if the farmer happens to be in debt, it is plain that since his yield per acre and the cost of tilling an acre remain practically the same, he is compelled to give more and more of his crop to pay yearly interest, and that it becomes more and more painfully difficult to save up the dollars that will be needed to pay off the principal when it comes due.

Albert Shaw, "William V. Allen: Populist—A Character Sketch and Interview," *Review of Reviews,* 10 (July, 1894), 39.

XII

A conservative denies the need for legislation on the farm problem.

FROM: The annual report of Secretary of Agriculture J. Sterling Morton, 1896.

J. STERLING MORTON of Nebraska was United States Secretary of Agriculture from 1893 until 1897. Although a Democrat and a West-erner, Morton had no sympathy for the various farmers' movements. In the 1870s as an editor, he opposed state regulation of railways. He was also conservative on the money question. During his tenure as Secretary he fought against what he called waste and paternalism. He opposed the distribution by his department of free pamphlets and seeds to farmers, and he regularly returned unspent a portion of his department's annual appropriation. In his final annual report, written at the depth of the Depression of 1893–1896, Morton rejected the idea that farmers were badly off.

Assuming the accuracy of Secretary Morton's figures on mortgages, in what ways might they be misleading, particularly with regard to the Western situation?

Since the census reported sharecropper plots in the South as separate farms, why would there be relatively few Southern farms listed as mortgaged?

THE farmers of the United States hold 72 out of each 100 farms—occupied by their owners—absolutely free from mortgages or other incumbrances. . . .

Out of each thousand farms in the United States only 282 are mortgaged, and three-fourths of the money represented by the mortgages upon the 282 farms was for the purchase of those farms or for money borrowed to improve those farms. And the prevalent idea that the West and the South are more heavily burdened with farm mortgages than the East and Northeast sections of the United States is entirely erroneous. . . .

The constant complaint by the alleged friends of farmers, and by some farmers themselves, is that the Government does nothing for agriculture. In conventions and congresses it has been proclaimed that the farmers of the country are almost universally in debt, despondent, and suffering. Largely these declarations are without foundation. Their utterance is a belittlement of agriculture and an indignity to every intelligent and practical farmer of the United States. The free and independent farmers of this country are not impoverished; they are not mendicants; they are not wards of the Government to be treated to annuities, like Indians upon reservations. On the other hand, they are the representatives of the oldest, most honorable, and most essential occupation of the human race. Upon it all other vocations depend for subsistence and prosperity. The farmer is the copartner of the elements. His intelligently directed efforts are in unison with the light and heat of the sun, and the success of his labors represents the commingling of the raindrops and his own sweat.

Legislation can neither plow nor plant. The intelligent, practical, and successful farmer needs no aid from the Government. The ignorant, impractical, and indolent farmer deserves none. It is not the business of

Report of the Secretary of Agriculture, 1896 (Washington: Government Printing Office, 1896), pp. xlv–xlvi.

Government to legislate in behalf of any class of citizens because they are engaged in any specific calling, no matter how essential the calling may be to the needs and comforts of civilization. Lawmakers can not erase natural laws nor restrict or efface the operation of economic laws. It is a beneficent arrangement of the order of things and the conditions of human life that legislators are not permitted to repeal, amend, or revise the laws of production and distribution.

XIII

A Secretary of Agriculture reports sixteen years of farm prosperity.

FROM: The annual report of Secretary of Agriculture James Wilson, 1912.

THE years between the Spanish-American War and World War I have come to be known as the "golden age" of American agriculture. As farm incomes rose during those years, the bitterness engendered by the long hardship abated. Throughout the period one man, James Wilson, was Secretary of Agriculture. Born in Scotland, Wilson migrated to the United States as a youth and settled on a farm in Iowa. Active both in agriculture and Republican politics, he was named by President McKinley to head the Department of Agriculture in 1897. Wilson continued to serve in that post under Presidents Theodore Roosevelt and William Howard Taft. In his final report Wilson described those prosperous years in glowing terms.

So far as he discussed the matter at all, to what did Secretary Wilson seem to ascribe the farmers' new prosperity?

How did Wilson's explanation of prosperity square with the idea that surplus production was the cause of low farm incomes during the late nineteenth century?

❧

MOST productive of all agricultural years in this country has been 1912. The earth has produced its greatest annual dividend. The sun and the rain and the fertility of the soil heeded not the human controversies, but kept on working in coöperation with the farmers' efforts to utilize them. The reward is a high general level of production. The man behind the plow has filled the Nation's larder, crammed the storehouses, and will send liberal supplies to foreign countries.

The prices at the farm are generally profitable, and will continue the prosperity that farmers have enjoyed in recent years. In spite of the lower total value of animals sold and slaughtered, the total crop value

Annual Reports of the Department of Agriculture, 1912 (Washington: Government Printing Office, 1913), pp. 11–12, 258.

is so far above that of 1911, and of any preceding year, that the total production of farm wealth is the highest yet reached by half a billion dollars.

Based on the census items of wealth production on farms, the grand total for 1912 is estimated to be $9,532,000,000. This unthinkable amount of wealth has been contributed to the Nation in one year by the soil and by the farmers' live stock. It is more than twice the value of the wealth produced on farms in 1899, according to the census, and it is about one-eighth more than the wealth produced in 1909.

During the past 16 years the farmer has steadily increased his wealth production year by year, with the exception of 1911, when the value declined from that of the preceding year. If the wealth produced on farms in 1899 be regarded as 100, the wealth produced 16 years ago, or in 1897, is represented by 84, and the wealth produced in 1912 by 202.1. During the 16 years the farmers' wealth production increased 141 per cent.

The array of figures that expresses the farmers' contribution to national wealth production testifies to the farmers' basic importance to the Nation. During the last 16 years the wealth production on farms, according to the census items, reached the grand total of more than $105,000,000,000. This stream of wealth has poured out of the farmers' horn of plenty, and in 16 years has equaled about three-quarters of the present national wealth. . . . . .

The record of 16 years has been written. It begins with a yearly farm production worth $4,000,000,000 and ends with $9,532,000,000. Then, farmers were loaded with debts that were a painful burden; prosperity followed and grew with unexampled speed. Then, the farmer was a joke of the caricaturist; now he is like the stone that was rejected by the builder and has become the head stone of the corner. Beginnings have been made in a production per acre increasing faster than the natural increase of population. There has been an uplift of agriculture and of country life.

XIV

An historian accounts for farm prosperity in the early twentieth century.

FROM: A monograph on reform trends from Populism to the New Deal.

THE return of farm prosperity after 1897 was caused by neither enactment of laws called for by farmer groups nor defeat of legislation favored by their opponents. New economic forces, not legislation, began to reverse the long downward trend of farm prices and incomes. The changes, since they involved no political defeat for either, made it possible for both gold standard men and inflationists to claim victory. Moreover, farmers learned that sometimes good can result from defeat. Hofstadter, an eminent modern historian, describes the changes that restored prosperous times to farmers until after World War I.

What was the "gold inflation" that Hofstadter writes of, and what caused it?

What important factors slowed the expansion of American agriculture after about 1890?

ONLY two years after McKinley and Hanna inflicted their overwhelming defeat on the forces of agrarianism, the American commercial farmer entered upon the longest sustained period of peacetime prosperity he has ever enjoyed. "There has never been a time," declared President Theodore Roosevelt's Commission on Country Life in 1909, "when the American farmer was as well off as he is today, when we consider not only his earning power, but the comforts and advantages he may secure." Thus the "final" victory of industrialism over the farmer was ironically followed by the golden age of American agriculture, to which agricultural interests later looked back nostalgically when they were defining a goal for the nation's farm policy.

How did all this agricultural well-being come to be, at a time when the agricultural population was shrinking before the advance of industrialism and urbanism? The answer is that the prosperity of the commercial farmers was achieved not only in spite of but in good part because of the rise of American industry and the American city. Not only this, but the political as well as the economic position of the farmer in the golden age of American agriculture became measurably stronger year by year as his numbers, relative to the urban sector, progressively grew smaller.

A vital part of the change came, of course, simply with the upturn in prices. The farmer's principal relief at first came from a detested source—gold. After 1897 the new international supplies of gold brought that inflationary movement which the farmers had tried to win with silver. The general price level, which had been sinking steadily for the thirty years before 1896, turned sharply upward in the closing years of the old century and continued to rise until the reaction after the first World War. In the United States wheat went from 72 cents a bushel in 1896 to 98 cents in 1909; corn from 21 cents to 57 cents; cotton from 6 cents to 14 cents a pound.

Richard Hofstadter, *The Age of Reform: From Bryan to F.D.R.* (New York: Alfred A. Knopf, 1959), pp. 109–111; © Copyright 1955 by Richard Hofstadter. Reprinted by permission of Alfred A. Knopf, Inc.

However, it was not only the gold inflation but the American city itself that saved the American farmer. During these very years of the golden age the farmer in most lines of production was rapidly losing a large part of his foreign market. What sustained his prosperity was the very thing that has been cited as evidence of his political submergence —the great increase of the urban population. In 1890, 5,737,000 American farms were supplying a domestic urban population of 22,100,000. Thirty years later there were only 711,000 additional farms, but there were 32,000,000 additional urban consumers. Relatively fewer but larger, more efficient, and more mechanized farms produced an increasing part of their total produce for the home market, and less for the foreign market, under far stabler and more advantageous conditions of transportation and finance than had prevailed in the past. True, the farm community was not expanding nearly as rapidly as it once had. But this slower and saner pace of expansion was itself a factor in rural well-being. And the surplus rural population found in the fast-growing cities an expansive safety valve. Many sons of farmers who were unable to accommodate themselves in the farm economy moved to the cities to find work or carve out careers.

The improved position of the commercial farmer led to a drastic change in dominant conceptions among farm organizations as to the methods of advancing their interests. The pre-war gold inflation of course put an end to the primacy of the money question that had been so characteristic of the agrarian thinking of the nineties. Where Greenback, Populist, and Bryanite panaceas, arising from a fixation on the quantity of money, had fostered legislative programs aimed above all at increasing the volume of currency, the new approach was aimed rather at decreasing and controlling the volume of the farm products themselves as a means of sustaining or raising prices.

FOR FURTHER THOUGHT

American businessmen and laborers sought, and to a degree found, solutions to their problems in organization. Through larger corporations and business combines and through labor unions, both were able to curtail excessive competition and to protect their incomes. Was organization an answer to the farm problem? What factors made effective organization of farmers difficult?

Economically, farmers and laborers were often in trouble during the late nineteenth century. What kept these two groups from uniting in a successful farmer-laborer political party?

Historians for many years spoke of the farm frontier as a "safety valve" against urban discontent and revolution. Why, in the late nineteenth century, might it be proper to speak of the city as a safety valve for agrarian discontent?

5. Politics in the Era of Economic Revolution, 1876-1896

HISTORIANS have traditionally considered the years from the end of the Civil War to the beginning of the twentieth century as a dismal, unprogressive period in domestic politics. Politicians and Presidents seemed second rate; personalities rather than great issues dominated presidential campaigns. The major political parties failed to respond meaningfully to the vastly significant economic changes examined in the three previous chapters, which suggest how modern America was being shaped by industrialization and urbanization. But politics did not keep pace with this modernization. American political parties did not, at least until 1896, really concentrate on basic issues in their efforts to appeal to the electorate. This lag in the political response to the economic revolution is the primary concern of this chapter.

The Reconstruction period between 1865 and 1877 established precedents for low level political performance during the postbellum generation. During the Johnson and Grant administrations, the prestige of the presidency declined precipitously. Lack of distinction in political leadership, as the Englishman James Bryce noted in his classic study, *The American Commonwealth* (1888), contributed to the poor quality of public life in the United States [I].

Prevailing concepts about the federal government and the presidency played a major role in characterizing American politics in this era. For example, most Americans still believed in the traditional Jeffersonian concept of limited government. Furthermore, the pre-Civil War Whig Party idea of the presidency (the President should carry out decisions made by Congress) persisted until almost the end of the century. All chief executives of the period accepted this generally restricted view of presidential prerogatives. This is not to say that these men were weak-willed; but there were no Jacksons, Polks or Lincolns in the White House in these years. The scholar Woodrow Wilson, later to serve as President himself, suggested in his study *Congressional Government* (1885) that another source of presidential problems was the gradual assumption of power by Congress [II]. These ingrained ideas contributed importantly to the political lag. They made it difficult for the parties to readjust their policies rapidly to an industrialized America.

The period was not completely devoid of discussion of substantive questions. Reformers maintained a constant if not always effective stream of agitation. Their earliest success was in the area of civil service reform. Industrialization contributed to expansion of federal activity, and the consequent increase in the number of federal employees emphasized the need for a merit system. Scandal during the Grant administration, patronage controversies when Rutherford B. Hayes was President, and the assassination of James A. Garfield in 1881 by a disappointed office seeker strengthened the hand of civil service reformers. With support from President Chester A. Arthur, they pushed through Congress in 1883 the Pendleton Act, establishing a civil service commission and a limited classified service. Grover Cleveland, the first President to serve a full term after passage of the act, faced a monumental task in resisting patronage demands, because he headed the first Democratic administration since 1861. Immediately before entering the presidency, Cleveland expressed his commitment to civil service reform in a letter to the prominent reformer George W. Curtis [III]. During his first administration, Cleveland exercised his legal option to expand the classified service. Even so, he disappointed some civil service advocates because he awarded many political jobs to faithful Democratic followers. Some of his critics, nonetheless, thought that he was a better choice for the presidency in 1888 than Benjamin Harrison. In a letter written during the 1888 campaign, Carl Schurz, a prominent Republican leader and civil service champion, explained why he would continue to support Cleveland over Harrison [IV]. After passage of the Pendleton Act and gradual expansion of the classified service, rare evidence of meaningful political response for those times, the issue of civil service reform receded into the background.

The malefactions accompanying the emergence of great industrial and financial empires in the form of pools, mergers, holding companies, and interlocking directorates stimulated demands for federal intervention and regulation (see Chapter Two). Farmer and labor groups were most vocal in their demand for government action (see Chapters Three and Four). But Congress passed only two major regulatory laws, the Interstate Commerce Act and the Sherman Antitrust Act, both poorly framed and ineffectively implemented before 1900. A Senate investigation of the nation's railroads, and the Supreme Court's decision in *Wabash* v. *Illinois* (1886), which ruled out state regulation of interstate railroads, preceded congressional approval of the Interstate Commerce Act in 1887. Shelby M. Cullom of Illinois, head of the Senate investigation, eloquently summarized the railroad problem in a Senate speech [V]. The Interstate Commerce Act and the weak Sherman Antitrust Act of 1890 did not represent effective responses by Congress to the economic revolution. Reflecting the general political temper, the executive and legislative branches of the federal government and an economically conservative Supreme Court were not yet willing to assume extensive regulatory functions.

The tariff also received attention from politicians, but again there was no fruitful approach to reform. Beginning with the Morrill Act of 1861, late nineteenth century tariffs were highly protective, based on the assumption that high rates would benefit American industry. Enemies of protection argued that the prevailing tariff structure contributed to the great power of industrialists and their tendency to ignore the public good. Neither major party seriously advocated substantial reduction during the period, but some concerned persons tried to awaken interest in tariff reform. President Cleveland, for example, demanded tariff reductions in a weighty State of the Union message in 1887. The Republican victory in 1888 eliminated Cleveland for the time being and made possible a substantial increase by the McKinley Tariff of 1890. Again President in 1893, Cleveland advocated tariff reform, only to be confronted in 1894 with the Wilson-Gorman Act, which represented neither reform nor significant reductions in its protective schedules. Cleveland explained his refusal to sign the law to a congressman from his own party [VI]. After William McKinley became President in 1897, the Republican-controlled Congress passed the Dingley Tariff, raising protectionist rates to the highest levels of the century. Members of Congress from both major parties resisted tariff reform when they thought it would adversely affect industries in their own districts. Many Americans in the late nineteenth century believed that tariff reform was one necessary response to the economic and social problems of industrialization. Failure to achieve such reform in the period was another example of the political lag.

Some historians consider Grover Cleveland the best President between Lincoln and Theodore Roosevelt. Certainly Cleveland did much to restore the prestige of the presidency. He was in some respects more of a reformer than his contemporaries in the presidential office, but Cleveland did not challenge the economic conservatism of the age. His use of federal troops to break the Pullman Strike of 1894 was revealing. This action and the lack of effective moves to solve the nation's financial problems after the Panic of 1893 helped split the Democratic party and contributed to Cleveland's declining popularity. Henry Adams' letter expressing his reaction to Cleveland's policy during the Pullman Strike conveys some of the flavor of the day [VII].

As Adams implied, by 1894 the money question had become the paramount issue in American politics. Advocates of cheap money after the Civil War championed both the expanded circulation of "greenback" currency and "free silver" as solutions to economic problems, particularly those of debtors. A new coinage law in 1873, which in effect had demonetized silver, angered cheap money supporters. Their views on this law were explained by the free silver champion William H. Harvey in *Coin's Financial School* (1894), a popular book widely used as a campaign document by the Populists and Democrats in 1896 [VIII]. The Bland-Allison Act of 1878 and the Sherman Silver Purchase Act of 1890 had provided only limited satisfaction to silver interests; the repeal of the latter law in October, 1893, demanded by the Cleveland administration as a partial solution to the declining gold reserve, aroused the free silver group and helped project the money question into the campaign of 1896.

The silverites captured the Democratic party in 1896, repudiated the Cleveland policies, nominated William Jennings Bryan of Nebraska for the presidency, and wrote a platform endorsing free silver. The Populist party (see Chapter Four) also accepted Bryan. The Republicans, with the stalwart William McKinley as their standard bearer, stood for the gold standard. The money planks in the Democratic and Republican platforms made clear the positions of the two major parties [IX]. President Cleveland, extremely disappointed with the candidate and platform of the Democratic convention, stoutly defended his own policies in a letter to a member of his cabinet [X]. From Bryan's analysis of the issue in his acceptance speech [XI] to the balloting in November, the Nebraskan tried to convince the voters that bimetallism was what the country needed. One of his strongest supporters, Governor John P. Altgeld of Illinois, summarized his ideas on the far-reaching issues in a major campaign address in mid-October, 1896 [XII].

With Bryan's defeat the free silver movement collapsed. Some analyses of the election of 1896 have emphasized the effective organization of the McKinley campaign and especially the influence of the vast amount of money raised in McKinley's behalf by Mark Hanna, the Republican campaign chairman. Undoubtedly this money played a role, but probably it is not the pivotal explanation for McKinley's victory. McKinley and the Republican party appealed to a majority of the voting public—the urban, industrial elements. The Populist-Democratic appeal was essentially rural, looking to the old America, while the Republicans presented a candidate and a program catering to the changes which had taken place in the preceding half-century. Although this is not to say that the Republican program was an adequate response to the needs of the country, the Republican party succeeded in associating itself with the *accomplishments* of the economic revolution. The political lag in the face of this revolution still existed. It was not until the Progressive Era and beyond that the federal government began to come to grips with modern America. EDITED BY ROGER R. TRASK

An English observer comments on the low tone of public life in the United States.

FROM: James Bryce's commentary on American politics and society, 1888.

THE Englishman James Bryce was a perceptive and widely read observer of the United States in the late nineteenth century. Bryce's work covered the national government, state governments, political parties, public opinion, and social institutions. While critical, Bryce showed admiration for the American commonwealth. In the selection below, he comments on the lack of distinction in the public service.

Could one conclude that his aristocratic bias made Bryce an unqualified observer of public life in the United States?

Can Bryce's comments be considered a valid explanation for American lack of progress in solving problems presented by the economic revolution?

THE tone of public life is lower than one expects to find it in so great a nation. Just as we assume that an individual man will at any supreme moment in his own life rise to a higher level than that on which he usually moves, so we look to find those who conduct the affairs of a great state inspired by a sense of the magnitude of the interests entrusted to them. Their horizon ought to be expanded, their feeling of duty quickened, their dignity of attitude enhanced. Human nature with all its weaknesses does show itself capable of being thus roused on its imaginative side; and in Europe, where the traditions of aristocracy survive, everybody condemns as mean or unworthy acts done or language held by a great official which would pass unnoticed in a private citizen. It is the principle of *noblesse oblige* with the sense of duty and trust substituted for that of mere hereditary rank.

Such a sentiment is comparatively weak in America. A cabinet minister, or senator, or governor of a State, sometimes even a President, hardly feels himself more bound by it than the director of a railway company or the mayor of a town does in Europe. Not assuming himself to be individually wiser, stronger, or better than his fellow-citizens, he acts and speaks as though he were still simply one of them, and so far from magnifying his office and making it honourable, seems anxious to show that he is the mere creature of the popular vote, so filled by the sense that it is the people and not he who governs as to fear that he should be deemed to have forgotten his personal insignificance. There is in the United States abundance of patriotism, that is to say, or a passion for the greatness and happiness of the Republic, and a readiness to make sacrifices for it. The history of the Civil War showed that this passion is at least as strong as in England or France. There is no want of an appreciation of the collective majesty of the nation, for this is the theme of incessant speeches, nor even of the past and future glories of each particular State in the Union. But these sentiments do not bear their appropriate fruit in raising the conception of public office, of its worth and its dignity. The newspapers assume public men to be selfish and cynical. Disinterested virtue is not looked for, is perhaps turned into ridicule where it exists. The hard commercial spirit which pervades the meetings of a joint-stock company is the spirit in which most politicians speak of public business, and are not blamed for speaking. Something, especially in the case of newspapers, must be allowed for the humorous tendencies of the American mind, which likes to put forward the absurd and even vulgar side of things for the sake of getting fun out of them. But after making such allowances, the fact remains that, although no people is more emotional, and even in a sense more poetical, in no country is the ideal side of public life, what one may venture to call the heroic element in a public career, so ignored by the mass and repudiated by the leaders. This affects not only the elevation but the independence and courage of public men; and the country suffers from the want of what we call distinction in its conspicuous figures.

II

A young scholar discusses the declining influence of the presidency.

FROM: Woodrow Wilson's book on *Congressional Government.*

In his first major book, Woodrow Wilson analyzed the American system of government. He paid particular attention to the gradual congressional assumption of prerogatives and power at the expense of the executive—hence the title of his work. In the passages here, Wilson discusses causes for the decline in the presidency and the concurrent assumption by Congress of the dominant role in the American government.

According to Wilson, how important was the personality of the President in determining the distribution of power between the executive and legislative branches?

If Wilson was correct, does his analysis help to explain the federal government's failure to act effectively on problems created by the nineteenth century economic revolution?

≈§

INDEPENDENTLY of experience . . . it might reasonably have been expected that the prerogatives of the President would have been one of the most effectual restraints upon the power of Congress. He was constituted one of the three great coordinate branches of the government; his functions were made of the highest dignity; his privileges many and substantial—so great, indeed, that it has pleased the fancy of some writers to parade them as exceeding those of the British crown; and there can be little doubt that, had the presidential chair always been filled by men of commanding character, of acknowledged ability, and of thorough political training, it would have continued to be a seat of the highest authority and consideration, the true centre of the federal structure, the real throne of administration, and the frequent source of policies. Washington and his Cabinet commanded the ear of Congress, and gave shape to its deliberations; Adams, though often crossed and thwarted, gave character to the government; and Jefferson, as President no less than as Secretary of State, was the real leader of his party. But the prestige of the presidential office has declined with the character of the Presidents. And the character of the Presidents has declined as the perfection of selfish party tactics has advanced.

It was inevitable that it should be so. After independence of choice on the part of the presidential electors had given place to the choice of presidential candidates by party conventions, it became absolutely necessary, in the eyes of politicians, and more and more necessary as time went on, to make expediency and availability the only rules of selection. As each party, when in convention assembled, spoke only those opinions which seemed to have received the sanction of the general voice, carefully suppressing in its "platform" all unpopular political tenets, and scrupulously omitting mention of every doctrine that might be looked upon as characteristic and as part of a peculiar and original programme, so, when the presidential candidate came to be chosen, it was recognized as imperatively necessary that he should have as short a political record as possible, and that he should wear a clean and irreproachable insignficance. "Gentlemen," said a distinguished American public man, "I would make an excellent President, but a very poor candidate." A decisive career which gives a man a well-understood place in public estimation constitutes a positive disability for the presidency; because

Woodrow Wilson, *Congressional Government: A Study in American Politics*, 7th ed. (Boston: Houghton, Mifflin and Company, 1890), pp. 41–47.

candidacy must precede election, and the shoals of candidacy can be passed only by a light boat which carries little freight and can be turned readily about to suit the intricacies of the passage.

I am disposed to think, however, that the decline in the character of the Presidents is not the cause, but only the accompanying manifestation, of the declining prestige of the presidential office. That high office has fallen from its first estate of dignity because its power has waned; and its power has waned because the power of Congress has become predominant. The early Presidents were, as I have said, men of such a stamp that they would under any circumstances have made their influence felt; but their opportunities were exceptional. What with quarreling and fighting with England, buying Louisiana and Florida, building dykes to keep out the flood of the French Revolution, and extricating the country from ceaseless broils with the South American Republics, the government was, as has been pointed out, constantly busy, during the first quarter century of its existence, with the adjustment of foreign relations; and with foreign relations, of course, the Presidents had everything to do, since theirs was the office of negotiation.

Moreover, as regards home policy also those times were not like ours. Congress was somewhat awkward in exercising its untried powers, and its machinery was new, and without that fine adjustment which has since made it perfect of its kind. Not having as yet learned the art of governing itself to the best advantage, and being without that facility of legislation which it afterwards acquired, the Legislature was glad to get guidance and suggestions of policy from the Executive.

But this state of things did not last long. Congress was very quick and apt in learning what it could do and in getting into thoroughly good trim to do it. It very early divided itself into standing committees which it equipped with very comprehensive and thorough-going privileges of legislative initiative and control, and set itself through these to administer the government. Congress is (to adopt Mr. Bagehot's description of Parliament) "nothing less than a big meeting of more or less idle people. In proportion as you give it power it will inquire into everything, settle everything, meddle in everything. In an ordinary despotism the powers of the despot are limited by his bodily capacity, and by the calls of pleasure; he is but one man; there are but twelve hours in his day, and he is not disposed to employ more than a small part in dull business: he keeps the rest for the court, or the harem, or for society." But Congress "is a despot who has unlimited time,—who has unlimited vanity,—who has, or believes he has, unlimited comprehension,—whose pleasure is in action, whose life is work." Accordingly it has entered more and more into the details of administration, until it has virtually taken into its own hands all the substantial powers of government. It does not domineer over the President himself, but it makes the Secretaries its humble servants. Not that it would hesitate, upon occasion, to deal directly with the chief magistrate himself; but it has few calls to do so, because our latter-day Presidents live by proxy; they are the executive in theory, but the Secretaries are the executive in fact. At the very first session of Congress steps were taken towards parceling out executive work amongst several departments, according to a then sufficiently thorough division of labor; and if the President of that day was not able to direct administrative details, of course the President of to-day is infinitely less able to do so, and must content himself with such general supervision as he may find time to exercise. He is in all every-day concerns shielded by the responsibility of his subordinates. . . . . .

I am inclined to think . . . that the enlarged powers of Congress are the fruits rather of an immensely increased efficiency of organization, and of the redoubled activity consequent upon the facility of action secured by such organization, than of any definite and persistent scheme of conscious usurpation. It is safe to say that Congress always had the desire to have a hand in every affair of federal government; but it was only by degrees that it found means and opportunity to gratify that desire, and its activity, extending its bounds wherever perfected processes of congressional work offered favoring prospects, has been enlarged so naturally and so silently that it has almost always seemed of normal extent, and has never, except perhaps during one or two brief periods of extraordinary political disturbance, appeared to reach much beyond its acknowledged constitutional sphere.

III

The President-elect expresses his ideas on civil service reform and party patronage.

FROM: Grover Cleveland's letter to George W. Curtis, December 25, 1884.

SHORTLY after his first election to the presidency, Cleveland wrote George W. Curtis, a leading civil service reformer, to explain his policies on appointment to public office. Cleveland made a clear commitment to enforcement of the Pendleton Act (1883) and rejected the idea that one who had served his party automatically deserved a government job. In office from 1885 to 1889, Cleveland remained interested in civil service reform, but he also appointed many Democrats to federal office. Early in his second term in 1893, he announced that he would decline all personal interviews with those seeking federal appointment unless he personally initiated the interview.

What was the meaning of Cleveland's reference to fears that his com-
ing to the presidency might "demonstrate that the abuses which have
grown up in the civil service are ineradicable"?

Do you think Cleveland weakened the position of his party by his
stand on patronage?

❧

YOUR communication dated December twentieth, addressed to
me on behalf of the National Civil Service Reform League, has been
received.

That a practical reform in the Civil Service is demanded, is abundantly established by the fact that a statute, referred to in your communication, to secure such a result, has been passed in congress with
the assent of both political parties; and by the further fact that a sentiment is generally prevalent among patriotic people, calling for the fair
and honest enforcement of the law which had been thus enacted. I
regard myself as pledged to this, because my conception of true Democratic faith and public duty, requires that this and all other statutes,
should be in good faith, and without evasion enforced, and because in
many utterances made prior to my election as President, approved by
the party to which I belong and which I have no disposition to disclaim,
I have in effect promised the people that this should be done.

I am not unmindful of the fact to which you refer, that many of
our citizens fear, that the recent party change in the National Executive,
may demonstrate that the abuses which have grown up in the Civil
Service are ineradicable. I know that they are deeply rooted, and that
the spoils system has been supposed to be intimately related to success
in the maintenance of party organization; and I am not sure that all
those who profess to be the friends of this reform will stand firmly
among its advocates, when they find it obstructing their way to patronage
and place.

But fully appreciating the trust committed to my charge, no such
consideration shall cause a relaxation on my part of an earnest effort
to enforce this law.

There is a class of government positions which are not within the
letter of the civil service statute, but which are so disconnected with
the policy of an administration, that the removal therefrom of present
incumbents, in my opinion, should not be made during the terms for
which they were appointed, solely on partisan grounds, and for the
purpose of putting in their places those who are in political accord
with the appointing power.

Grover Cleveland Papers (Washington: The Library of Congress, 1958), Microfilm
Series 2, Reel 3.

But many now holding such positions have forfeited all just claim to retention, because they have used their places for party purposes, in disregard of their duty to the people, and because, instead of being decent public servants, they have proved themselves offensive partisans, and unscrupulous manipulators of local party management.

The lessons of the past should be unlearned; and such officials, as well as their successors, should be taught that efficiency, fitness, and devotion to public duty are the conditions of their continuance in public place, and that the quiet and unobtrusive exercise of individual political rights, is the reasonable measure of their party service.

If I were addressing none but party friends, I should deem it entirely proper to remind them that though the coming Administration is to be Democratic, a due regard for the people's interest does not permit faithful party work to be always rewarded by appointment to office; and to say to them that while Democrats may expect all proper consideration, selections for office not embraced within the Civil Service rules, will be based upon sufficient inquiry as to fitness, instituted by those charged with that duty, rather than upon persistent importunity or self-solicited recommendations, on behalf of candidates for appointment.

IV

Carl Schurz evaluates the candidates on their commitment to civil service reform, 1888.

FROM: A letter from Carl Schurz to Thaddeus C. Pound, September 15, 1888.

As Secretary of the Interior in the Hayes administration, Carl Schurz fought diligently for comprehensive civil service reform in the entire executive branch. In 1884, he helped lead the insurgent "Mugwump" group out of the Republican party because of opposition to presidential candidate James G. Blaine, whose political honesty had been questioned. Schurz and the Mugwumps supported the Democratic nominee, Grover Cleveland. In this letter to a Republican representative from Wisconsin, who had urged him to campaign for Benjamin Harrison, Schurz explained why he had to support Cleveland again in 1888.

Given his criticism of Cleveland, was Schurz justified in supporting him?

Would party loyalty have been a more effective course for Schurz in 1888? Would he have been a more useful fighter for civil service reform within his own party?

ꜩ

IN condemning the concessions to the spoils element in the Democratic party made by President Cleveland in violation of his own original program, I go as far as his severest critic among the friends of reform. With my experience of public life, I cannot join in any of the excuses or palliations which have been offered for them. I do not think, for instance, that, had he unflinchingly done those things which he had given the country reason to expect of him, he would have been a "President without a party." The American people love that manly courage which, in keeping good faith and in righting wrongs, does not shrink from defying great odds. The spectacle of a President telling his party friends that neither flattery nor threats could tempt him to abandon a single iota of his word, either in letter or spirit, would have stirred the noblest impulses of the American heart. His very enemies would have been compelled to do homage to the intrepidity of his rectitude. The party organization, seeing that it could not command him, would have been obliged to follow his leadership, for it could not have sacrificed such a President without ruining itself. He might indeed have lost the support of some of its worst elements, but he would have gained on the other side the full confidence and aid of a much larger number of patriotic men who stood ready, without regard to political antecedents, to rally around a thoroughgoing reformer. His party would then have been morally as well as numerically stronger than it is to-day. This, I think, would have been the result; but even if such expectations had not been entirely fulfilled, certain it is that by the example of such conduct President Cleveland would have rendered a far greater service to the cause of healthy politics and good government in America than by anything else he has done or could have done.

In view of the departures from the standards set up by himself, the extent and significance of which have, perhaps, not fully come to President Cleveland's own consciousness, I can well understand the feelings and reasoning of those of our independent friends who, after having supported Mr. Cleveland in 1884, now, on account of his failings as a civil service reformer, oppose his reelection. I am very far from questioning the sincerity of their motives when they argue that such shortcomings should not be permitted to pass with impunity. But I differ from them in answering the important question, whether, if they succeeded in punishing Mr. Cleveland, they would not at the same time punish the country still more.

The main consideration is, after all, how the public interest in the largest sense can be best served. Concerning administrative reform, we have seen enough of political life to know that, as to their devotion to

Frederic Bancroft, ed., *Speeches, Correspondence and Political Papers of Carl Schurz,* IV (New York and London: G. P. Putnam's Sons, 1913), 511–514.

the spoils system, there is no difference between the working politicians in the Republican and those in the Democratic party. Both will occasionally yield to a demand for reform from fear, or to make political capital, or shout for it when in opposition; but both hate it at heart and will exert their whole influence against it whenever they feel at liberty to do so. There are exceptions, but not many, on either side. It is true, a larger number of friends of reform have been associated with the Republicans than with the Democrats. But nobody will pretend that they control the nominations or the actual policy of the party. It was, no doubt, owing to the pressure of Democratic partisans that President Cleveland practically gave up a very important portion of his reform program. So it had, no doubt, been owing to the pressure of Republican partisans that President Grant in his time threw overboard the whole system, examination, rules and all. And it is certain that the efforts President Cleveland really did make in the way of reform found no countenance among Republican politicians. It is equally certain that a Republican victory now would be followed by a "clean sweep," with all that the term implies, involving not only all Democratic officeholders, good and bad, outside of the classified service, but the Republicans left in office by President Cleveland, too, as Republicans who consented to remain in place under a Democratic Administration are especially hateful to Republican politicians.

Is it reasonable to expect that Mr. Harrison, if elected, would oppose such a "clean sweep" with greater courage and firmness than was shown by Mr. Cleveland? Mr. Harrison is, in point of personal character, no doubt vastly preferable to Mr. Blaine. But neither his professions nor his antecedents stamp him as a man who would resist the demands of the influential politicians of his party. He would on the contrary, to the extent of his power, meet them, as he asked his demands to be met under a previous Republican Administration. The cause of civil service reform would, therefore, have to hope rather less from Mr. Harrison than from Mr. Cleveland.

But, if I rightly understand the attitude of the Republican party, it is really Mr. Blaine, not Mr. Harrison, whom we are invited to put into power. Mr. Blaine is vociferously proclaimed, not only as the "greatest statesman," as the "real leader of the Republican party," but also as the "Premier," the "head of the Republican Administration" that is to be. That Mr. Harrison's Administration shall be under Mr. Blaine's control seems to be taken for granted, without any conspicuous dissent. Mr. Harrison is so pointedly consigned to the role of second man that his position as a candidate appears grotesque in the extreme. It is an entirely new thing in our Constitutional history that one person is to be elected President of the United States for the very purpose of permitting the Presidential power to be wielded by another.

V

Senator Shelby Cullom claims that the railroads
"are imbued with . . . an intelligence that neither slumbers nor
sleeps."

FROM: A speech in the Senate, April 14, 1886.

SHELBY M. CULLOM, Republican Senator from Illinois, was the principal sponsor of an interstate commerce bill introduced in Congress in 1886 and finally signed into law by President Cleveland in 1887. This act, although not effectively enforced immediately, was the first important federal regulatory legislation passed in response to the nineteenth century economic revolution. At the end of a long speech in which he summarized the main features of the bill, Cullom commented about railroads and their influence in American life.

What specific grievances against railroads did Cullom express? Were they basically economic?

Was Cullom right in suggesting that the railroads endangered the personal liberty of individual Americans?

⋘

I DO not expect that the passage of this bill and the appointment of any five gentlemen who might be named under its provisions for its enforcement will at once bring the millennium to American transportation. For forty years a constant struggle of wits has been going on between the grasping corporations and Legislatures endeavoring to restrain them, and to-day we are confronted with successful, legalized wrongs remaining uncontrolled and unredressed. But we shall have done our duty when we shall have done our utmost to the future security of the people. I do not believe that this bill will accomplish radical results, but it is a step in the right direction, both for the people and for honest railroad management. For many years a contest between the safe-maker and the burglar has been waged. Each failure of the safe to withstand its robber has begotten improvements believed to be final, and each in turn has yielded to human cunning and ingenuity. But it is not for the safe-maker to stop in his endeavors. If this bill becoming a law should fail utterly to supply a remedy, another attempt must be made. If it is partially successful, we shall have accomplished something and new remedies will be suggested by its partial failure.

THE COMPLAINT OF THE PEOPLE

An examination of the report and testimony will not show that railroad corporations are making too much money, or that the average

Congressional Record, 49th. Congress, 1st. Session, pp. 3477–3478.

rates of transportation are too high. On the other hand they have been in the main unprofitable, and transportation between competing points in America is the cheapest in the world. The complaint of the people is of discrimination, uncertainty, and secret injury. The complaint of investors is that two-sevenths of the capitalized investment is water, and that through inside combinations the masters of Wall Street are able to realize vast profits upon railroad wreckage and the depreciation of railroad property, as well as upon their prudent conduct and honest management. A great stride toward personal liberty was believed to have been made when our Government was organized with the prohibition of entail; but the sovereignty of trunk lines and railroad systems, imperishable as they are, present a more dangerous *imperium in imperio* for our consideration than the largest entailed interests of the world.

RAILROAD SERVANTS, NOT MASTERS

Railroads are beneficent servants, but they must not become masters. The dwarf has grown large enough for us to impose restrictions upon his growth, else the old fable will be illustrated in practical life. If unchecked he bids fair to develop into an Afrite of gigantic stature and overwhelming and malignant influence. Railroads are no longer dull, insensate things. They are imbued with intelligence, and an intelligence that neither slumbers nor sleeps. They are no longer joint stock companies alone; they are dynasties.

They are already outlined, and in a few years if not supervised and controlled by legislation they will have become as firmly fixed in their grasp upon continued power, commercial, social, and political, as the Hapsborgs, the Hohenzollerns, or the Guelphs. These reigning houses were born of force. They were the triumph of the strong over the weak. These modern dynasties will have been born of law and of concession and will be the triumph of the creature over the creator. . . . . .

SPECIAL PRIVILEGES FOR NONE—EQUAL RIGHTS FOR ALL

Hitherto content has come to the plain people of our land, to the mechanic, to the farmer, to the artisan, because, as he sat by his hearth noting the progress of his fellows who had outstripped him in life's race, his eye turned to the bright boy and the laughing girl with a knowledge that to them America offered every possibility of culture, wealth, and power. He knew that the history of the men whom America had delighted to honor had shown that from the humblest beginnings nothing restricted or directed the development of the American citizen outside of himself. To-day he sees the price of his labor determined not from his surroundings. He sees his village built up or destroyed by a foreign will. He sees the value of his little property decreased and that of the property of his fellow in an adjoining village increased without the action of either and beyond the control of any. He sees his neighbor, by secret arrangement with the railroad company, increasing his store with no extra labor or display of energy or ability, while his fellows are correspondingly depressed.

These things it is the object of this measure to correct.

All the American citizen has asked in the past or will ask in the future is a fair chance; no odds of the Government, but its protection, for which his life is pledged, and its schools, for which his money is paid. Special privileges for none, equal rights for all.

VI

Grover Cleveland explains his reasons for refusing to sign the Wilson-Gorman Tariff.

FROM: A letter from Grover Cleveland to Representative Thomas C. Catchings, August 27, 1894.

IN his annual message in December, 1887, President Cleveland made an impassioned plea for tariff reform. Although the House of Representatives later passed the Mills bill, the Senate bottled up the legislation and Cleveland's defeat at the polls in November, 1888, killed it. The congressional response to Cleveland's request for tariff reform in his second term was the Wilson-Gorman Act of 1894, which Cleveland refused to sign but did not veto. Responding in a letter to a Democratic congressman who urged him to sign the bill, Cleveland explained why he could not do so.

Why did Cleveland believe tariff reform was needed?

How valid was Cleveland's reasoning regarding the effect of tariff reductions on raw materials?

☙

SINCE the conversation I had with you and Mr. Clarke of Alabama a few days ago in regard to my action upon the Tariff bill now before me, I have given the subject further and most serious consideration. The result is, I am more settled than ever in the determination to allow the bill to become a law without my signature.

The New York Times, August 28, 1894.

When the formulation of legislation which it was hoped would embody Democratic ideas of tariff reform was lately entered upon by the Congress nothing was further from my anticipation than a result which I could not promptly and enthusiastically endorse.

It is, therefore, with a feeling of the utmost disappointment that I submit to a denial of this privilege.

I do not claim to be better than the masses of my party, nor do I wish to avoid any responsibility which, on account of the passage of this law, I ought to bear as a member of the Democratic organization. Neither will I permit myself to be separated from my party to such an extent as might be implied by my veto of tariff legislation, which, though disappointing, is still chargeable to Democratic effort. But there are provisions in this bill which are not in line with honest tariff reform, and it contains inconsistencies and crudities which ought not to appear in tariff laws or laws of any kind. . . .

And yet, notwithstanding all its vicissitudes or the bad treatment it received at the hands of pretended friends, it presents a vast improvement to existing conditions. It will certainly lighten many tariff burdens that now rest heavily upon the people. It is not only a barrier against the return of mad protection, but it furnishes a vantage ground, from which must be waged further aggressive operations against protected monopoly and Governmental favoritism.

I take my place with the rank and file of the Democratic Party who believe in tariff reform and who know what it is, who refuse to accept the results embodied in this bill as the close of the war, who are not blinded to the fact that the livery of Democratic tariff reform has been stolen and worn in the service of Republican protection, and who have marked the places where the deadly blight of treason has blasted the counsels of the brave in their hour of might.

The trusts and combinations—the communism of pelf—whose machinations have prevented us from reaching the success we deserved, should not be forgotten nor forgiven. We shall recover from our astonishment at their exhibition of power, and if then the question is forced upon us whether they shall submit to the free legislative will of the people's representatives, or shall dictate the laws which the people must obey, we will accept and settle that issue as one involving the integrity and safety of American institutions. . . . . .

I cannot be mistaken as to the necessity of free raw materials as the foundation of logical [and] sensible tariff reform. The extent to which this is recognized in the legislation already secured is one of its encouraging and redeeming features, but it is vexatious to recall that, while free coal and iron ore have been denied us, a recent letter of the Secretary of the Treasury discloses the fact that both might have been made free by the annual surrender of only about $700,000 of unnecessary revenue.

I am sure that there is a common habit of underestimating the importance of free raw materials in tariff legislation, and of regarding them as only related to concessions to be made to our manufacturers. The truth is, their influence is so far-reaching that, if disregarded, a complete and beneficent scheme of tariff reform cannot be successfully inaugurated.

When we give to our manufacturers free raw materials we unshackle American enterprise and ingenuity, and these will open the doors of foreign markets to the reception of our wares and give opportunity for the continuous and remunerative employment of American labor.

With materials cheapened by their freedom from tariff charges, the cost of their product must be correspondingly cheapened. Thereupon justice and fairness to the consumer would demand that the manufacturers be obliged to submit to such a readjustment and modification of the tariff upon their finished goods as would secure to the people the benefit of the reduced cost of their manufactures, and shield the consumer against the exaction of inordinate profits.

It will thus be seen that free raw materials and a just and fearless regulation and reduction of the tariff to meet the changed conditions would carry to every humble home in the land the blessings of increased comfort and cheaper living.

The millions of our countrymen who have fought bravely and well for tariff reform should be exhorted to continue the struggle, boldly challenging to open warfare and constantly guarding against the treachery and half-heartedness in their camp.

Tariff reform will not be settled until it is honestly and fairly settled in the interest and to the benefit of a patient and long-suffering people.

VII

Henry Adams comments on the Pullman Strike, Grover Cleveland, and the gold-bugs.

FROM: A letter from Henry Adams to Elizabeth Cameron, July 13, 1894.

HENRY ADAMS, novelist and historian, was a pungent observer of Washington politics and society after he moved to the capital in 1877. A master letter writer, one of his most frequent correspondents was Elizabeth Cameron, the wife of Senator Donald Cameron, the Republican leader of Pennsylvania. In this letter to Mrs. Cameron, Adams comments on President Cleveland's use of federal troops to suppress the Pullman Strike and Senate approval of his action.

How would you characterize Adams' personal political and economic views?

What was the basis for his conclusion that the workingman was a political failure?

Who was Eugene Debs and what was his role in the Pullman Strike?

THE last week has been more than usually awkward for politicians. Cleveland has won another colossal victory for his friends the gold-bugs; a greater than his silver triumph, for he has settled the working-man forever. Now that the gold-bug has drunk blood, and has seen that the government can safely use the army to shoot socialists, the wage-question is as good as settled. Of course we silver men will be shot next, but for the moment, the working-men are worse off than we. Of course, too, the Senate has unanimously approved of Cleveland. I hope your husband was not there, for, to my mind, the men who endorsed Cleveland made the gravest kind of a blunder. The proof is that the House did not dare do it. Bellamy Storer introduced the Resolution, but so many members of both parties came to him to beg him to desist, that he had to do so. . . . Of course every gold-bug in the country, and all the newspapers are radiant and violent in support of Cleveland. Indeed I am very much inclined to think that his second great victory settles everything. The gold-bug has got us cold. For my part, I do not object. I never think it good sense to try to reverse the processes of nature, and my idea of politics is to hasten rather than retard results. Silver is really in the interests of money, and would prolong indefinitely the money-lenders' reign, whereas gold is fatal to it. Were you, in your former lives, ever acquainted with one Midas, a Greek banker, who has typified the gold-bug for three thousand years? If not, look him up in your Ovid, in the 11th Book of *Metamorphoses*, lines 90 to 190. '*Ille male usurus*'—that outrageous usurer—turned everything to gold, and had asses ears; two infallible signs of a banker. Bacchus kindly gave him free silver, and saved his life and ears. I am no Bacchus, and, if possible, would prefer to take his life and cut off his ears.

Your husband had better keep dead quiet now, till things take another turn. He is really helpless, and at most can only keep his head above water till time shall show whether we are to have a chance once more. Debs has smashed everything for the present. The working-man is so brilliant a political failure—so suicidal a political ally, that until he is dead and buried, the gold-bug must rule us. George M. Pullman

Worthington Chauncey Ford, ed., *Letters of Henry Adams (1892–1918)* (Boston and New York: Houghton Mifflin Company, 1938), pp. 52–53. Reprinted by permission.

and Andrew Carnegie and Grover Cleveland are our Crassus and Pompey and Caesar,—our proud American triumvirate, the types of our national mind and ideals. We are under a sort of terror before them. The Senate bows down, and even I, who want not so much as a protective duty on my books, think life easier if I hold my tongue and let Midas's ears alone.

VIII

A free-silver publicist examines the "Crime of 1873."

FROM: "Coin" Harvey's influential book of 1894.

WILLIAM H. HARVEY, a Chicago publisher of free-silver literature, printed the first edition of his own *Coin's Financial School* in 1894. Widely read and reprinted many times, it became the major free-silver document in the campaign of 1896. Harvey created "Coin," a fictitious character, who set up a financial school at the Art Institute of Chicago and presented six lessons on the money question. Coin made many of his main points in response to questions from the audience. In the excerpt here from the first day's lesson, Coin discussed the so-called "Crime of 1873," the demonetization of silver.

How convincing were Coin's arguments? How sound were they economically?

Do you think this method of presenting a basic issue would be effective in a modern presidential campaign?

∽§

"WE now come to the act of 1873," continued COIN. "On February 12, 1873, Congress passed an act purporting to be a revision of the coinage laws. This law covers 15 pages of our statutes. It repealed the *unit* clause in the law of 1792, and in its place substituted a law in the following language:

"That the gold coins of the United States shall be a one-dollar piece which at the standard weight of twenty-five and eight-tenths grains *shall be the unit of value.*

"It then deprived silver of its right to unrestricted free coinage, and destroyed it as legal tender money in the payment of debts, except to the amount of five dollars.

"At that time we were all using paper money. No one was handling silver and gold coins. It was when specie payments were about to be resumed that the country appeared to realize what had been done. The

William H. Harvey, *Coin's Financial School* (Chicago: Coin Publishing Company, 1894), pp. 15–19.

newspapers on the morning of February 13, 1873, and at no time in the vicinity of that period, had any account of the change. General Grant, who was President of the United States at that time, said afterwards, that he had no idea of it, and would not have signed the bill if he had known that it demonetized silver.

"In the language of Senator Daniel of Virginia, it seems to have gone through Congress 'like the silent tread of a cat.'

"An army of a half million of men invading our shores, the warships of the world bombarding our coasts, could not have made us surrender the money of the people and substitute in its place the money of the rich. A few words embraced in fifteen pages of statutes put through Congress in the rush of bills did it. The pen was mightier than the sword.

"But we are not here to deal with sentiment. We are here to learn facts. Plain, blunt facts.

"The law of 1873 made gold the *unit* of values. And that is the law to-day. When silver was the unit of value, gold enjoyed *free coinage,* and was legal tender in the payment of all debts. Now things have changed. Gold is the unit and silver does not enjoy free coinage. It is refused at the mints. We might get along with gold as the unit, if silver enjoyed the same right gold did prior to 1873. But that right is now denied to silver. When silver was the unit, the unlimited demand for gold to coin into money, made the demand as great as the supply, and this held up the value of gold bullion."

Here Victor F. Lawson, Jr., of the Chicago *Evening News,* interrupted the little financier with the statement that his paper, the *News,* had stated time and again that silver had become so plentiful it had ceased to be a precious metal. And that this statement believed by him to be a fact had more to do with his prejudice to silver than anything else. And he would like to know if that was not a fact?

"There is no truth in the statement," replied COIN. "On page 21 of my Handbook you will find a table on this subject, compiled by Mulhall, the London statistician. It gives the quantity of gold and silver in the world both coined and uncoined at six periods—at the years 1600, 1700, 1800, 1848, 1880, and 1890. It shows that in 1600 there were 27 tons of silver to one ton of gold. In 1700, 34 tons of silver to one ton of gold. In 1800, 32 tons of silver to one ton of gold. In 1848, 31 tons of silver to one ton of gold. In 1880, 18 tons of silver to one ton of gold. In 1890, 18 tons of silver to one ton of gold.

"The United States is producing more silver than it ever did, or was until recently. But the balance of the world is producing much less. They are fixing the price on our silver and taking it away from us, at their price. The report of the Director of the Mint shows that since 1850 the world has produced less silver than gold, while during the first fifty years of the century the world produced 78 per cent more silver than gold. Instead of becoming more plentiful, it is less plentiful. So it is less, instead of more. . . . . .

"At the time the United States demonetized silver in February, 1873, silver as measured in gold was worth $1.02. The argument of depreciated silver could not then be made. Not one of the arguments that are now made against silver was then possible. They are all the bastard children of the crime of 1873."

IX

The Democrats and Republicans disagree on silver and gold in the campaign of 1896.

FROM: Party campaign documents of 1896.

WHILE issues of substance were not often carefully debated in presidential campaigns between the end of the Civil War and 1900, the free silver question received wide attention in the Bryan-McKinley contest of 1896. The money planks in major party platforms set the direction of the debate, and the subsequent campaign concentrated to a high degree on the money question.

What were the major differences between the Democratic and Republican statements?

How did the two platforms differ on the effects of the gold standard?

᳁

THE DEMOCRATIC MONEY PLANK

RECOGNIZING that the money question is paramount to all others at this time, we invite attention to the fact that the Federal Constitution named silver and gold together as the money metals of the United States, and that the first coinage law passed by Congress under the Constitution made the silver dollar the monetary unit and admitted gold to free coinage at a ratio based upon the silver-dollar unit.

We declare that the act of 1873 demonetizing silver without the knowledge or approval of the American people has resulted in the appreciation of gold and a corresponding fall in the prices of commodities produced by the people; a heavy increase in the burden of

Democratic Campaign Book. Presidential Election of 1896 (Washington: Hartman & Cadick, Printers, 1896), pp. 3–4.

taxation and of all debts, public and private; the enrichment of the money-lending class at home and abroad; the prostration of industry and impoverishment of the people.

We are unalterably opposed to monometallism which has locked fast the prosperity of an industrial people in the paralysis of hard times. Gold monometallism is a British policy, and its adoption has brought other nations into financial servitude to London. It is not only un-American but anti-American, and it can be fastened on the United States only by the stifling of that spirit and love of liberty which proclaimed our political independence in 1776 and won it in the War of the Revolution.

We demand the free and unlimited coinage of both silver and gold at the present legal ratio of 16 to 1 without waiting for the aid or consent of any other nation. We demand that the standard silver dollar shall be a full legal tender, equally with gold, for all debts, public and private, and we favor such legislation as will prevent for the future the demonetization of any kind of legal-tender money by private contract.

We are opposed to the policy and practice of surrendering to the holders of the obligations of the United States the option reserved by law to the Government of redeeming such obligations in either silver coin or gold coin.

THE REPUBLICAN MONEY PLANK

THE Republican party is unreservedly for sound money. . . . It caused the enactment of a law providing for the redemption [resumption] of specie payments in 1879. Since then every dollar has been as good as gold. . . . We are unalterably opposed to every measure calculated to debase our currency or impair the credit of our country. . . . We are therefore opposed to the free coinage of silver, except by international agreement with the leading commercial nations of the earth . . . which agreement we pledge ourselves to promote, and until such agreement can be obtained the existing gold standard must be maintained. All of our silver and paper currency must be maintained at parity with gold, and we favor all measures designated to maintain inviolable the obligations of the United States, of all our money, whether coin or paper, at the present standard, the standard of the most enlightened nations of the earth.

Official Proceedings of the Eleventh Republican National Convention Held in the City of St. Louis, Mo., June 16, 17, and 18, 1896 (Reported by James Francis Burke of Pittsburg, Pa., Official Stenographer, 1896).

X ───

President Cleveland criticizes the Democratic platform and candidate in 1896.

FROM: A letter from Grover Cleveland to Hoke Smith, August 4, 1896.

CLEVELAND was disgusted with the results of the Democratic convention in 1896. The platform, dominated by the free silver plank, repudiated most policies and programs of the Cleveland administration. William Jennings Bryan, the party nominee and darling of the free silver forces, was totally unacceptable to Cleveland. Cleveland's Secretary of the Interior, Hoke Smith, supported Bryan in his own newspaper, the Atlanta *Journal*. While Smith liked neither the platform nor the candidate, he feared that widespread repudiation of Bryan would split the Democratic party in Georgia and lead to Republican control there. Cleveland responded to Smith's explanation of his course with the following letter, which lucidly expressed his reaction to the decisions of the Democratic convention.

How fair was Cleveland's criticism of Smith's stand? Was he right to give precedence to national over state political considerations?

Was Cleveland genuinely concerned about the money issue, or did his personal feelings determine his position?

⮐

I HAVE determined to say to you frankly that I was astonished & much disappointed by your course & that I am by no means relieved by the reasons you present in justification of it. When you addressed the Citizens of your State so nobly and patriotically, you were discussing the Silver question alone; & when you assured them that you intended to support the nominee of the National Convention you could certainly have intended no more than to pledge yourself that in case you were overruled by the Convention *in the question under discussion* you would accept your defeat & support the platform & candidates which represented that defeat. This—considering your strong expressions on the silver question, your earnest advocacy of sound money & your belief in its transcendent importance—was going very far.

You surely could not have intended to promise support to a platform directly opposed not only to sound money, but to every other safe & conservative doctrine or policy, and framed in every line & word in condemnation of all the acts & policies of an administration of which you have from the first, been a loyal, useful, & honorable member. You

Grover Cleveland Papers (Washington: The Library of Congress, 1958), Microfilm Series 2, Reel 95.

could not have intended a promise to uphold candidates, not only pledged to the support & advancement of this destructive & un-Democratic platform, but whose selection largely depended upon the depth & virulence of their hatred of our administration. I say "our" Administration because I have constantly in mind the work we have done, the patriotism that has inspired our every act, the good we have accomplished & the evil we have averted in the face of the opposition of the vicious forces that have temporarily succeeded in their revolt against every thing good & glorious in Democratic faith & achievement.

It is due to our country men & to the safety of the Nation that such an Administration should not be discredited or stricken down. It belongs to them & should be protected and defended, because it is their agency devoted to their welfare & safety. None can defend it better than those who constitute it, & know the singleness of purpose & absolute patriotism that have inspired it. You say, "While I shall not accept the platform, I must support the nominees of the Chicago Convention." I cannot see how this is to be done. It seems to me like straining at a gnat & swallowing a camel.

The vital importance of the issues involved in the national campaign & my failure to appreciate the inseparable relation between it & a State contest, prevents me from realizing the force of your reference to the "local situation." I suppose much was said about the "local situation" in 1860.

I am perfectly satisfied that you have been influenced in the position you have taken, by the same desire to do exactly right, that has guided you in all your acts as a member of the Cabinet.

You know how free my association with my official family has been, from any attempt to influence personal action & how fully that association has been characterized by perfect confidence and a spirit of unreserved consultation & frankness.

In this spirit I now write. I have no personal grievance that any one need feel called on to even notice. My only personal desire is to make as good a President as possible during the residue of my term, & then to find retirement and peace; but I cannot believe that I will do my duty to my country men and party—either as President or citizen, by giving the least aid & comfort to the nominees of the Chicago Convention or the ideas they represent.

XI

Bryan discusses honest money in his acceptance speech, 1896.

FROM: Bryan's speech accepting the Democratic nomination, August, 1896.

WILLIAM JENNINGS BRYAN, with endorsement from the Populist and National Silver parties as well as the Democrats, referred to the money question in almost all of his six hundred speeches in the campaign of 1896. His formal acceptance of the Democratic nomination at New York's Madison Square Garden in August, 1896 illustrates this emphasis. Bryan touched on the major points he made repeatedly on the money question throughout the electoral contest. As the campaign progressed, he concentrated increasingly on this basic issue.

How convincing are Bryan's economic ideas?

Is there any basis for suggesting that Bryan encouraged class conflict?

⋙

NOW let me ask you to consider the paramount question of this campaign—the money question. It is scarcely necessary to defend the principle of bimetallism. No national party during the entire history of the United States has ever declared against it, and no party in this campaign has had the temerity to oppose it. Three parties—the Democratic, Populist, and Silver parties—have not only declared for bimetallism, but have outlined the specific legislation necessary to restore silver to its ancient position by the side of gold. The Republican platform expressly declares that bimetallism is desirable when it pledges the Republican party to aid in securing it as soon as the assistance of certain foreign nations can be obtained. Those who represented the minority sentiment in the Chicago Convention opposed the free coinage of silver by the United States by independent action, on the ground that, in their judgment, it "would retard or entirely prevent the establishment of international bimetallism, to which the efforts of the Government should be steadily directed." When they asserted that the efforts of the Government should be steadily directed toward the establishment of international bimetallism, they condemned monometallism. The gold standard has been weighed in the balance and found wanting. Take from it the powerful support of the money-owning and the money-changing classes and it cannot stand for one day in any nation in the world. It was fastened upon the United States without discussion before the people, and its friends have never yet been willing to risk a verdict before the voters upon that issue.

There can be no sympathy or co-operation between the advocates of a universal gold standard and the advocates of bimetallism. Between bimetallism—whether independent or international—and the gold standard there is an impassable gulf. Is this quadrennial agitation in favor of

William J. Bryan, *The First Battle: A Story of the Campaign of 1896* (Chicago: W. B. Conkey Company, 1896), pp. 320–322.

international bimetallism conducted in good faith, or do our opponents really desire to maintain the gold standard permanently? Are they willing to confess the superiority of a double standard when joined in by the leading nations of the world, or do they still insist that gold is the only metal suitable for standard money among civilized nations? If they are in fact desirous of securing bimetallism, we may expect them to point out the evils of a gold standard and defend bimetallism as a system. If, on the other hand, they are bending their energies toward the permanent establishment of a gold standard under cover of a declaration in favor of international bimetallism, I am justified in suggesting that honest money cannot be expected at the hands of those who deal dishonestly with the American people.

What is the test of honesty in money? It must certainly be found in the purchasing power of the dollar. An absolutely honest dollar would not vary in its general purchasing power; it would be absolutely stable when measured by average prices. A dollar which increases in purchasing power is just as dishonest as a dollar which decreases in purchasing power. . . .

It cannot be successfully claimed that monometallism or bimetallism, or any other system, gives an absolutely just standard of value. Under both monometallism and bimetallism the Government fixes the weight and fineness of the dollar, invests it with legal tender qualities, and then opens the mints to its unrestricted coinage, leaving the purchasing power of the dollar to be determined by the number of dollars. Bimetallism is better than monometallism, not because it gives us a perfect dollar—that is, a dollar absolutely unvarying in its general purchasing power—but because it makes a nearer approach to stability, to honesty, to justice, than a gold standard possibly can. Prior to 1873, when there were enough open mints to permit all the gold and silver available for coinage to find entrance into the world's volume of standard money, the United States might have maintained a gold standard with less injury to the people of this country; but now, when each step toward a universal gold standard enhances the purchasing power of gold, depresses prices, and transfers to the pockets of the creditor class an unearned increment, the influence of this great nation must not be thrown upon the side of gold unless we are prepared to accept the natural and legitimate consequences of such an act. Any legislation which lessens the world's stock of standard money increases the exchangeable value of the dollar; therefore, the crusade against silver must inevitably raise the purchasing power of money and lower the money value of all other forms of property.

Our opponents sometimes admit that it was a mistake to demonetize silver, but insist that we should submit to present conditions rather than return to the bimetallic system. They err in supposing that we have reached the end of the evil results of a gold standard; we have not reached the end. The injury is a continuing one, and no person can say how long the world is to suffer from the attempt to make gold the only standard money. The same influences which are now operating to destroy silver in the United States will, if successful here, be turned against other silver-using countries, and each new convert to the gold standard will add to the general distress. So long as the scramble for gold continues, prices must fall, and a general fall in prices is but another definition of hard times.

XII

Governor Altgeld of Illinois expresses his views on the issues in the campaign of 1896.

FROM: Speech at Cooper Union, New York City, October 17, 1896.

JOHN PETER ALTGELD, whose parents brought him to the United States at the age of three months, was governor of Illinois when President Cleveland used federal troops to break the Pullman Strike in 1894. In 1896, as one of the primary silverite leaders in the Democratic party, he played a major role in drafting the Democratic platform and selecting William Jennings Bryan as his party's nominee. In the campaign speech from which the passage below is taken, Altgeld reviews the events at Pullman and then summarizes what he thought were the far-reaching questions in the campaign of 1896. Altgeld fell with Bryan; he lost his 1896 bid for reelection as governor of Illinois.

To what was Altgeld referring in his remarks about the Supreme Court?

What was the "British monetary policy" Altgeld spoke about?

◦S

NO campaign ever made in this country involved so many far-reaching questions as this one does. Questions, every one of which goes to the foundation of free government and affects the perpetuity of our institutions.

First—The question whether the people have surrendered the right of self-government into the hands of the Supreme Court of the United States, and whether the courts are thus placed above criticism and their acts exempt from that scrutiny which every patriotic and intelligent man should give to the acts of the other branches of government.

Second—Whether both the Constitution and the traditions of the

John P. Altgeld, *Live Questions* (Chicago: Geo. S. Bowen & Son, 1899), pp. 687–688.

government shall henceforth be ignored and the President shall be conceded the power of sending federal troops at his pleasure into any neighborhood in the United States or a thousand neighborhoods at one time; troops who will not be subject to the civil authorities nor to the local authorities; who are under instructions from Washington; whether this can be done not only without the request of the local authorities, but in defiance of them?

Third—Whether the people of this country and especially the laboring masses who do not have much of a voice in the selection of judges shall recognize and thus perpetuate the system of governing by injunction, which does away with government by law, does away with trial by jury, does away with trial according to the forms of law and substitutes the caprice, whim, prejudice or passion of a judge for all these, making him at once legislator, judge and to a certain extent executioner?

Fourth—Whether we shall dissolve in boodle, bribery and corruption. Whether the men who have grown great as lobbyists shall rule this land. Whether we shall declare to the world scoundrelism is in the end the loftiest form of patriotism. It is a remarkable fact that those men and those influences whose slime is dissolving our institutions are all helping Mr. Hanna. Everything within their reach is being prostituted. Where they can, they degrade the religious press and defile the pulpit. They have dragged the American flag in the mire by using it as an advertising sheet for McKinley and Hobart. In Chicago it is a fitting coincidence that most of the buildings from which the flag is thus degraded do not pay their fair share of taxes. Wave the flag and plunder the public, is the gospel of McKinleyism.

Fifth—Whether the British monetary policy shall be made perpetual so that the toiling and producing masses of this country will be reduced in their purchasing power; will be reduced ,in the end to a lower plane of civilization; will be reduced in the end to the conditions of the men who till the fields of Europe or the Valley of the Nile?

FOR FURTHER THOUGHT

Why were the Democrats of 1896 less successful than the Republicans in identifying their party with the accomplishments of the economic revolution?

Is there any basis for assuming that the major parties, given the temper and situation of the times, could have avoided the political lag of the late nineteenth century? How can the lag be explained?

Was the performance of American political parties between 1876 and 1896 atypical in comparison to other periods in the nation's history? Is a political lag unusual?

6. The Shaping of Urban Society, 1865-1914

AN amazing growth of the world's cities marked the last half of the nineteenth century. In the United States this urban development varied in rate of increase from decade to decade, but by 1914 it was clearly apparent that the old agrarian way of life and thought was rapidly diminishing.

From the opening of the Erie Canal in 1825 to the completion of the transcontinental railroads, improved means of communication were the major factors in this change. Villages and town located at strategic points along the arteries of transportation attracted new commerce, industries, and people. Inland cities such as Chicago, St. Louis, Minneapolis-St. Paul, and Omaha profited especially from the new technologies, and the strategic location of a railroad line or possibly a great bridge such as the Eads Bridge at St. Louis might mean the difference between prosperity and urban decline.

Meanwhile, immigration, the natural internal increase of city populations, and a growing flight from the farm were shaping a new urban society in the United States.

The process of America's urban growth stimulated surprised analysis by 1900. Each ambitious community had its own "boomers," but statisticians recognized that the significant forces behind urban growth were availability of industrial opportunities and the myriads of people-demanding supporting services encouraged by the new industries [I].

Social and cultural attractions also encouraged urban growth. The alleged mysteries and excitements of the city, the passion for "the crowd, the hum, the shock of men," drew the hopeful millions from quiet rural hamlets. The city, some hypothesized, was a Darwinian environment wherein talent formerly slumbering in rural countrysides might be stimulated toward leadership and achievement in the ceaseless turmoil of urban competition and opportunity [II]. For contrary to agrarian mythology, it was the city which supposedly contributed the higher ratio of the nation's leaders [III].

For increasing swarms of imaginative young people such as Hamlin Garland's rustic heroine, Rose Dutcher, the city was an unbelievable and thrilling gateway to adventure and a career [IV]. But those who remained behind in the quiet byways of America's countrysides often suspected the urban colossus and lamented its influence on their sons and daughters. The city became the subject of a new American folklore declaiming the joys of country living and contrasting the lurking dangers of urban greed, vice, and personal failure [V].

Indeed, the rapid growth of cities seriously complicated the problems of administering, supervising, inspecting, and regulating the conditions of urban living. Paramount was the problem of housing the city's businesses and citizens. Metal-framed "skyscrapers" and hydraulic elevators to service them helped businessmen meet the dilemma of increasingly expensive urban land. But the problems of housing for the working classes were less readily solved. The masses who could not escape to the city's fringes huddled miserably in the run-down houses of its core [VI]. Spiraling land costs also encouraged the division of old quarters until every dusty attic and dismal cellar seemed to return an income for distant owners. Privacy, fresh air, light, pure water, and even decency were wanting in the spreading urban slums. Respectable people, however, tended to think in terms of the self-help ethic (see Chapter One) and to rationalize the human consequences of slum living as the primary cause of the slum itself. The real problems of the slum thus escaped even the Social Darwinist-minded vestrymen of New York's most distinguished and pious slum-lord, old Trinity Church [VII].

Inadequate housing, a population uprooted from the disciplines of conventional family life, and the uncertainties of urban living contributed to the grimmer problem of crime. Congestion offered both instruction and opportunity for crime and vice. The glittering contrasts of fashionable shops and stench-filled hovels, the impersonality of city life, the drifting educationless youth together presented a scarcely submerged threat of social revolution to conservatives already made uneasy by the rumblings of European socialisms [VIII]. An immediate response was the augmentation of police forces and the enhancing of the role of the "detective" in an effort to match the increasing sophistication of urban lawlessness [IX].

City congestion was a product of the high cost of land and the unhappy ratio between time and commuting distance. Horse cars, introduced during the 1850s, were slow but convenient, and their jostling gregariousness offered new insights into urban social manners. By the 1870s the fast elevated steam trains opened up the suburbs to more fortunate workingmen at the cost of diverting public attention from the problems of those unable to flee the slums. In 1883 the magnificent 1,595 foot span of the Roebling great suspension bridge arched the East River to unite Brooklyn to New York City, a communications triumph which made uneasy holders of franchises for services now technologically obsolescent [X]. The economic stakes involved in such urban projects were enormous, and roving monopolists drew upon ready purses and amenable politicians to seize and consolidate urban transit lines to the alarm of reformers and the inconvenience of their customers [XI].

A major result of the urbanizing of the United States was the Progressive Movement which dominated much of city, state, and national politics from about the turn of the century to World War I. The city had always been the natural habitat of a commercial and professional middle class possessing a strong sense of civic responsibility. Alarmed by the threat of the new industrial plutocracy to its own prestige and influence, this group provided leadership in the bitter battles for reforms in city government. It questioned dubious 999-year trolley franchises and introduced municipal home-rule, new techniques of urban government such as "city manager" plans, and a tighter watch over the city treasury.

Progressivism moved to the arena of state-level politics, exposing corrupt alliances between business and politics more sordid than those lampooned by Mark Twain in *The Gilded Age* (see Chapter One). It pressed for such instruments of "direct democracy" as the initiative and referendum, the direct election of Senators, primary elections, and even the recall of judicial decisions. Its demands for "social justice" resulted in legislation bettering the lot of women and children, abused labor, ignored slum youth, and even the socially outcast. Progressivism in an era when politics and the idea of "spoils" enjoyed a costly partnership introduced the concepts of expertism and efficiency into many branches of government with the help of universities, civil service reforms, and regulatory commissions (see Chapter Eight).

Presidents Theodore Roosevelt and Woodrow Wilson, both with either urban or state government experience, became the expositors of Progressivism on the national scene. Responding to popular reform pressures, they demanded the divorcement of big business from politics, pressed the battle against monopoly, introduced pure food and drug legislation, and sought to restore government accountability to its citizens. Originating as a reform movement in cities, Progressivism even influenced American foreign policy. It is true that its White, Anglo-Saxon, Protestant ethic of racial and moral superiority tended to foster brief imperialist ventures. But Progressivism also suggested an open honesty in international politics of the kind sought by Wilson at the time of the World War (see Chapter Nine).

Urbanism has proved to be an irresistible economic and social force in our recent history. Today 200 million Americans occupy but one per cent of the nation's land. The agrarian tradition grows dimmer in the minds of young people whose lives have evolved in the city and its suburbs. But many of the old problems of congestion, crime, slum dwelling, and municipal political ineptitude have again grown serious. The "challenge of the city" or confronts Americans today in an often startling reflection of those amazing years of urban expansion between 1865 and 1914. EDITED BY HUGO A. MEIER

I

Rising school enrollments prompt an official opinion about the process of urban growth.

FROM: The annual report of the United States Commissioner of Education, 1896.

THE continuing expansion of America's cities reflected statistically in many areas of urban life, among them education. William T. Harris, the United States Commissioner of Education, reported in 1896 that the causes of such urban growth lay especially in "the unprecedented advance made in the last century in the invention and use of machinery," which tended to concentrate people in cities. He also traced the steps by which this process converted rural hamlets into great cities.

What changes in technology probably contributed most to the shift of industry to the cities?

Describe the circumstances which determine whether a rural village stagnates or grows into a city.

THE single constant factor observable in the statistics of city schools is progressive increase in numbers. It is fitting, therefore, that an examination be made into the facts and conditions of growth of the cities themselves in order to arrive at a clear understanding of the growth of the schools. . . . . .

The same agency, machinery, at the same time that it has lessened the number of men required for a given amount of farm work, has provided for the surplus laborers by transferring to the city many of the former occupations of the farm; the manufacture of implements, spinning, weaving, and the like were formerly the work of the farmer and his family. But with the use of improved tools, which are not available to the farmer, and with the help of the steam engine these things may now be done in the city so much more cheaply and expeditiously that the farmer finds it to his interest to confine himself almost wholly to the

Report of the Commissioner of Education for the Year 1894–1895, I (Washington: Government Printing Office, 1896), 3–4, 6–7.

cultivation of the soil and the production of the raw material, and to buy manufactured products from the town. Thus it happens that not only is labor highly specialized and manufacturing divorced from agriculture, but the importance and volume of trade and transportation are vastly augmented. Other changes in this general direction conduce to the concentration of people in the cities, in which nearly all occupations not directly concerned with the production of raw material may be pursued more conveniently and advantageously than in the sparsely settled rural communities.

The aggregation of people in close contact with each other in itself gives rise to new needs that must be met by the establishment of other industries, giving employment to still more people, who must also live in the cities. The same density of population makes possible greater combinations for education, business, or amusement than would be practicable in the country. The graded school, the daily newspaper, the library, the theater, the opera, and many other agencies that add to the pleasure of living and to the cultivation of the mind attain their highest development in the city, and some of them can exist nowhere else. Such attractions lure men to the communities in which they exist and indirectly lead to the multiplication of industries, for men unable to find a place in those already existing invent new ones in order to be near the attractions they desire, and by presenting novelties create a demand for them. Thus cities increase of their own momentum, and in their development grow from mere appendages to surrounding agricultural regions into great centers of dominating influence. . . . . .

. . . The following therefore may be taken as a type of the growth of American cities.

Agriculture is usually the only industry open to the first permanent settlers in a new country. The difficulties of obtaining supplies and the impossibility of profitable manufacture or trade when the population is sparse compel the settler to rely upon his own exertions in tilling the soil for the simple necessities of life. He therefore chooses for his home the place promising the richest return for his labor. The most desirable lands are thus first occupied, then the less desirable. Later comes the store for the exchange of products and the sale of articles not produced on the farm. Then simple mechanical industries, as a blacksmith shop, a mill, or a wagon shop, are established; a church and school are built, a post-office opened, and a village is begun. If the community is prosperous the village speedily grows. New stores are added, a weekly newspaper begun, more churches are built, and other industries are started. Under favorable conditions, such as proximity to a navigable river or railroad, and especially if at the junction of two or more transportation lines, the growth is all the more sure and steady. If the conditions for manufacturing are also especially favorable, further development into city is reasonably certain. The first articles manufactured are generally those required in the immediate neighborhood, but gradually the field is broadened and goods are sold in distant communities less favorably situated for the manufacture of those particular articles, special facilities in transportation making a desirable center of distribution, and proximity to mines or to great forests equally insuring development. . . . . .

The city absorbs an undue share of foreign immigration, and its population grows proportionally much faster than that of the country, because comparatively few persons are needed for farm work, and, as a rule, that number is all but supplied when the building of the city is scarcely begun. . . .

This illustrates the growth typical of American cities. The country is dotted over with communities in all the various stages of development, and each year a considerable number of them attain the size and importance sufficient to justify them in being considered as cities in all discussions of urban questions. It is to these new cities to a large extent that the wonderful urban growth shown by the censuses is due.

11

A population expert evaluates the advantages of urban life and the role of the city in "natural selection."

FROM: A pioneering statistical study of nineteenth century cities, 1899.

THE groundwork for the study of urban history was laid at the turn of the century when accelerating urbanism spurred sociological and statistical analysis of the rise and social characteristics of cities. A major study was Adna Ferrin Weber's *The Growth of Cities in the Nineteenth Century.* Appointed by Governor Theodore Roosevelt to New York State's Bureau of Labor Statistics, Weber pioneered in introducing workmen's compensation laws. He assesses here the relevancy of urban advantages to the currently popular Darwinian "natural selection" theory.

Compare the relative advantages of urban over country life as seen by Adna Weber around 1900 with the situation today. What changes may have shifted the balance since then?

Does the city in its physical and social environments exercise any significant influence as an agent of "natural selection"?

SOCIAL CAUSES—To enumerate the social advantages that the cities possess as compared with the country would demand too much

Adna Ferrin Weber, *The Growth of Cities in the Nineteenth Century: A Study in Statistics,* Volume XI in Columbia University Studies in History, Economics and Public Law (New York: The Macmillan Company, 1899), pp. 218–222, 439–442, 444–445.

space, but most of them will be found to be embraced in the following classification:

(1) Educational. The city alone must be the residence of those who study art, medicine, music, etc. Even in the matter of primary education, city advantages are superior to those of the rural districts, though not to those of the villages. . . .

(2) Amusements. The opera, philharmonic concerts, art exhibits etc., may be classed as educational advantages or mere amusements, but there are many other forms of recreation afforded by the city and not by the country, which come under the head of amusements alone.

(3) The standard of living. The desire for a higher standard of life, for purely material comforts and luxuries, brings many people to the city. Food is to be procured at prices almost as low as in the country, and in vastly greater variety; while everything else is cheaper. The buyer enjoys a larger consumer's rent, as the economists say; that is he can buy at prices much below those he would be willing to give if pressed, thus deriving a surplus of enjoyment. Then there are conveniences to be had in the city which in many cases could not be obtained in the country, on account of the small numbers to bear the heavy expenses. . . .

(4) Intellectual Associations. The village is dull not only to the man pursuing light amusements, but to him who seeks cultivated associations, for in these days the cities are the centers of intellect as of wealth. Even the college town with its intellectual atmosphere is to many high-minded people less stimulating than the city, where intellectual ability is so much more varied.

(5) Such are some of the advantages of city life; some of them are modern, and some are as old as civilization. Not the least important factor in city growth is gregariousness or the social instinct itself, which appears to be stronger than ever before in these days of restlessness. . . Another thing to be reckoned with is the passion for "the crowd, the hum, the shock of men," among those who have once lived in the city One of the trying difficulties of social workers in their efforts to improve the housing conditions of the tenement population is the strong desire of these poor people to be among their associates, and their absolute refusal to settle in more comfortable homes in the country or in the suburbs. . . .

(6) Finally, we have to take into consideration the forces which in recent times have spread a knowledge of the advantages of city life among all classes of the community. Education has a great deal to do with it, especially the half-education which prevails in the rural districts and gives the farmers' boys a glimpse of a more attractive life without teaching them how to attain such a life at home. Then the news

paper comes in to complete the enchantment, with its gibes against the "hayseed" and "country bumpkin." Thus the spread of information, made possible by nineteenth-century improvements in communication, creates a distaste for country life, and more especially for rural life; while easier travel enables young men lightly to abandon the distasteful life. . . . . .

Socially, the influence of the cities is similarly exerted in favor of liberal and progressive thought. The variety of occupation, interests and opinions in the city produces an intellectual friction, which leads to a broader and freer judgment and a great inclination to and appreciation of new thoughts, manners, and ideals. City life may not have produced genius, but it has brought thinkers into touch with one another, and has stimulated the divine impulse to originate by sympathy or antagonism. As the seat of political power, as the nursery of the arts and sciences, as the center of industry and commerce, the city represents the highest achievements of political, intellectual and industrial life. The rural population is not merely conservative; it is full of error and prejudice; it receives what enlightenment it possesses from the city. Nor is the small city free from the same reproach; while it performs the useful function of an intermediary between the progressivism, liberalism, radicalism of the great city, and the conservatism, bigotry, of the country, it is the chief seat of the pseudo-bourgeois Philistine. . . . Americans of the present generation are destined to see this provincialism vanish before the powerful influences of large cities, which the introduction of manufactures and commerce on a large scale will in a short time produce. The South will be brought into contact with the current of world-thought. To the negro race justice will at length be accorded, and a stronger feeling of fraternity toward the North will grow up, strengthening the bonds of patriotism. . . . . .

But the highest social service performed by the cities will not be realized until we have made clear to ourselves their function in the process of natural selection. Otto Ammon's comparison of this process of natural selection in human society with that of horse-breeding is not flattering to a human being's sense of dignity; but he expresses the facts when he likens cities to folds (*Pferche*) into which the most desirable bloods are brought and nourished on a superior diet. Inside the fold are divisions to secure the concentration of the breeder's attention upon the very few superior animals. These divisions in the cities are the social classes. . . .

The city is the spectroscope of society; it analyzes and sifts the population, separating and classifying the diverse elements. The entire progress of civilization is a process of differentiation, and the city is the greatest differentiator. The mediocrity of the country is transformed by the city into the highest talent or the lowest criminal. Genius is often born in the country, but it is brought to light and developed by the city. On the other hand, the opportunities of the city work just as powerfully in the opposite direction upon the countrymen of an ignoble cast; the boy thief of the village becomes the daring bank robber of the metropolis. . . .

. . . Even if the "fittest" members of society did perish earlier in the struggle for existence in the city than in the country, it would be open to doubt if society would not gain more by their residence in the city where they can find scope for their abilities than in the country without opportunities for performing the highest social service of which they are capable. But with the modern combination of city business life and rural residence, or at least open-air holidays and recreation periods, and the opportunities that cities alone offer for the carrying on of athletic sports and games, the best blood of the race is not liable to extinction.

III

Who's Who in America suggests that American leaders are more likely to come from urban rather than rural backgrounds.

FROM: "City Boys Versus Country Boys," an item in *Science,* 1909.

NOT only was the rate of growth of cities outstripping that of the country, but sociologists were challenging the myth that rural America was the source of national greatness and personal success. Adna Weber had suggested the role of the city in natural selection of the "fittest" for leadership. Others sought statistical proof by rummaging through data supplied by sources such as *Who's Who in America,* foreshadowing the more sophisticated "quantitative approaches" to historical research increasingly popular today.

Is the writer's use of Who's Who in America *a reliable method for proving his thesis of urban priority in leadership creation?*

What suggestions for additional testing of the thesis can you offer?

What precautions in handling statistics should historians observe?

🔊

. . . DOES the farm produce more than its share of leading Americans? Such a question must be answered on a statistical, impartial, and as far as possible, scientific basis. It is first necessary to determine who are the "leaders in every phase of activity in this country." I have turned to

Frederick Adams Woods, "Discussion and Correspondence," *Science,* n.s. 29 (April 9, 1909), 577–579. Reprinted by permission.

"Who's Who in America" to answer this question. This book has already been successfully used in several sociological studies, and has great value as a starting point for such researches. The editor doubtless tries to be as impartial and comprehensive as possible; but its greatest value to one who wishes to answer a question similar to the present discussion, is that here he finds a list of names prepared by some one else, without any idea or bias in relation to the investigator's present problem. Thus the first, and one of the most important requirements is obtained, the subjective element is eliminated. . . . . .

The leaders of to-day are about fifty years old on the average, so we must go back a half century and picture American population as it was then distributed. According to the census of 1860, there were 5,072,256 persons living in cities of over 8,000 inhabitants, out of a total population of 31,443,321, or 16.1 per cent. This standard of 8,000 or more is the one arbitrarily taken by the census bureau as constituting a city, and is so used to illustrate the growth of urban populations. There were ninety-six such cities, and a list of them is given in the "Annual Cyclopedia" for 1861. It is easy then to see if these cities have done better or worse than might be expected in producing leading men. Under initial A in "Who's Who in America," we find 128 born in cities out of 433, or 29.6 per cent. as against the 16.1 per cent. expected.

Under initial B, we find 404 out of 1,477, or 27.5 per cent.

Under initial C, we find 362 out of 1,143, or 31.7 per cent.

Under initial D, we find 213 out of 676, or 31.6 per cent.

Under initial E, we find 97 out of 273, or 35.6 per cent.

For the sake of being on the safe side I have added all the unrecorded birthplaces to the suburban and rural, and yet the latter fail to produce their proper quota in every single group, and in fact every little group of fifty or a hundred taken at random alphabetically will show the same result.

It seems unnecessary to carry investigation further to establish the fact that the urban beats the non-urban by nearly two to one. The towns, villages and farms should have produced more than five times as many leaders as the cities. They have failed to produce more than about twice as many. Thus the entire non-urban which should have given rise to about 85 per cent. of the total has only produced about 70 per cent. . . . .

Now, as to its bearing on the question of heredity. It is an easily verified fact that talent tends to be drawn by, and to locate itself in the great centers of human activity. If we turn to the geographical index in the back part of our same biographical reference volume, we find that the great cities, New York, Chicago, Boston, etc., show two or three times as many names as would be expected merely from their populations. I think no one will question the fact that there has been a migration and selection of the most able men, especially the ambitious and gifted young men, towards the large cities and away from the small towns and farms. This change is in process at present, and must have been going on for some time. Thus there is every reason to suppose that by the year 1860 (if not very much earlier than this) there had already taken place a part at least of this same phenomenon. So that the distribution of talent was then somewhat as it is to-day, concentrated about the cities. Now if mental traits are inherited, the cities must show a higher proportionate birth of talent than the country, and our observed facts are only what we might expect.

Of course it is impossible here to separate the question of environment, which may be more favorable in the city, as some contend, or less favorable, as others sometimes think, or be the slight and almost unmeasurable force which I, myself, shall be content to hold it, until some one has succeeded in measuring it.

Mental heredity, on the other hand, has been measured, and the results are in substantial agreement.

IV

Novelist Hamlin Garland portrays the magic lure of the big city for rural young people.

FROM: "Her First Conquest," a chapter in Garland's *Rose of Dutcher's Coolly,* 1895.

HAMLIN GARLAND deserted farm life in 1884 to pursue a literary career in Boston and Chicago as debunker of the homespun agrarian myth. His short stories and novels presented the often pathetic story behind the statistics of the rural exodus to the cities. In *Rose of Dutcher's Coolly,* a novel of 1895, Garland gave voice to the lure of the city for rural young people who, abandoning dull country towns and isolated farms, confronted for the first time the mystery, the diversity, and the excitement of the metropolis.

What changes in the political and economic history of the United States from 1865 to 1900 made rural life less congenial?

Are the reactions of Rose Dutcher to Chicago still typical of young people moving into the big city?

≈§

THE next day Rose went to town alone. The wind had veered to the south, the dust blew, and the whole terrifying panorama of life in

Hamlin Garland, *Rose of Dutcher's Coolly* (Chicago: Stone and Kimball, 1895), pp 203–207.

the streets seemed some way blurred together, and forms of men and animals were like figures in tapestry. The grind and clang and clatter and hiss and howl of the traffic was all about her. . . . . .

So it was—the wonderful and the terrifying appealed to her mind first. In all the city she saw the huge and the fierce. She perceived only contrasts. She saw the ragged newsboy and the towering policeman. She saw the rag-pickers, the street vermin, with a shudder of pity and horror, and she saw also the gorgeous show windows of the great stores. She saw the beautiful new gowns and hats, and she saw also the curious dress of swart Italian girls scavenging with baskets on their arms. Their faces were old and grimy, their voices sounded like the chattered colloquies of monkeys in the circus.

It all seemed a battlefield. There was no hint of repose or home in it all. People were just staying here like herself, trying to get work, trying to make a living, trying to make a name. They had left their homes as she had, and though she conceived of them as having a foot-hold she could not imagine them having reached security. The home-life of the city had not revealed itself to her.

She made her way about the first few blocks below Water street, looking for Dr. Herrick's address. It was ten o'clock, and the streets were in a frenzy of exchange. The sidewalks were brooks, the streets rivers of life which curled into doors and swirled around mountainous buildings.

It was almost pathetic to see how helpless she seemed in the midst of these alien sounds. It took away from her the calm, almost scornful, self-reliance which characterized her in familiar surroundings. Her senses were as acute as a hare's and sluiced in upon her a bewildering flood of sights and sounds. She did not appear childish, but she seemed slow and stupid, which of course she was not. She thought and thought till she grew sick with thought. She struggled to digest all that came to her, but it was like trampling sand; she apparently gained nothing by her toil.

The streets led away into thunderous tunnels, beyond which some other strange hell of sound and stir imaginatively lay. The brutal voices of drivers of cabs and drays assaulted her. The clang of gongs drew her attention, now here, now there, and her anxiety to understand each sound and to appear calm added to her confusion.

She heard crashes and yells that were of murder and sudden death. It was the crash of a falling bundle of sheet iron, but she knew not that. She looked around thinking to see some savage battle scene.

She saw women with painted faces and bleached hair whom she took to be those mysterious and appalling women who sell themselves to men. They were in fact simple-minded shop girls or vulgar little housewives with sad lack of taste.

Every street she crossed, she studied, looking both up and down it, in the effort to see some end of its mystery. They all vanished in lurid, desolate distance, save toward the lake. Out there she knew, the water lay serene and blue.

This walk was to her like entrance into war. It thrilled and engaged her at every turn. She was in the center of human life. To win here was to win all she cared to have.

V

A folk poet reminds expatriate rural sons and daughters that there are two ends to the road to the city.

FROM: "The Road to Boston," a poem by Sam Walter Foss, 1892.

By no means every American followed Rose Dutcher's enchanted path to the city. And some of those who did trudged wearily back home again with disappointed promises and sometimes lurid tales of city life. Trapped in some dismal urban tenement, others ruefully agreed with the nostalgic appeals of popular folk poet Sam Walter Foss, author of America's favorite, "House By the Side of the Road," that life back on the farm often had more to offer young people than did the unceasing competition of the city.

What contrasting images of country versus city life does Foss present? What might have been Rose Dutcher's reaction to the poem?

Of all the verse or folk songs you have read and perhaps memorized, what proportion sentimentalized rural life? Life in the city?

THE ROAD TO BOSTON

The little road goes past my house, goes winding like a snake,
Climbs up the hills of hemlock, and winds through swamps of brake,
It leaps the sweeping river and climbs the mountain height,
Bends down into the valley, and goes glimmering out of sight. . . . . .

My boys and girls when they grew up, they felt the heavy load
Of this quietude and dulness—and they traveled down the road,
And they wound across the rivers, and far o'er the mountains gray,
To the biggest street in Boston, two hundred miles away.

And many men among the hills hear Boston's distant roar,
For the biggest street in Boston passes every farmhouse door,
And the distant roar and rumble comes like magic to the ear,
And thousands travel down the road, pass on, and disappear.

Sam Walter Foss, *Back Country Poems* (Boston: Potter Publishing Company, 1892), pp. 26–27.

But my boys they write from Boston that, for feet that waded through
The early fields of clover and the daisies and the dew,
The stones are hard and cruel there on Boston's biggest street,
And are pressed each day and hour by a horde of tired feet.

And that men are cold and selfish, each one busy with his plan
To climb to wealth and power o'er his prostrate fellow-man;
That the few have ease and comfort, and the many toil and die,
Shut in by brick and granite from the sunlight and the sky.

And I write my children letters; tell them that their father still,
Still is toiling by the roadside on the green and quiet hill,
And to come away from Boston, with its cruel noise and roar,
For the biggest street in Boston passes by their father's door!

VI

*A United States Commissioner of Labor analyzes
the urban working classes and their shelter.*

FROM: Commissioner Carroll Wright's report of 1895.

RAPID population growth in the nineteenth century stimulated careful
sociological studies of urban problems in Great Britain and elsewhere.
American investigators, taking their cue from such analyses, sought the
basis for social groupings within the city and their relationship to housing, crime, and city services. Among such analysts was Carroll D. Wright,
a pioneer in objective research on labor problems and first United States
Commissioner of Labor. Wright concluded in a careful report of 1895
that solutions to the housing problems of the working class must be
largely economic in approach.

*Compare working class groupings and their housing problems in 1895
with those in the city today. What factors account for any noticeable
differences?*

*How might a present-day liberal receive the Commissioner's sugges-
tions for alleviating the condition of the lowest stratum of urban working
class society?*

*Of what value are comparative studies such as Wright's parallel inter-
est in English experience? Does this method apply also to history?*

IT will be obvious to a careful reader of the preceding pages that
differentiation of the great mass included under the somewhat indefinite
term of working people is a necessary preliminary to the statement of

*Eighth Special Report of the Commissioner of Labor: The Housing of the Working
People* (Washington: Government Printing Office, 1895), pp. 439–443.

conclusions. In the first place there is the artisan element. Members of this class are in receipt of fair wages. As a rule, they are steady, thrifty, and socially ambitious. They are good tenants, and persons who make house ownership their business are very glad to have them. . . .

The next step in the gradation is occupied by individuals who have not mounted quite so high in the social scale. One section has been unfortunate, and through sickness or other misfortune has grown deeply in debt or become discouraged in the effort to maintain a fair standard of existence. The other includes those prone to be lazy and careless, and those who are not particularly intelligent or ambitious or are possessed of bad habits. Both sections are somewhat irregular as rent payers, the latter figuring especially as rent jumpers. They are not desirable tenants, and usually they have difficulty in finding fair accommodation. . . . . .

The third section includes the incorrigible, the drunkard, the criminal, the immoral, the lazy, and the shiftless. These do not pay rent if they can avoid it. They ruin any property in which they take shelter, and can consequently only get the lowest sort of accommodation. They hate discipline, and, as Lord Shaftesbury significantly remarks, they have hardly any domestic or civilized feelings. Further, says he, "I believe that nothing has led more to misery of every sort, moral and physical, than burying those people in holes where nobody saw them, and they saw nobody, except those who lived immediately around them." There must be an entire change of policy on the part of governing bodies toward this class. Lord Provost Russell of Edinburgh goes so far as to say that they should be driven from their hiding places into municipal lodging houses, where they could be under police control, the sexes separated, and the children placed in institutions where they might grow up useful members of society. The concurrence of these distinguished authorities, both of whom have experienced a lifelong interest in the housing of the poor, and have had, therefore, every opportunity for mature judgment, would seem to furnish weighty reasons for reform in the current treatment of the lowest social strata. To the possible cry against breaking up the family it is only necessary to answer that the bulk of such people are unmarried, that they have not even a moderate standard of domestic life, and that to them the word "home" has no proper meaning. The only prospect of reducing the number of the submerged is to strike at the root of the matter by removing the children from environments where there is everything to drag down and nothing to uplift. Happily, the increasing strictness of sanitary enforcement is driving this class more and more into lodging houses. . . . . .

A way, however, seems to be opening up wherein the elements just mentioned do not largely enter. For the workingman's purposes space is measured by time not by distance. Underground and overhead electric transportation means the lessening of distances, and brings a large range of territory within living areas which hitherto has been outside possible consideration. The effect of rapid transit ought normally to be that artisans, or the higher earning portion of working people, will more and more house themselves in the suburbs of cities, where they may purchase homes upon reasonable conditions. Widening habitable areas to workingmen in cities would not only relieve congestion of population, but it must in time reduce the demand for houses in those spots where massing most frequently occurs, consequently reducing rents so that those with lower earnings might then find fair accommodation at reasonable rates. . . . . .

The problem of the housing of working people includes sanitary, economic, and ethical issues of the highest importance, but a final solution can only be wrought out along economic lines.

VII
  Respectable Trinity Church proves to be one of New York City's least respectable "slum-lords."

FROM: "The Tenements of Trinity Church," a magazine article by Charles Edward Russell, 1908.

In 1908, Charles Edward Russell, a well-known socialist and early "muckraker," rocked polite society by exposing New York's historic Trinity Church as a grinding slum-lord in a clerical collar. The city's enormous growth had converted an inheritance of a colonial grant of land into urban assets estimated to approach $100,000,000. Here was an excellent example of the principle of the "unearned increment" in land value preached earlier by single-tax reformer Henry George. It was popular to condemn slum dwellers such as those in Trinity's tenements as the social misfits of natural selection. It was less pleasing to learn that "respectable people" were profiting from the very slum environment guaranteed to keep the inmates unfit.

How did Trinity Church's economic interests demonstrate Henry George's thesis of "poverty within progress?"

The sociologist E. A. Ross in Sin and Society *demanded that religion pay at least as much attention to "social sins" as it did to individual sins. How might this apply to Trinity Church and its vestrymen?*

✑

. . . WHEREVER you walk in this dreadful region, [Hudson Park area of New York City's lower West Side] you find something that Trinity owns, and, as a rule, it is something that you know she ought not to own. . . . . .

. . .[T]his is the wealth that the sheer growth of New York has made for Trinity; and this is the fortune that by the managers of this remarkable church is guarded with a strange secrecy and care. . . .

What? Expressed in wretched, rotten, old tenement-houses? Yes. Expressed in hundreds of such tenement houses. . . . . .

It appears, therefore, that while the charities established by Trinity since 1857 are trying to lead men upward, the Trinity tenements, with an irresistible force, are crushing men downward; and we are therefore presented at once with a very memorable spectacle of the contradictions and inconsistencies of this our mortal state. . . . . .

. . . Profit, much profit, very great profit, lies in property of this sort; it yields much to the golden stream. These are houses that old-time tenants built on land had from Trinity on short leases. When the leases expired, Trinity, following a consistent and profitable policy, refused to grant renewals—to the late tenants. It also refused to purchase the house that the tenant had built. The tenant, therefore, was confronted with this situation: he could tear his house down brick by brick and cart it away to the dump or the river; or he could abandon it (as it stood) to Trinity, sometimes for nothing, sometimes for a nominal sum. These are houses, therefore, in which the investment of Trinity was almost nothing, possibly an average of $200 each, and now from these same houses she gathers $40 or $50 a month for rent, paying out nothing for repairs. . . . . .

. . . When the building was new and clean, it might have been a tolerable place in which to house horses—temporarily; say for a day. It was never, at any time, a tolerable place in which to house human beings. For fifty or sixty years it has been unfit for anything except burning. How would you like to draw an income from the maintaining of such a place? You would want to have the money disinfected before it touched your hand, would you not? Lest into your presence it bear some odor of the rear tenement, or some bacteria from the interior bedrooms, or from the filthy courts. . . . . .

The good gentlemen of the vestry have strong and steady nerves; they are not easily worried; they are not likely ever to die of heart failure. I know that they have large and well-grounded philosophies and rest steadfastly upon the belief that a Special Providence watches over the tenement-house region. I know this must be so because otherwise they would never be able to sleep, under the terror that the condition of their tenement-houses must inspire. . . . . .

And how about the rest of use that are not obliged to lead our lives in such surroundings, but are still our brothers' keepers? I know that there is a belief more or less widespread among us that tenement-house dwellers do not have feelings like ours. They are differently constituted, their fibres are different, their ganglia are of another material; so by a merciful provision they do not feel the pangs of poverty nor mind dirt, darkness, and squalor. We should mind such things, but these people do not, because of some great difference in their physical and mental make-up. In fact, they are said to be very happy in the station to which Providence has assigned them, and we really should let them live on in their cellars and back rooms so long as tuberculosis and typhoid will allow. . . . . .

How comes it that the Astor Estate, owner of hundreds of tenements, has pursued for years one settled policy of improvement for the benefit of the tenants, and the Trinity tenants have been left to shift for themselves? The Astor Estate maintains no charities; it has no missions, no hospitals, no beds, and no Sunday-school excursions; yet I am perfectly certain that the balance of actual good in the world is in its favor; I am perfectly certain that to obliterate one court that breeds tuberculosis is better than to spend $70,000 a year on organ music, and that to provide a tenement with fire-escapes is better than to preach a sermon of remote and genteel theology. . . . . .

Ah, yes, blessings on the Sunday-school excursions, blessings on the trade-schools, blessings on the parochial schools, blessings on the fruit and flower missions, blessings on the organ music, blessings on the chapel guilds, blessings on the contributions for the poor of St. John's. Beautiful, indeed, are all these things. But while they keep their wonted way, the mill of the tenement-house goes on crushing, and the products of the crushing stare us in the face with ugly questions, not to be answered with Sunday-school excursions.

VIII

A growing urban "proletariat" brings lawlessness to the cities and uneasiness to conservative citizens.

FROM: A popular book about New York City's "dangerous classes," 1872.

POST Civil War riots, labor violence, and urban crime triggered fears about the new "dangerous classes" of the city. Charles Loring Brace, the reformer who in 1853 had founded New York's pioneering Children's Aid Society, popularized the term with good intentions. Conservatives, however, recalled the threats of revolution in the Communist Manifesto of 1848 and worried whether the United States had generated its own urban proletariat in the Marxian sense. Middle class opinion preferred to link the "dangerous classes" with inherited degeneracy, vice, and crime rather than with the class struggle. The roots of the problem actually lay in poverty, ignorance, and restricted economic opportunity for the apparently unassimilable urban masses.

What is a "proletarian"? Did the United States ever possess a proletariat in the Marxian Communist sense?

What aspects of city life tended to aggravate the alleged American tendency toward violence?

What are the sociological origins of city "gangs"? How would you rate the comparative significance of race and environment and heredity as sources of gang behavior?

ᦥ

"THE PROLETAIRES OF NEW YORK"

. . . THE intensity of the American temperament is felt in every fibre of these children of poverty and vice. Their crimes have the unrestrained and sanguinary character of a race accustomed to overcome all obstacles. They rifle a bank, where English thieves pick a pocket; they murder, where European *proletaires* cudgel or fight with fists; in a riot, they begin what seems about to be the sacking of a city, where English rioters would merely batter policemen, or smash lamps. The "dangerous classes" of New York are mainly American-born, but the children of Irish and German immigrants. . . . . .

There are thousands on thousands in New York who have no assignable home, and "flit" from attic to attic, and cellar to cellar; there are other thousands more or less connected with criminal enterprises; and still other tens of thousands, poor, hard-pressed, and depending for daily bread on the day's earnings, swarming in tenement-houses, who behold the gilded rewards of toil all about them, but are never permitted to touch them.

All these great masses of destitute, miserable, and criminal persons believe that for ages the rich have had all the good things of life, while to them have been left the evil things. Capital to them is the tyrant.

Let but Law lift its hand from them for a season, or let the civilizing influences of American life fail to reach them, and, if the opportunity offered, we should see an explosion from this class which might leave this city in ashes and blood.

"THE NINETEENTH-STREET GANG OF RUFFIANS"

SEVENTEEN years ago, my attention had been called to the extraordinarily degraded condition of the children in a district lying on

Charles Loring Brace, *The Dangerous Classes of New York and Twenty Years Among Them* (New York: Synkoop and Hallenbeck, 1872), pp. 27, 29, 317–318.

the west side of the city, between Seventeenth and Nineteenth Streets, and the Seventh and Tenth Avenues. A certain block, called "Misery Row," in Tenth Avenue, was the main seed-bed of crime and poverty in the quarter, and was also invariably a "fever-nest." Here the poor obtained wretched rooms at a comparatively low rent; these they sub-let, and thus, in little, crowded, close tenements, were herded men, women, and children of all ages. The parents were invariably given to hard drinking, and the children were sent out to beg or to steal. Besides them, other children, who were orphans, or who had run away from drunkards' homes, or had been working on the canal-boats that discharged on the docks near by, drifted into the quarter, as if attracted by the atmosphere of crime and laziness that prevailed in the neighborhood. These slept around the breweries of the ward, or on the hay-barges, or in the old sheds of Eighteenth and Nineteenth Streets. They were mere children, and kept life together by all sorts of street-jobs—helping the brewery laborers, blackening boots, sweeping sidewalks, "smashing baggages" (as they called it), and the like. Herding together, they soon began to form an unconscious society for vagrancy and idleness. Finding that work brought but poor pay, they tried shorter roads to getting money by pettey [*sic*] thefts, in which they were very adroit. Even if they earned a considerable sum by a lucky day's job, they quickly spent it in gambling, or for some folly.

The police soon knew them as "street-rats;" but, like the rats, they were too quick and cunning to be often caught in their petty plunderings, so they gnawed away at the foundations of society undisturbed.

IX

The gentle arts of "clubbing" and pocket-picking suggest that a policeman's life in the "Gay Nineties" was busy if not always happy.

> FROM: *Darkness and Daylight,* an "inside story" of New York's slum life, 1892.

THE city, as Adna Weber pointed out, sharpened the wits of its citizens regardless of class. Labor strikes, vice, and crime converted some neighborhoods into asphalt jungles and required highly organized police services and sophisticated new techniques for enforcing the law. In a realistically illustrated volume on the "lights and shadows of New York life" published in the nineties, Col. Thomas W. Knox, an experienced newspaperman, contributed insights into how the reliable policeman's "billy" and his twenty-two inch long "nightstick" served the cause of law and order in city streets. Meanwhile, new versions of old crimes such as picking pockets challenged the defensive skills of citizens and policemen alike as described by Thomas Byrnes, widely known New York detective.

Why should policemen, supposedly themselves members of the working class, have "a great antipathy to labor strikes"?

In what ways would urban growth encourage not only an increase in criminal activity, but also in the variety of crimes?

COL. THOMAS W. KNOX: *WHEN CLUBBING IS NECESSARY.*

THEY [the police] are instructed not to use unnecessary violence in the discharge of their duty. Notwithstanding this, they have frequently been charged with a free use of the club on occasions when it was not needed. With some officers there is doubtless a temptation to wield the club when milder measures might answer just as well. Much depends upon the surroundings and the character of the offender; in the dangerous parts of the city he is justified in employing severity under circumstances that would be reprehensible in other portions.

"As to clubbing," said an old officer, "there is no doubt that some of the men lose their temper sooner than others do, and then use the club unjustifiably. The club is put into the hands of a policeman for use, so that he thinks logically he has a right to use it when necessary. Now, it is absolutely necessary to use it sometimes, unless the officer is willing to sacrifice his life. In some parts of the city, especially in the Fourth Ward, we have perfect devils to deal with. Within the last week no less than half a dozen of my men have come into the station with their clothes actually torn off them."

Every citizen has a right of complaint when he thinks an officer has gone beyond his duty, and he can be sure that the case will receive a searching investigation at the hands of the Commissioners. . . . . .

During the strike of the employees of the Third Avenue Surface Railway Company a mob assembled at the corner of Third Avenue and Fifty-ninth Street, where there was a large quantity of building-material. The police formed in a solid phalanx extending across the avenue, and when the order to advance was given they moved with a solid front in perfect alignment. The mob greeted them with a shower of bricks, and several policemen fell stunned to the ground. But the lines closed, the men, armed with their heavy night clubs, were ordered to charge, and they obeyed the order with the promptness of a military

Helen Campbell, ed., *Darkness and Daylight; or, Lights and Shadows of New York Life* (Hartford, Conn.: A. D. Worthington and Company, 1892), pp. 511–513, 708–709.

detachment. With their powerful weapons, which never miss fire and require no reloading, they fell upon the mob, and in less time than it takes to tell the story there were a dozen rioters stretched on the pavement, and the rest of the mob was in full flight in all directions where flight was possible. The police carried out the orders of their superiors with the efficiency of soldiers of the regular army.

The police have a great antipathy to labor strikes and the disorder that accompanies them, and when they come in contact with a striking mob they are not tender in their ways of handling it.

THOMAS BYRNES: *HOW PICKPOCKETS OPERATE IN A CROWD*

WHEN a mob of pickpockets start out to "work a crowd" on a horse-car or a railroad train, they break into twos. The part of one is to ascertain the location of the victim's money. He gets alongside the man whose pocket is to be picked, and with rapid movement he dexterously passes his fingers over every pocket. His touch is so delicate that it enables him to locate the prize and to ascertain its character, whether a roll, a purse, or a pocket-book. The surging of the crowd, especially on a railroad train, accounts to the suspicious traveler for the occasional jostling he receives. The most common receptacle for the pocket-book is the left trousers pocket. When the victim is selected, the second man plants himself squarely in front of him, while the other crowds up behind him on the right side. The operator in front, under cover of a newspaper or coat thrown over his arm, feels the pocket, and if the victim is a straight-backed man, in standing position, he finds the opening of the pocket drawn close together. In such case it is dangerous to attempt the insertion of the hand. A very low-toned clearing of the throat, followed by a gutteral noise, is the signal for his confederate to exert a gentle pressure upon the victim's right shoulder. This is so gradually extended that the traveler yields to the pressure without knowing it, and without changing the position of his feet. This throws the lips of the pocket conveniently open for the operator in front, who does not insert his hands to draw the book out but works upon the lining. He draws it out a little at a time without inserting his fingers more than half way. Should this process of drawing the contents of the pocket to its mouth be felt by the victim, another low clearing of the throat gives the sign to the confederate, and the game is dropped. If the victim's suspicions are not aroused, the pickpocket continues at his work of drawing the lining out until the roll of bills or pocket-book is within reach of his deft fingers. The successful completion of the undertaking is indicated by a gentle chirrup, and the precious pair separate from their victim to ply the same tricks upon the next one.

X
_____

*Horse-cars, elevated trains, and suspension bridges
extend the boundaries of America's big cities.*

FROM: Reports on urban transit by an English novelist and two New
York newspapers, 1862, 1878, 1883.

A MAJOR need of big city living was improved transportation. The
horse-drawn omnibus and streetcar introduced Americans to mass transit
before the Civil War, and with it came the hectic and often rude public
manners supposedly peculiar to big cities. English novelist Anthony
Trollope graphically described the change in manners after confronta-
tions with the mobile American female in her streetcar habitat. In the
1870s elevated steam railways sped service and helped ease congestion.
But it was the opening of the Brooklyn Bridge in 1883 which symbolized
America's reliance on technology to extend city boundaries and speed
urban movement even at the cost of the rapid obsolescence of existing
services.

*Which modern technological changes have been most significant in
making the modern city a feasible place in which to live and work?*

*What new problems of urban organization and administration were
introduced by the technological expansion of city boundaries?*

ANTHONY TROLLOPE: *AMERICAN HORSE-CARS AND FEMALE PASSENGERS.*

THE street cars are manned with conductors, and, therefore, are
free from many of the perils of the omnibus, but they have perils of their
own. They are always quite full. By that I mean that every seat is
crowded, that there is a double row of men and women standing down
the center, and that the driver's platform in front is full, and also the conductor's platform behind. That is the normal condition of a street car in
the Third Avenue. You, as a stranger in the middle of the car, wish to be
put down at, let us say, 89th Street. In the map of New York now before
me, the cross streets running from east to west are numbered up north-
ward as far as 154th Street. It is quite useless for you to give the number
as you enter. Even an American conductor, with brains all over him, and
an anxious desire to accommodate, as is the case with all these men, cannot remember. You are left therefore in misery to calculate the number of
the street as you move along, vainly endeavouring through the misty
glass to decipher the small numbers which after a day or two you perceive to be written on the lamp posts.

But I soon gave up all attempts at keeping a seat in one of these
cars. It became my practice to sit down on the outside iron rail behind,

Anthony Trollope, *North-America* (Philadelphia: J. B. Lippincott and Company, 1862),
pp. 212–213, 215–216.

and as the conductor generally sat in my lap I was in a measure protected. As for the inside of these vehicles the women of New York were, I must confess, too much for me. I would no sooner place myself on a seat, than I would be called on by a mute, unexpressive, but still impressive stare into my face, to surrender my place. From cowardice if not from gallantry I would always obey; and as this led to discomfort and an irritated spirit, I preferred nursing the conductor on the hard bar in the rear. . . . . .

. . . The woman, as she enters, drags after her a misshapen dirty mass of battered wirework, which she calls her crinoline, and which adds as much to her grace and comfort as a log of wood does to a donkey when tied to the animal's leg in a paddock. Of this she takes much heed, not managing it so that it may be conveyed up the carriage with some decency, but striking it about against men's legs, and heaving it with violence over people's knees. The touch of a real woman's dress is in itself delicate; but these blows from a harpy's fins are as loathsome as a snake's slime. If there be two of them they talk loudly together, having a theory that modesty has been put out of court by women's rights. But, though not modest, the woman I describe is ferocious in her propriety. She ignores the whole world around her as she sits; with a raised chin and face flattened by affectation, she pretends to declare aloud that she is positively not aware that any man is even near her. She speaks as though to her, in her womanhood, the neighborhood of men was the same as that of dogs or cats. They are there, but she does not hear them, see them, or even acknowledge them by any courtesy of motion. But her own face always gives her the lie. In her assumption of indifference she displays her nasty consciousness, and in each attempt at a would-be propriety is guilty of an immodesty. . . . She looks square at you in the face, and you rise to give her your seat. You rise from a deference to your own old convictions, and from that courtesy which you have ever paid to a woman's dress, let it be worn with ever such hideous deformities. She takes the place from which you have moved without a word or a bow. She twists herself round, banging your shins with her wires, while her chin is still raised, and her face is still flattened, and she directs her friend's attention to another seated man, as though that place were also vacant, and necessarily at her disposal. Perhaps that man opposite has his own ideas about chivalry. I have seen such a thing, and have rejoiced to see it.

NEW YORK *DAILY TRIBUNE: STEAM IN SIXTH AVENUE,* MAY 1, 1878.

THE first trip over the Gilbert Elevated Railway from Trinity Church to Central Park, was made yesterday. There were four cars containing 200 passengers, among them Dr. Gilbert, the projector of the road. . . .

. . . Not a jar or jolt was felt by the passengers as the train sped smoothly toward Central Park. Pushing along the avenue at the level of the second-story windows, it was difficult even for persons most familiar with the first-story features of the busy thoroughfare to realize just where they were. It seemed as if one were travelling through some unknown street in a strange city. A few landmarks, however, had a familiar look—the Jefferson Market Court House, Macy's store, Booth's Theatre, the Masonic Temple, and the Forty-second Street Reservoir.

The partially finished platforms at Ninth, Fourteenth, Twenty-third and Forty-second-sts. were thronged with spectators, as were also the windows of the houses. Nearly every one had a friendly look for the pioneer train. A few wagged their heads or shook their fists good-naturedly. At the Sixth Avenue car stables two or three hostlers were noticed energetically calling "whoa" and clinging to the bits of horses that exhibited no symptoms of fright, except pricking up their ears. The curtains were drawn closely down in the window of the office of the company as the triumphant train moved past. . . .

Within the car hilarity and congratulations prevailed whenever the absorbed passengers turned from the windows and realized the circumstances in which they were placed. Then there burst forth such exclamations as "No more hanging onto straps," "No more blockades, filthy straw, frozen feet and crowded horse cars."

The trip to Fifty-ninth-st. was made in seventeen minutes, including a delay of one minute at Sixth-ave. and Amity-st. It is expected that the same distance will ordinarily be run by through trains in twelve minutes, and by way trains in twenty-two minutes.

THE NEW YORK TIMES: CROSSING THE NEW BRIDGE, MAY 26, 1883.

THE gray-haired book-keeper of the Union Ferry Company was asked what the effect of the bridge travel had been upon the receipts of the company during the day. "I should think it had reduced them 10 per cent., perhaps more. We cannot tell until to-morrow." A policeman who has been on duty at the Fulton ferry for years declared that one-half of the wagon traffic had certainly been diverted to the bridge during the day. "Why, it's like a funeral around here now," said he. . . . There has hardly been a morning in the history of the ferries that some delay was not caused by the volume of traffic. Yesterday morning not a wagon had to wait. Throughout the day it was the same. The ferry-boats went over and came back about half loaded as to vehicles. "A great deal of this traffic over the bridge, passenger and wagon, is stimulated by curiosity," said the gray-haired book-keeper. "Much of it will soon come back to us. We see no reason to feel uneasy. The ferry-boat offers a few minutes' rest to man and beast. On the bridge it is a continual 'move on.' " The drivers of the Fulton ferry stages express no fears as to any permanent injury to their business. . . . . .

Mr. Lyon, President of the Third-avenue line of street cars, when asked what the company intended to do in view of the opening of the bridge, said: "We are not going to give up one foot of the ground to which we are entitled. The Third-avenue road was authorized by the Legislature long before the Brooklyn bridge was thought of, and we have the right of way by virtue of precedence of our claim over the Brooklyn bridge. If the bridge finds that we are in its way, there is one thing for it to do. It can sink itself and pass under the railroad. What we want is, not to restrict our privileges, but to enlarge them."

XI

An enterprising financial "Titan" buys street railways, tunnels, and Chicago politicians.

FROM: "A Matter of Tunnels," a chapter in Theodore Dreiser's novel, *The Titan*, 1914.

WITH the multiplication of the administrative responsibilities of municipal governments, small-spirited politicians thrived as dispensers of franchises and other special privileges to businessmen eager to service the needs of city living. Theodore Dreiser, one of the first realist American novelists, pictured this lucrative cooperation in *The Titan*, suggested by the career of a Chicago transit monopolist of the 1880s. Frank Cowperwood, the novel's non-hero, moves into that city in quest of new street railway franchises after a term in prison and financial exploits in Philadelphia. In "A Matter of Tunnels," Cowperwood shrewdly assesses the needs and opportunities of public transportation in Chicago and the convenient venality of local politicians.

Is there anything essentially "dishonest" in the transaction between Cowperwood and McKenty—or was it simply shrewd business?

In which new essentially urban-oriented enterprises were opportunities for able early-comers especially promising?

⋐ξ

. . . COWPERWOOD, with a now splendid scheme in his mind, one day invited John J. McKenty, over to his house to dinner on a social pre-

Theodore Dreiser, *The Titan* (New York: World Publishing Company, 1914), pp. 172–176. Reprinted by permission of the World Publishing Company.

text. When the latter, accompanied by his wife, had arrived, and Aileen had smiled on them both sweetly, and was doing her best to be nice to Mrs. McKenty, Cowperwood remarked:

"McKenty, do you know anything about these two tunnels that the city owns under the river at Washington and La Salle streets?"

"I know that the city took them over when it didn't need them, and that they're no good for anything. That was before my time, though," explained McKenty, cautiously. "I think the city paid a million for them. Why?"

"Oh, nothing much," replied Cowperwood, evading the matter for the present. "I was wondering whether they were in such condition that they couldn't be used for anything. I see occasional references in the papers to their uselessness."

"They're in pretty bad shape, I'm afraid," replied McKenty. "I haven't been through either of them in years and years. The idea was originally to let the wagons go through them and break up the crowding at the bridges. But it didn't work. They made the grade too steep and the tolls too high, and so the drivers preferred to wait for the bridges. They were pretty hard on horses. I can testify to that myself. I've driven a wagon-load through them more than once. The city should never have taken them over at all by rights. It was a deal. I don't know who all was in it. Carmody was mayor then, and Aldrich was in charge of public works."

He relapsed into silence, and Cowperwood allowed the matter of the tunnels to rest until after dinner when they had adjourned to the library. There he placed a friendly hand on McKenty's arm, an act of familiarity which the politician rather liked.

"You felt pretty well satisfied with the way that gas business came out last year, didn't you?" he inquired.

"I did," replied McKenty, warmly. "Never more so. I told you that at the time." The Irishman liked Cowperwood, and was grateful for the swift manner in which he had been made richer by the sum of several hundred thousand dollars.

"Well, now, McKenty," continued Cowperwood, abruptly, and with a seeming lack of connection, "has it every occurred to you that things are shaping up for a big change in the street-railway situation here? I can see it coming. There's going to be a new motor power introduced on the South Side within a year or two. You've heard of it?"

"I read something of it," replied McKenty, surprised and a little questioning. He took a cigar and prepared to listen. Cowperwood, never smoking, drew up a chair.

"Well, I'll tell you what that means," he explained. "It means that eventually every mile of street-railway track in this city—to say nothing of all the additional miles that will be built before this change takes place—will have to be done over on an entirely new basis. I mean this cable-conduit system. These old companies that are hobbling along now with an old equipment will have to make the change. They'll have to spend millions and millions before they can bring their equipment up to date. If you've paid any attention to the matter you must have seen what a condition these North and West Side lines are in."

"It's pretty bad; I know that," commented McKenty.

"Just so," replied Cowperwood, emphatically. "Well, now, if I know anything about these old managements from studying them, they're going to have a hard time bringing themselves to do this. Two to three million are two to three million, and it isn't going to be an easy matter for them to raise the money—not as easy, perhaps, as it would be for some of the rest of us, supposing we wanted to go into the street-railway business."

"Yes, supposing," replied McKenty, jovially. "But how are you to get in it? There's no stock for sale that I know of."

"Just the same," said Cowperwood, "we can if we want to, and I'll show you how. But at present there's just one thing in particular I'd like you to do for me. I want to know if there is any way that we can get control of either of those two old tunnels that I was talking to you about a little while ago. I'd like both if I might. Do you suppose that is possible?"

"Why, yes," replied McKenty, wondering; "but what have they got to do with it? They're not worth anything. Some of the boys were talking about filling them in some time ago—blowing them up. The police think crooks hide in them."

"Just the same, don't let any one touch them—don't lease them or anything," replied Cowperwood, forcefully. "I'll tell you frankly what I want to do. I want to get control, just as soon as possible, of all the street-railway lines I can on the North and West Sides—new or old franchises. Then you'll see where the tunnels come in."

He paused to see whether McKenty caught the point of all he meant, but the latter failed.

"You don't want much, do you?" he said, cheerfully. "But I don't see how you can use the tunnels. However, that's no reason why I shouldn't take care of them for you, if you think that's important."

"It's this way," said Cowperwood, thoughtfully. "I'll make you a preferred partner in all the ventures that I control if you do as I suggest. The street-railways, as they stand now, will have to be taken up lock, stock, and barrel, and thrown into the scrap heap within eight or nine years at the latest. You see what the South Side company is beginning to do now. When it comes to the West and North Side companies they won't find it so easy. They aren't earning as much as the South Side, and besides they have those bridges to cross. That means a severe inconvenience to a cable line. In the first place, the bridges will have to be rebuilt to stand the extra weight and strain. Now the question arises at once—at whose expense? The city's?"

"That depends on who's asking for it," replied Mr. McKenty, amiably.

"Quite so," assented Cowperwood. "In the next place, this river traffic is becoming impossible from the point of view of a decent street-car service. There are waits now of from eight to fifteen minutes while these tows and vessels get through. Chicago has five hundred thousand population to-day. How much will it have in 1890? In 1900? How will it be when it has eight hundred thousand or a million?"

"You're quite right," interpolated McKenty. "It will be pretty bad."

"Exactly. But what is worse, the cable lines will carry trailers, or single cars, from feeder lines. There won't be single cars waiting at these draws—there will be trains, crowded trains. It won't be advisable to delay a cable-train from eight to fifteen minutes while boats are making their way through a draw. The public won't stand for that very long, will it, do you think?"

"Not without making a row, probably," replied McKenty.

"Well, that means what, then?" asked Cowperwood. "Is the traffic going to get any lighter? Is the river going to dry up?"

Mr. McKenty stared. Suddenly his face lighted. "Oh, I see," he said, shrewdly. "It's those tunnels you're thinking about. Are they in any shape to be used?"

"They can be made over cheaper than new ones can be built."

"True for you," replied McKenty, "and if they're in any sort of repair they'd be just what you'd want." He was emphatic, almost triumphant. "They belong to the city. They cost pretty near a million apiece, those things."

"I know it," said Cowperwood. "Now, do you see what I'm driving at?"

"Do I see!" smiled McKenty. "That's a real idea you have, Cowperwood. I take off my hat to you. Say what you want."

"Well, then, in the first place," replied Cowperwood, genially, "it is agreed that the city won't part with those two tunnels under any circumstances until we can see what can be done about this other matter?"

"It will not."

"In the next place, it is understood, is it, that you won't make it any easier than you can possibly help for the North and West Side companies to get ordinances extending their lines, or anything else, from now on? I shall want to introduce some franchises for feeders and outlying lines myself."

"Bring in your ordinances," replied McKenty, "and I'll do whatever you say. I've worked with you before. I know that you keep your word."

"Thanks," said Cowperwood, warmly. "I know the value of keeping it. In the mean while I'll go ahead and see what can be done about the other matter. I don't know just how many men I will need to let in on this, or just what form the organization will take. But you may depend upon it that your interests will be properly taken care of, and that whatever is done will be done with your full knowledge and consent."

"All very good," answered McKenty, thinking of the new field of activity before them. A combination between himself and Cowperwood in a matter like this must prove very beneficial to both. And he was satisfied, because of their previous relations, that his own interests would not be neglected.

"Shall we go and see if we can find the ladies?" asked Cowperwood, jauntily, laying hold of the politician's arm.

FOR FURTHER THOUGHT

Does the American experience support the argument that the true index of the quality of a nation's greatness is the condition of its cities?

Is urban development today significantly different in process, speed of change, and direction of trends from that of the nineteenth century city? What may the city of A.D. 2000 be like?

Of what special usefulness to historians are the knowledge and use of statistical procedures? In what areas of historical research might such procedures prove especially useful? Where are they of little or no help?